IRELAND AND THE GREAT WAR

The Lees Knowles Lectures 1998, given at Trinity College, Cambridge

This book explores the impact, both immediate and in its longer historical perspective, of the First World War upon Ireland across the broadest range of experience – nationalist, unionist, Catholic, Protestant – and in civilian social, economic and cultural terms, as well as purely military.

Underscoring the work is a belief that the Great War is the single most central experience in twentieth-century Ireland and that the events of the war years, whether at home in Dublin during the Easter Rising or at the European battlefront, constitute a 'seamless robe' of Irish experience. The book also explores cultural responses to the war and its commemoration since 1918, up to the dedication of the Irish 'Peace Tower' in Belgium in November 1998. It argues that identifying and exploring the Irish Great War experience can contribute to the contemporary Irish peace process.

KEITH JEFFERY is Professor of Modern History, University of Ulster. His publications include *A Military History of Ireland*, edited with Thomas Bartlett (1996, paperback 1997).

IRELAND AND THE GREAT WAR

KEITH JEFFERY

CAMBRIDGE
UNIVERSITY PRESS

PUBLISHED BY THE PRESS SYNDICATE OF THE UNIVERSITY OF CAMBRIDGE
The Pitt Building, Trumpington Street, Cambridge, United Kingdom

CAMBRIDGE UNIVERSITY PRESS
The Edinburgh Building, Cambridge CB2 2RU, UK   www.cup.cam.ac.uk
40 West 20th Street, New York, NY 10011–4211, USA   www.cup.org
10 Stamford Road, Oakleigh, Melbourne 3166, Australia
Ruiz de Alarcón 13, 28014 Madrid, Spain

First published 2000

Printed in the United Kingdom at the University Press, Cambridge

Typeface Monotype Imprint 10.5/13.5pt   *System* QuarkXPress™   [SE]

A catalogue record for this book is available from the British Library

ISBN 0 521 77323 7 hardback

Dedicated to my Irish great-uncles who served in the Great War:

NICHOLAS ENGLAND
born Portadown, County Armagh, 1886; died France, August 1918
58th Battalion Canadian Infantry

ROBERT ENGLAND
born Portadown, County Armagh, 1894; died British Columbia, 1985
Royal Canadian Regiment

ROBERT SIMPSON HACKETT
born Dublin, 1885; died British Columbia, 1951
Canadian Machine Gun Corps

WILLIAM LUMLEY HACKETT
born Dublin, 1888; died France, November 1918
Canadian Machine Gun Corps

Contents

List of illustrations viii
Acknowledgements xi
List of abbreviations xiv

Introduction 1

1 Obligation: 'Irishmen remember Belgium'
Enlisting for war service 5

2 Participation: Suvla Bay, the Somme and the Easter
Rising
The military experience of the war, abroad and at home 37

3 Imagination: onlookers in France
Irish cultural responses to the war 69

4 Commemoration: 'turning the 11th November into
the 12th July'
Irish politics and the collective memory of the war 107

Bibliographical essay: recent writing about Ireland and the
First World War 144

Notes 157
Bibliography 180
Index 196

Illustrations

TABLE

1 Recruits raised in Ireland for the war, for each six-month period
   7

PLATES

Illustrations not otherwise acknowledged are from the author's
collection.

1.1 Recruiting leaflet: 'Irishmen remember Belgium' 11
1.2 Recruiting poster: 'What will your answer be?' (courtesy of the
     National Library of Ireland) 13
1.3 Recruiting poster: 'Irishmen avenge the Lusitania' (courtesy of
     the National Library of Ireland) 17
1.4 Anti-recruiting poster (courtesy of the National Library of
     Ireland) 25
1.5 Picture postcard: 'Ye thocht Oi was going to be a
     thraitor' 27
1.6 Women workers at Lambkins tobacco factory, Cork (courtesy of
     the *Examiner*) 29
1.7 'For Us!', by William Conor (Linenhall Library, Belfast, and
     with the permission of Mrs Kay Dalzell) 34
1.8 The family of William Lumley Hackett 36
2.1 *Off: the Ulster Division*, by William Conor (photograph
     reproduced by kind permission of the Trustees of the National
     Museums and Galleries of Northern Ireland, and Mrs Kay
     Dalzell) 40

2.2 Irish Guards in the trenches at Wytschaete (copyright the Father
F. M. Browne, SJ Collection/The Irish Picture Library) 43

2.3 The Grand Place, Iper/Ypres (copyright the Father
F. M. Browne, SJ Collection/The Irish Picture Library) 46

2.4 Destruction in Dublin, Easter 1916 52

2.5 16th and 10th (Irish) Division memorial crosses in France and
Macedonia (courtesy of the Somme Association) 60

2.6 A page from *Ireland's Memorial Records* (1923) 62

2.7 Rudyard Kipling (copyright the Father F. M. Browne, SJ
Collection/The Irish Picture Library) 66

3.1 *Peace*, by Mainie Jellett (by permission of Michael Purser) 72

3.2 *Men of the West*, by Seán Keating (courtesy of the Hugh Lane
Municipal Gallery of Modern Art, Dublin) 77

3.3 *The Thinker on the Butte de Warlencourt*, by Sir William
Orpen (courtesy of Pyms Gallery, London, and Mrs Kit Casey)
80

3.4 *Armistice Night, Amiens*, by Sir William Orpen (courtesy of
Pyms Gallery, London, and Mrs Kit Casey) 82

3.5 *The Studio Window, 7 July 1917*, by Sir John Lavery
(photograph reproduced by kind permission of the Trustees of
the National Museums and Galleries of Northern Ireland, and
by courtesy of Felix Rosenstiel's Widow & Son Ltd, London, on
behalf of the estate of Sir John Lavery) 84

3.6 *To the Unknown British Soldier in France* (original version), by
Sir William Orpen (with the permission of the Imperial War
Museum, London, and Mrs Kit Casey) 87

3.7 *To the Unknown British Soldier in France* (final version), by Sir
William Orpen (with the permission of the Imperial War
Museum, London, and Mrs Kit Casey) 89

3.8 Front cover of *Thoughts from Flanders* by Harry Midgley
(1924) 103

4.1 Title page and frontispiece of Cyril Falls's *History of the 36th
(Ulster) Division* (1922) 108

4.2 Irish National War Memorial, Islandbridge (copyright *Country
Life* Picture Library) 120

4.3 Irish National War Memorial, Islandbridge (copyright *Country
Life* Picture Library) 122

4.4 Irish cavalry passing the cenotaph erected to the memory of

Michael Collins and Arthur Griffith (courtesy of the National Library of Ireland) 124

4.5   Cork war memorial (detail) 130

4.6   Unveiling of Longford war memorial, 27 August 1925 (British Pathe Library) 132

4.7   Somme memorial mural, Monkstown, County Antrim 134

4.8   Island of Ireland Peace Tower, Mesen/Messines, Belgium 141

Acknowledgements

The Lees Knowles lectures on 'some period of Military History or on some other subject connected with the study of Military Service' are the result of a benefaction given by Sir Lees Knowles (1857–1928) to Trinity College, Cambridge (his old college). This book is based on the lectures I delivered during the Michaelmas term of 1998 under the title '"For the freedom of small nations": Ireland and the Great War', and my first debts of gratitude are to Sir Lees Knowles himself and to the Master and Fellows of Trinity College Cambridge for inviting me to be the Lees Knowles Lecturer for the period 1998/9. While resident in Cambridge for five weeks in 1998, I was entertained by the college with wonderful hospitality, organised in particular by Dr Boyd Hilton and Professor Robert Neild. But I also must thank the Master, Professor Amartya Sen, and the Junior Bursar, Paul Simm, who both went out of their way to ensure that I felt at home in Trinity during my stay.

An older Trinity College debt which I owe is to the late Professor Jack Gallagher, my research supervisor, who took me on even though I came from the rival neighbouring college of St John's. I like to think that the topic of my lectures is not so very distant from his own interests. He was himself a part of the Irish diaspora, once a soldier in the British army, and always a sharp observer of the points at which the grand sweep of history comes up against the idiosyncrasies and eccentricities of real people.

My colleagues at the University of Ulster have been extremely tolerant of my obsession with the First World War and its memorials, some of which is evident in the writing that follows. The University has been most generous with its support for my research, and I would particularly like to thank Tom Fraser and Alan Sharp for their constant encouragement. Paul Arthur and Alan Bairner offered much friendly criticism, of which some was constructive. My students, on whom for some years I have inflicted a specialised course on 'Ireland and the Great War', have allowed me to test out my ideas on them. A recent graduate, Sylvia Carr, generously shared some of her material on women's war work with me.

A great host of other people have helped me along the way, only some of whom I can thank individually. Jane Leonard has always shared her enthusiasm and special knowledge of the subject. At a late stage Marie Therese Flanagan assisted with her linguistic skills. I owe other debts to Tom Bartlett, Philip Ollerenshaw, Tony Hart, Linda Longmore and Dermot Lucey, editor of *Times Past*, journal of the Ballincollig Community School Local History Society. Although much of the text that follows draws on the work of academic historians, as I have noted in the bibliographical essay, we owe much to the work of enthusiasts outside the sphere of professional scholarship. Above all, we are indebted to Kevin Myers of the *Irish Times*, who (almost single-handedly it seems) created and has sustained a lively public interest in Ireland's engagement with the Great War.

I have been privileged to visit some of the battlefields of the Western Front with real experts, including Peter Simkins, late of the Imperial War Museum, and Piet Chielens of the 'In Flanders Fields' Museum at Iper/Ypres. I was introduced to Piet by Jacquey Visick, whose intelligent and penetrating interest in the Great War has been a particular inspiration. Further afield I profited greatly from a year's sabbatical (partly funded by a research grant from the British Academy) spent in Australia at the Australian National University, where Ken Inglis was a marvellous colleague, and the Australian Defence Force Academy, where Robin Prior's companionable good advice was often to the point. I particularly remember a very congenial lunch at the Arts Café, Canberra, on 21 May 1998, with Robin and Sally Visick where the basic scheme for these lectures was drawn up. Joan

Beaumont, Peter Dennis, Brian Kennedy, Chris Pugsley and Trevor Wilson also assisted in ways that were not just academic. In New Zealand, Eric Pawson, Jock Phillips and Simon Swaffield helped me understand the legacy of the war in that country.

I would like to acknowledge the particular help I had with illustrations from Bruce Arnold, Alan Hobart (Pyms Gallery), Michael Kenny (National Museum of Ireland), Ron Saunders (British Pathe), Carol Walker (Somme Association) and Tony Feenan of the University of Ulster whose technical expertise was indispensable. The help of Sally Visick (and Designs Matter) with pictures was just a tiny fraction of the support she gave. Bill Davies at Cambridge University Press not only came to all the lectures, but also has been an exemplary editor, as has Karen Anderson Howes, who meticulously copy-edited the text.

Finally, I must thank my mother and my late father, who constantly encouraged me and helped in many practical ways, not least by photographing war memorials throughout Ireland and elsewhere. My cousin Bob Hackett in Canada provided some valuable information about his father Bert Hackett's war service. The dedication of the book speaks for itself, and I still treasure the correspondence and conversations I had with my great-uncle Robert England who went over the top at Vimy Ridge in 1917 and was twice wounded in the conflict. In old age he recalled the 'forgotten deeds of long-lost valiant men'. But, through his professional involvement with the civil re-establishment of war veterans, he also knew well that the impact, and the cost, of war is not confined to the battlefield.

Abbreviations

GOC	general-officer-commanding
GPO	General Post Office
ICA	Irish Citizen Army
IFS	Irish Free State
IRA	Irish Republican Army
IRB	Irish Republican Brotherhood
IWM	Imperial War Museum
NAI	National Archives of Ireland
PRO	Public Record Office (Kew)
UVF	Ulster Volunteer Force

Introduction

In recent years there has been a significant growth of historical interest concerning Ireland and the First World War. Indeed, it may not be too strong to argue that there has been a historiographical revolution involving the ways in which we regard the Great War years in Ireland. Scholars have begun to modify that 'national amnesia' which F. X. Martin identified in 1967 as applying to nationalist Ireland's involvement with the war.[1] The volume of published work has steadily expanded, led, above all, by that of David Fitzpatrick at Trinity College, Dublin.[2] Although we are not yet absolutely embarrassed with the richness of Irish Great War studies, much has now been done, enough, at any rate, to enable us to look intelligently and with a more informed perspective than hitherto on the period. I have drawn heavily on my own work on the impact of the war on Ireland, especially in cultural terms, and also on that of many other scholars who have helped to illuminate this once shadowy corner of Ireland's modern history. My intention with these lectures, however, in keeping with their public nature, was not just to synthesise this scholarship and (one might hope) advance the academic study of the topic, but also to reach out to a wider, less specialised audience.

The historiography of early twentieth-century Ireland has conventionally been dominated, for quite understandable reasons, by accounts of the often violent conflict between nationalism and unionism; by the clash of soldiers fighting for one side or the other. One of the merits of time passing, of a longer historical perspective, is that we need not necessarily see the Irish soldiers of the Great War and the immediately following years as no more than diametrically opposed contending groups. Certainly they fought against each other in 1916 and after, and certainly their *differences*, above all else, were emphasised during those years. But now, over eighty years on, that the sharp political divergence of that time appears to matter less than it did, we can begin to perceive some of the common factors and impulses which made those Irish people act as they did.

To be sure, paths diverged during the war, and *because* of the war, but if we view the development of 'advanced nationalism', the outbreak of the Easter Rising in 1916 and so on not as some completely separate narrative distinct from the world war, but as an integral part of essentially the same story, then the Great War itself becomes the single most central experience of twentieth-century Ireland, not just, nor least, for what happened at the time, but in its longer-term legacy and the meaning which we can draw from it today. In the matters of enlistment and mobilisation, of fighting and suffering casualties, it seems to me that the separate experiences of Redmondites, unionists and advanced nationalists actually constitute a series of 'parallel texts', in which the similarities might be more significant than the differences, great though they were in political terms. So it is, too, with the cultural responses to the events of these years, and the longer-term commemoration of the conflict, a fact clearly demonstrated by the recent conjunction of a new Irish First World War memorial in Flanders with the current Northern Ireland 'peace process'.

There is, too, a parallel to be drawn between August and September 1914 and 22 May 1998, when the overwhelming majority of people in Ireland, north and south, nationalist and unionist, Catholic and Protestant, voted in favour of the 'Good Friday Agreement', settled a few weeks before. Not since the early months of the Great War had everyone on the island of Ireland (so far as we can tell) been so unequivocally behind the same political objective. In both cases only a tiny, eccentric collection of irreconcilables dissented from the majority. So, there may be merit in looking back to and exploring that shared experience, to probe its meaning and see if it has anything to say to us today.

The late autumn of 1998 was also a particularly apt time to address the subject of Ireland and the Great War. The timetable of the lectures was deliberately designed so that the third lecture, 'Imagination', was delivered on Wednesday 11 November, the eightieth anniversary of the armistice and the day on which the Irish 'Peace Tower' at Mesen/Messines was dedicated. The human cost of the Great War was much in mind as I prepared and delivered the lectures, as was that of our thirty years' conflict in Northern Ireland. Fatally obsessed with *difference*, in Ireland we too often fail to perceive the similarities of our predicament, upon which we must build if any lasting 'peace' is to be established on our island. By identifying and exploring those similarities in the context of the Great War and its legacy, I hope in some small way to contribute to the process by which we can come to live peaceably with our neighbours, both in Ireland and throughout the wider archipelago.

There are private as well as public motives for this work. Among my earliest memories is one of my grandmother weeping in the kitchen at home. It was, I was told, the anniversary of the death of her twin, Uncle Willie, in France in November 1918. It is an illustration of both how recent and how remote the First World War is that this memory is of about forty years ago, more or less the same period of time between then and the end of the war. At an intimate, family level I have been exploring the events which caused my grandmother such pain. I have been seeking to explain what extraordinary circumstances took

Uncle Willie from his emigrant's life in Canada to that 'corner of a foreign field' in France, and to examine the private, as well as the public, legacy of that family tragedy, just one amongst so very many.

1 Obligation: 'Irishmen remember Belgium'

Enlisting for war service

In the late 1960s a well-meaning and diligent but unsophisticated military historian (and I hope that is not a tautology) called Henry Harris, a retired British army major, wrote a pioneering account of Irish units in the First World War. For the first time, declared G. A. Hayes-McCoy, the doyen of Irish military history, their story was told 'as one continuous narrative'.[1] In this book and in a chapter on Irish recruitment (commissioned, significantly enough, for a volume of essays on the 1916 Rising) Harris, following an impressive but deeply flawed review of statistical evidence, contended that some 500,000 Irishmen had enlisted in the British forces during the war.[2] In fact, the *minimum* number of Irishmen whom he claimed were *known* to have served was 'nearly 300,000', but he compared that with what he called the number of 'known dead', 49,435, who were recorded in the eight volumes of *Ireland's Memorial Records* produced in 1923 under the auspices of the Irish National War Memorial. There was, he averred, '*no* doubt about the number of dead' and, since 'statistics of casualties for the Great War show a ratio of 1:10 for deaths to the total numbers engaged', the figure for Irish enlistment must approach (at least) the magic figure of half a million individuals.

The estimates of Irish enlistment made by historians have varied quite considerably, from Edmund Curtis's 100,000 in 1936[3] to Harris's half a million thirty years later.

5

The reasons for these variations may lie not only in the
'casual manner' in which the figures have frequently been
compiled – as J. J. Lee has complained[4] – but also because
of political considerations which underlie any examination
of the period. In short, and to put it crudely, commentators
sympathetic towards unionism may tend to boost the
figures, as, perhaps, will some seeking to relegitimise
Redmondite constitutionalism; more extreme nationalists
may seek to reduce or at least belittle them. David
Fitzpatrick's careful, and I think reliable, calculations give
us a figure of about 210,000 as Ireland's 'aggregate male
contribution to the wartime forces'. This, however, does
not include natives of Ireland who joined units in Britain,
the empire or the USA.[5]

Even before conscription was applied in Great Britain,
Ireland's response to the call for recruits was less enthu-
siastic than in other parts of the United Kingdom.
Nevertheless, recent research (by Patrick Callan, David
Fitzpatrick and others) has shown that Ireland was not so
dramatically out of kilter with other parts of Britain and
the empire as has sometimes been assumed. Reporting on
recruitment during the first three months of the war (to 4
November 1914), Lord Midleton told the House of Lords
in January 1915 that Scotland had produced the best
returns of 237 recruits for every 10,000 population. In
England, industrial and urban areas had provided more
men than purely agricultural regions. Lancashire, for
example, had 178, while London and the home counties
had returned 170 men per 10,000. The figure for Ulster,
Dublin, Wicklow, Carlow and Kildare was 127. By contrast, that for the west of England was 88 and for East
Anglia, 80, but the agricultural districts of southern
Ireland produced only 32.[6]

During the first eighteen months of the war (to the end
of February 1916), when voluntary enlistment applied
throughout the United Kingdom, Irish recruitment fell off
quite dramatically, but in almost exactly the same proportions as in England, Scotland and Wales. For Ireland,

Table 1   *Recruits raised in Ireland for the war, for each six-month period*

PERIOD	TOTAL	INDEX
4 August 1914 to February 1915	50,107	100
February 1915 to August 1915	25,235	50
August 1915 to February 1916	19,801	40
February 1916 to August 1916	9,323	19
August 1916 to February 1917	8,178	16
February 1917 to August 1917	5,609	11
August 1917 to February 1918	6,550	13
February 1918 to August 1918	5,812	12
August 1918 to 11 November 1918 (3½ months)	9,845	20
Total	140,460[a]	

Note:

[a] This figure differs slightly from that of Fitzpatrick, who suggests that about 144,000 recruits were raised during the war. The balance of Fitzpatrick's total of 210,000 is made up of the 58,000 existing Irish regulars and reservists in 1914 and several thousand officers not otherwise included in the statistics (Fitzpatrick, 'Militarism in Ireland', pp. 386, 388).

Source: Callan, 'British recruitment in Ireland', p. 49.

Patrick Callan has calculated a six-monthly recruiting index for the whole war (see table 1). If the first six-month period – the peak period for voluntary enlistments – is 100, the second is 50 and the third 40. Despite the fact that the recruiting response for Ireland as a whole was worse than that for the rest of the United Kingdom, the rate of decline was very similar. The British index figures for the first three periods of six months are 100, 50 and 39.[7] From February 1916 (before the Easter Rising) there was a further sharp drop in Irish recruiting, with only half as many men enlisting between February and August 1916 as had done so during the previous six months. After this the Irish returns dip still further, the lowest point being reached during February–August 1917, with a recruiting index of just 11. Thereafter recruiting picked up slightly over twelve months, and then quite markedly in the last three-and-a-half months of the war, from August to 11 November 1918. More men joined up during this short period than had done so during February–August 1916. Partly this was in response to a special voluntary recruiting effort, which if successful was to be a possible alternative to conscription.[8]

The remarkable response to the 1918 recruiting campaign casts some doubt on there being an unequivocally direct correlation between recruitment and political opinion. Army officials in Ireland certainly believed that social and economic factors were more important than political atmosphere. Even more basic considerations constrained recruitment. In the spring of 1918 one observer reported that 'without in any way discounting the very live National Feeling in Ireland today, the fear of conscription is the ordinary elementary fear of the average healthy human being of being tortured and killed'.[9] In 1918, moreover, Irishmen were encouraged to enlist in non-combatant branches of the armed services based at home. The army, too, seems to have been held in low regard, an attitude which had perhaps grown up since the 1916 Rising, but also one which displayed a healthily pragmatic appreciation of the risks accompanying enlistment. In 1918, 56 per cent of the recruits went to the Royal Air Force – attracted, among other things, by the labouring and technical opportunities, with only 36 per cent to the army, and the rest to the Royal Navy.[10]

There is no way of telling for certain whether the pattern of voluntary recruitment in Great Britain would have followed that of Ireland had conscription *not* been introduced, but the available evidence suggests that the Irish experience after February 1916 may not have been wholly unrepresentative of the voluntary spirit of service throughout the United Kingdom. The progressive (though not consistently so) unwillingness of Irishmen to serve Britain and, by extension, the empire may say as much about contemporary attitudes to the war throughout the British Isles as it does about political circumstances in Ireland. It would be unwise to argue that the growth of separatist nationalism, and the concomitant alienation of much Irish political opinion from the British link, had *no* effect on recruitment, but that effect may have been less than has hitherto generally been supposed. Nevertheless, any explanation of the causes of enlistment has to explain not just the 50,000 who joined up in the first six months of the war, but the 90,000 who enlisted in the succeeding forty-five months.

For us, with the crystal clarity of hindsight, and in an age when such factors as patriotism and duty no longer have the power they apparently once had, the voluntary enlistment of adult males to participate in the Great War seems an irrational and crazy act. A staple of popular perceptions of the Great War is of great crowds of men and women across Europe clamouring for war in the late summer of 1914, and the men flocking in droves to the colours. We see these poor devils as being duped in some way, bamboozled into joining up by the chauvinistic, emotional blackmail of cynical political leaders. The men enlisted, as Philip Orr suggests, 'in a surge of naive patriotism',[11] and we might feel that the epithet 'naive' is itself redundant in this context.

When considering the question of enlistment the first thing to remember about Ireland is that all the Irishmen (like all the Australians and, with some qualification, all the Indians[12]) who joined up were volunteers. Some Irish Great War memorials differ from British ones in that they commemorate men who *willingly* gave their lives. The Irish did not *have* to go, certainly in any legal sense. We should, therefore, not underestimate the rationality of their decision to enlist. These men were not wholly ignorant, or unintelligent, or insensitive, and we insult them and their memory by sweepingly categorising them as dupes. They may have been foolish (and even that is debatable), but they were not all fools. This is despite Tom Kettle's poetic assertion to the contrary in his poignant and

well-known sonnet, 'To My Daughter Betty', written on 4
September 1916, five days before his own death in action
on the Somme:

> Know that we fools, now with the foolish dead,
> Died not for flag, nor King, nor Emperor,
> But for a dream, born in a herdsman's shed,
> And for the secret Scripture of the poor.[13]

But Kettle also here touches precisely on the matter of
motivation, to which I want to turn.

The question of why men joined for service in the First
World War remains a most important and difficult one. It is
clear, however, that no monocausal explanation will suffice.
The process of enlistment is complex and the forces impel-
ling men to take the king's shilling cover a spectrum which
encompasses low as well as high causes: venal and valiant,
selfish and selfless. We are inclined to forget (though John
Grigg, Trevor Wilson and Brian Bond have tried to remind
us[14]) that among the motives for enlistment there was a
widely accepted moral justification for going to war against
Germany. It has been described as the war for Big Words:
King, Country, Freedom, Duty, Democracy, Liberty, and
Civilisation (as in the inscription on the victory medal
awarded to all British servicemen: 'The Great War for
Civilisation 1914–1919'). Clearly these Big Words are
useful, perhaps essential, to political leaders; it is the
vocabulary that they habitually use in times of great
national crisis. But in the summer and autumn of 1914 it
may have been that these words did not operate merely at a
high rhetorical level. There is evidence that concepts of
national duty and high moral motivation had real meaning
among those crowds of volunteers pressing to get into the
recruiting offices.

Tom Kettle, poet, scholar, philosopher, sometime
Nationalist MP, who when war broke out had been in
Belgium buying guns for the nationalist Irish Volunteers,
noted that men (including himself) went because the cause
was a just one. It was the cause of small nations, Serbia and

Figure 1.1   This recruiting leaflet, dating probably from the autumn of 1914, exhorted volunteers to 'join the Irish Army Corps today . . . Your place is on the Battlefield and no true Irishman should be sought or found elsewhere.'

Belgium, which Austria and Germany had outraged, and which Britain and its allies had taken up. And this made it right for Ireland to fight on England's side. 'This war is without parallel. Britain, France and Russia enter it', he said with more enthusiasm than accuracy, 'purged from their past sins of domination.'[15] 'Irishmen', exhorted an early wartime recruiting pamphlet, 'Remember Belgium!' Noting the deplorable, 'Hunnish' atrocities which had been reported to a shocked population back home, the pamphlet further asserted that 'What has happened in Belgium might by now be taking place in Ireland but for the British Fleet and the Allied Armies.'[16] 'The war', argued the *Cork Free Press*, 'is against military despotism and in defence of the integrity of small nations. "Louvain" and "Rheims" alone [both places devastated during the German advance] are cries which would stir the blood of Catholic Irishmen.'[17] Though he stopped short of explicitly encouraging Irishmen to enlist, the Catholic primate, Cardinal Logue, denounced 'the barbarism of the Germans in burning Rheims Cathedral'.[18] 'Ireland', said the *Westmeath Examiner*, 'is at war with the forces of despotism.'[19]

Early in September 1914 the veteran Nationalist MP William O'Brien told a meeting in Cork that 'in fighting England's battle in the particular circumstance of [the] war . . . they were fighting the most effective battle for Ireland's liberty'.[20] In the north, too, the link was made with 'gallant little' (though not perhaps in this case Catholic) Belgium. Some verses with an apparent English provenance, were published in the *Newtownards Chronicle*:

> Think, from our cliffs the eye can almost see
> Fair Belgian homes go up in smoke and flame.
> Unless you fight to keep your homeland free,
> She too must know the agony and shame.[21]

As we have seen, it was not just the army recruiting authorities who linked Ireland and Belgium, but Irish Nationalists too. In mid-September 1914 not only was the British Expeditionary Force retreating from the Belgian

Figure 1.2 An early example of the 'What did you do in the war, father?' type of poster. It reminds us that Irishmen fought for freedom in 1915 as well as 1916.

town of Mons in some disarray, but on 18 September the third Irish Home Rule Bill became law, although its operation was suspended for the duration of hostilities. No one, or almost no one, soldier or politician, anticipated that the war would drag on for as long as it did. Not just the war, but also the fraught journey to Home Rule, might be 'over by Christmas'.

The formal, legal achievement of devolution was crucial for John Redmond, leader of the Irish Parliamentary Party and the dominant nationalist politician of the day, and it enabled him to pledge the Irish Volunteers – already committed to home defence – fully to the war effort in a speech at Woodenbridge, County Wicklow, on 20 September. 'The interests of Ireland – of the whole of Ireland – are at stake in this war', he declared: true and prophetic words indeed. He drew out the grand causes, the Big Words:

> The war is undertaken in defence of the highest principles
> of religion and morality and right, and it would be a

disgrace for ever to our country, and a reproach to her
manhood, and a denial of the lessons of her history, if
young Ireland confined their efforts to remaining at home
to defend the shores of Ireland from an unlikely invasion,
and shrunk from the duty of proving on the field of battle
that gallantry and courage which has distinguished our
race all through its history.[22]

While drawing on Ireland's alleged special military
prowess, Redmond, with his call to 'young Ireland', also
neatly worked in an allusion to the radical, revolutionary
tradition. For a long time it was unfashionable to admire
Redmond, though Paul Bew, *inter alios*, has done much
sympathetically to reconstruct what he calls 'the project of
"Redmondism"'.[23] Perhaps we should give him the benefit
of the doubt and allow that the speech at Woodenbridge,
this 'fateful speech',[24] was not mere political flannel, but
that he, and thousands of others, actually believed that the
cause of Ireland was worth fighting for in Flanders and in
France. Writing ten years after the event, the Protestant
nationalist Stephen Gwynn asserted that by supporting
the war effort the Redmondites were not only sealing the
'compact' of Home Rule but also 'doing their best to lessen
the difficulties with Ulster'.[25] This theme – perhaps aspiration would be the better word – of the reconciling power of
common war service is one which we shall encounter again.
Indeed, it has survived into the 1990s.

Redmond's Woodenbridge speech also confirms how,
even for constitutional nationalists, England's – and the
empire's – extremity was Ireland's opportunity. If on a
high public level the offer of Irish recruits was apparently
unconditional, in practical terms the need to secure political advantage remained strong. Redmond did not sud-
denly cease being a party leader with the onset of war. Nor,
of course, did Sir Edward Carson, the Unionist leader. It
is clear that, despite their public protestations of loyalty,
during August 1914 both leaders 'were intent on using
their volunteers to exercise pressure on the government in

their own favour'.[26] Redmond, as we have seen, held off calling unconditionally for recruits until the Home Rule bill was safely passed. In mid-August Carson had said that the Ulster Volunteer Force could immediately provide two divisions for foreign service, but only if the measure were postponed. Unlike the Nationalists, however, the Unionists were hoisted with their own patriotic petard. As David and Josephine Howie have noted, 'the war had greatly weakened the Unionists' bargaining position, for their patriotism prevented them from renewing their threat of civil war in Ulster'.[27] Events in Belgium proved decisive. The perilous military situation caused by the powerful German advance during the last week of August enabled the British prime minister, Herbert Asquith, to force the issue with Carson and secure an unconditional offer of Ulster recruits for Lord Kitchener's 'New Army' – the mass volunteer force which the secretary for war raised following the outbreak of the conflict.

The cause of Ulster itself was also adduced in justifying support for the war, though it was on the whole less explicitly expressed than that of Ireland. Unionism, after all, was already a practical demonstration of common cause with the rest of the United Kingdom, and the war amply provided unionists in Ireland, north and south, with an opportunity to subsume their efforts in the wider national enterprise. Yet the potential benefits for the province were not lost, for example in another piece of doggerel published in October 1914:

> And wherever the fight is hottest,
> And the sorest task is set,
> ULSTER WILL STRIKE FOR ENGLAND –
> AND ENGLAND WILL NOT FORGET.[28]

For Ulstermen there was an additional debt of honour to be repaid. The 'Curragh incident' of March 1914, when British officers had resigned their commissions rather than (as they thought) coerce Ulster into Home Rule, provided a supplementary reason why unionists should enlist. 'The

Army stood by us in our darkest hour', wrote Belfast linen merchant Adam Duffin to Edward Carson, 'and we must stand with them and for the Empire now.' This, he added, being a businessman, 'is not only the most patriotic course but the most politic'.[29] Carson may have agreed, and throughout the first month of the war strove to secure political advantage from the promise of loyalist recruits. Publicly, however, on 7 September he declared that 'we do not seek to purchase terms by selling our patriotism . . . England's difficulty is our difficulty.'[30]

Another factor stimulating enlistment was urgent military need. Some evidence of both United Kingdom and Irish enlistments challenges the 'surge of naive patriotism' analysis. Although (as every schoolchild knows) there was a 'rush to the colours' at the start of the Great War, Peter Simkins has stressed that in the United Kingdom the recruiting peak for the whole war was not the beginning of August 1914, but the last week of the month and the first two weeks of September, that is to say, after the news of the headlong retreat from Mons had arrived back home. How do we explain this curious fact? Perhaps it was a keen apprehension of possible defeat that drew the greatest number to the colours in the early weeks of the war.

In his definitive study of 'Kitchener's armies', Simkins also counsels that we should not get the initial recruiting surge out of proportion. Only about one-third of the volunteers who enlisted in the British forces during the First World War – that is, between the start of the war and January 1916 when conscription was introduced in Great Britain – actually joined up in August and September 1914. Simkins has concluded that the bulk of volunteers for Kitchener's 'New Armies' were motivated 'by a sense of duty and obligation rather than missionary zeal'.[31] While these may not be mutually exclusive categories, the pattern of Irish recruitment does suggest something more complex than a simple – or simplistic – Pavlovian response to some martial and patriotic tocsin.

Figure 1.3 A dramatic poster produced in May 1915 by the Central Council for the Organisation of Recruiting in Ireland which oversaw propaganda from 1914 to October 1915, when it was replaced by the more professionally based Department of Recruiting in Ireland.

In the Royal Munster Fusiliers district, with recruiting offices in Cork, Limerick, Tralee and Kinsale, the highest weekly total was returned in the third week of the war, with the second and fifth weeks following closely behind.[32] In this district, moreover, enlistments for the first three months of 1915 were 12 per cent higher than for the last three months of 1914.[33] Also reinforcing Peter Simkins's emphasis of the extent to which recruiting was sustained after the initial surge are David Fitzpatrick's calculations of average Irish daily enlistment rates. These show that, while the highest daily average was indeed in August 1914, and the broad trend was downwards, the decline was by no means unremitting. Recruitment dipped significantly (by some 20 per cent) after August 1914, but picked up again from February to April 1915, with a further peak in September 1915. A decline in enlistments in late 1917 was followed by an increase in the spring of 1918.[34] Irish responses were also affected by the problems and delays in creating specifically 'Irish' and 'Ulster' divisions – there was more hesitation regarding the former than the latter – and do not precisely reflect Peter Simkins's findings. Yet, while Irish enlistments may not unambiguously be seen as a response to the *urgent* military need posed by the retreat from Mons, the figures seem to reflect at least some response to non-urgent and continuing military need, again suggesting that enlistment was perhaps a more rational phenomenon than has been allowed in the past.

Economic rationality is a staple explanation of Irish recruitment to the British armed services. 'Hundreds of working-class Dubliners, signing up largely for economic reasons', writes Myles Dungan, 'were among the 45,000 men who joined the various battalions of the Dublin Fusiliers over the four years of the conflict.'[35] For those who 'took the king's shilling', it is argued that the money is the important component of the contract, not whose it is. Soldiering is simply another job, steadier than most, if occasionally rather more hazardous. In a society with a high incidence of emigration, the army offered a kind of assisted passage away from home, but one with steady employment and a pension at the end. If this were the case in peacetime, then maybe it applied in war as well. There is certainly evidence to confirm the importance of the economic factor. Jim Donaghy in Derry was laid off from the linen mill where he worked during the first week of the war so he decided to enlist.[36] At the other end of the island, as calculated in Thomas Dooley's intensely absorbing study, James English, a labourer of Wexford, found that, with separation allowances, he and his family were 154 per cent better off once he was soldiering.[37] Some recruiting calls explicitly emphasised the value of army pay and dependants' allowances.[38]

Economic analyses can fit the geographical pattern of military recruitment in both peace- and wartime, where urban centres, with readier numbers of unskilled unemployed men, always recruit better than rural areas. Economic causes – secular factors – ostensibly providing a 'scientific' explanation, are attractive to many historians for they bypass the difficulties presented by more intangible influences. If it be simply a matter of labour supply and demand, then we need not tiptoe gingerly into the minefield of more subjective sentimental, emotional or (God forbid) psychological motivations.

James Connolly had himself served in the British army and, as befits a socialist revolutionary, he argued that British colonial exploitation had so depressed employment and wages in Ireland that men had no alternative to joining up. It was simply 'economic conscription'. 'Fighting at the front today', he asserted in 1915, 'there are many thousands whose soul revolts against what they are doing, but who must nevertheless continue fighting and murdering because they were deprived of a living at home, and compelled to enlist that those dear to them might not starve.'[39]

The economic case seems plausible, and common sense suggests that it must have some role to play, yet David Fitzpatrick, in a typically penetrating article, has concluded that the pattern of Great War recruitment in

Ireland 'cannot be understood through the logic of economic rationality'. Among the occupational groups *most*
likely to join up were men (especially in Ulster) from the
relatively prosperous shipbuilding industry. Far from
enlistments being heaviest among those with *in*secure
employment prospects, Fitzpatrick concluded that 'collective pressures for enlistment were particularly effective in
industries with stable and well-organised work forces'. He
also examined the relative propensity of Catholics and
Protestants to join up and found that there was little evidence to support the contemporary Unionist assertion that
Catholic Nationalists as a group were reluctant to enlist.
What he did find was that men, both Catholic and
Protestant, in industrialised Ulster as a whole were more
likely to enlist than those from the rest of Ireland. He also
discovered that previous service in either the Ulster
Volunteers or the Irish Volunteers tended to dispose men
towards joining up. His overall conclusion, therefore, was
that before 1916 – though less so after – 'the readiness of
individuals to join the colours was largely determined by
the attitudes and behaviour of comrades – kinsmen, neighbours, and fellow-members of organizations and fraterni-
ties', rather than by economic, religious or political
factors.[40]

Fitzpatrick's work suggests that we shall have to contemplate some other factors – social and sentimental considerations, even psychological pressures. Perhaps there are Big
Words here, too, though not quite the same ones as in the
grand, patriotic discourse already noted, but important
words all the same: excitement, adventure, friendship,
comradeship, 'mateship' (the vital force that the journalist
and military historian Charles Bean identified as particularly distinguishing the close cohesion and spirit of the all-
volunteer Australian soldiers). There is that sense of
invulnerable enterprise which propels young men – and
their *youth* is really important – almost lightheartedly to
war: an impulse captured with exceptional resonance by
Samuel Hynes in *The Soldiers' Tale*. 'War', he writes,

'brings to any society its electric, exhilarating atmosphere, and young men rush to join in it, however grim the stories of war they have read and accepted as the truth.'[41]

Wallace Lyon was one young Irishman who enlisted in the Leinster Regiment at the start of the war. A Protestant (from the Church of Ireland) who had been educated at a Jesuit school (Belvedere College in Dublin), he had worked for the British American Tobacco Company in India before the war. 'Personally', he recalled, 'I cannot claim to have been actuated by any excess of loyalty to King and Country. I had enjoyed pig sticking in India, and I thought it would be great fun to try my hand at the Uhlans.'[42] Tom Barry, who became a celebrated IRA leader in West Cork, was similarly enthused to enlist. In June 1915 he 'decided to see what this Great War was like'. He was then in his '17th year', a late adolescent. Indifferent to Redmond's appeal that joining up would help secure Home Rule, 'not influenced by the lurid appeal to fight to save Belgium or small nations . . . I went to the war for no other reason than that I wanted to see what war was like, to get a gun, to see new countries and to feel a grown man'.[43] 'Among the motives at work', maintained Dorothy Macardle ('hagiographer royal to the Republic'[44]) were 'the natural vitality of Irish youth and inherent love of adventure'.[45] There is more than a hint here of that powerful mythic figure, the 'fighting Irishman', as there is in Redmond's Woodenbridge speech, when he spoke of 'that gallantry and courage' which had distinguished 'our race' all through its history.

The recruiting authorities in Ireland certainly exploited the supposed Irish martial tradition, though with varying success. In his entertaining though perhaps not wholly reliable memoirs, Sir Henry Robinson, executive head of the Irish Local Government Board, complained that recruiting in Ireland was 'rather badly handled. The war pictures, cinemas and posters were simply terrifying.' Battlefield scenes, he thought, were more likely to dissuade than attract recruits. 'Proper, attractive posters . . . might have made a considerable difference.' For example, 'the picture of the Irish Guards in France, instead of showing a lot of careworn men seen through fire and smoke', should have 'portrayed a number of laughing young soldiers sitting outside a cafe with girls on their knees and brimming goblets of porter on the table beside them'.[46]

One recruiting pamphlet, in fact, approached Robinson's diverting ideal: *Ireland's Cause*, which unusually had parallel texts in Irish and English. Herein the soldier's life and comforts were attractively outlined. Good and regular meals, it declared, were provided in the most unpromising circumstances: 'even in the blackest days of the retreat from Mons the commissariat performed miracles and served hot meals to the weary soldiers. Meal-time is a jolly time in the Army, and dissatisfied men are unknown.' A page entitled 'the Soldier at the Front' was unexpectedly matched with an illustration of soldiers boxing and playing football. John Redmond, who visited the battle-zone in November 1915, was quoted on the high quality of the trenches and the 'enormous improvements' that had been made in them since the winter of 1914–15. Most had boarded floors, others were of brick; and although in really wet weather it was 'impossible to prevent them turning into a morass of mud and water', the men were provided 'with long indiarubber boots, which go right up over their thighs like fishing waders'. Quoted from a speech at his home town of Waterford in December 1915, Redmond reported that he had 'met every Irish regiment at the front'. All they asked of Ireland, he said, was 'that Ireland should stand by them' and, bearing mind the slackening flow of recruits from home, send them 'such reserves as are necessary to keep those regiments at their full strength, *and to keep them Irish regiments*'.[47]

Sustained purity of Irishness was not, for the most part, a problem which affected the Irish Volunteers, though when we look at enlistment on the separatist, republican side of the nationalist movement we find many similarities with that for service in the British armed forces. But here we also find a historiographical paradox. What appears to be, if not a *surge*, at least a growing impulse of 'naive patriotism' – what else is motivating Patrick Pearse and his colleagues? – is by and large accepted as if it were a perfectly normal and understandable state of affairs. Yet the parallels seem close. If the recruits for the Great War are advancing *en masse* like lemmings to military disaster, so too are the Irish Volunteers of 1914 and 1915, although in much, much smaller numbers. By early 1916 there were about 146,000 of the former (of whom 95,000 had joined up since August 1914) as compared with about 5,000 of the latter. The precise number who rallied to the separatist side remains conjectural; the various estimates put forward have been, no doubt, as influenced by emotional and political considerations as the figures for enlistment in the British forces. Henry Harris's chapter-title-cum-estimate, 'The *other* half million' (emphasis added), characterises these servicemen as distinct and separate from the mass of Irish people, and seems to imply that an equivalent number stayed behind and took the republican nationalist side. But at no stage did the numbers of Volunteers of whatever stripe, reach 200,000, let alone 500,000.

There is a mirror image here, and while we may try to recover the rationality of enlistment in the British forces, or at least explore the possibility of there being a rational dimension to the process, we can also investigate the same zone of rationality as it affected republicans willingly choosing (they were all volunteers as well) to fight for their cause.

'Just cause' was certainly taken as self-evident by the republicans who split from Redmond after the Woodenbridge speech in September 1914, forming the Irish Volunteers, as opposed to Redmond's National Volunteers. At the first convention of the (schismatic) Irish Volunteers, on 25 October 1914, Eoin MacNeill declared that 'the issue between Mr Redmond and ourselves' was 'clear and simple'. Repudiating Redmond's conflation of Ireland, Belgium and the British decision to go to war,

MacNeill said that the issue was whether the Irish Volunteers were 'pledged to the cause of Ireland, of all Ireland, and of Ireland only', or were 'bound to serve the Imperial Government in defence of the British Empire'.[48] The following spring Patrick Pearse bluntly stated 'we have no desire, no ambition but the integrity, the honour, and the freedom of our native land. We want recruits', he continued, 'because we are sure of the rightness of our cause.'[49]

Pearse was particularly invigorated by the martial courage displayed in the war. In December 1915 he proclaimed that 'the last sixteen months have been the most glorious in the history of Europe. Heroism has come back to the earth.' The basis of this heroism, he argued, was patriotism, which underpinned 'Belgium defending her soil', just as much as 'Turkey fighting with her back to Constantinople'. And, in a much-quoted passage, we seem to find Pearse exulting in the blood sacrifice of the war: 'It is good for the world that such things should be done. The old heart of the earth needed to be warmed with the red wine of the battlefields.'[50] While Pearse's bloodthirsty tone went rather further than political wisdom (or even good taste) might allow – James Connolly said they were the words of 'a blithering idiot'[51] – he was certainly not alone in believing that the end justified the means. In this he was at one with John Redmond. Others had already asserted that war could be spiritually uplifting. 'War', announced a prominent Belfast Methodist early in the conflict, 'is a kind of purgatory. It is a painful but salutary remedy for softness, slackness and sensuality.'[52] At the end of 1914 James Bennett Keene, Church of Ireland Bishop of Meath, while noting the grievous costs of the war, echoed the theme of purification. 'We believe', he said, 'that this fiery trial will prove to be a purifying discipline. If it lead to a moral and spiritual renewal of our nation the loss will end in gain.'[53]

The demands throughout the United Kingdom for more and more men to feed the apparently insatiable needs of the Western Front had an impact in Ireland in early 1916 when

Figure 1.4 A satirical Sinn Fein treatment of a John Redmond recruiting poster first issued in 1915.

the introduction of conscription in Great Britain drove some fervently nationalist Irishmen back home. Michael Collins, for example, left his job at the Guaranty Trust Company in London, saying he was going 'to join up'. Because of this he got an extra week's pay (which he donated to the Irish Republican Brotherhood) and promptly crossed over to Ireland. There he met up with a group of like-minded activists, 'the refugees', who had also returned to Ireland to avoid conscription and had set up camp at Count Plunkett's home, Larkfield, in Kimmage, County Dublin.[54]

There is, too, an economic dimension to recruitment on the physical-force wing of Irish nationalism. Paul Bew has observed that the particular strength of radical republicanism lay in Dublin and gained support in 1915–16 at a time when unemployment in the city remained high.[55] Unlike Belfast, much of Dublin's industry was of a non-essential character – distilling, brewing, biscuit manufacture and building – and a slackening of economic activity enhanced the potential for social and political unrest. Some of the same collective social factors identified by David Fitzpatrick which carried Ulster and National Volunteers into the British forces obviously worked in a similar fashion to carry a significant number of Irish Volunteers on to the Dublin streets at Easter 1916, even after Eoin MacNeill had officially cancelled the planned operation.

Whether the republican rebels exemplify the 'fighting Irish' or not, many of them were certainly young men imbued with a spirit of adventure. Onlookers remarked on the youth of the rebels. James Stephens noted that among the rebels holding St Stephen's Green 'were some who were only infants – one boy seemed about twelve years of age. He was strutting [in] the centre of the road with a large revolver in his small fist.' St John Ervine, the manager of the Abbey Theatre and who was in Dublin during the Rising, characterised the Volunteers as a mixture of 'middle-aged' labourers, 'young clerks and shop assistants

Begorra, but ye thocht Oi was going to be a thraitor.

Figure 1.5 This picture postcard, no. 5010 in the English firm Bamforth & Company's 'War Cartoons' series, was sent from Ballykinlar army camp, County Down, on 18 September 1914 by John Dillon, a recruit in the 15th Royal Irish Rifles. His unit went over the top on the first day of the Somme, but Dillon survived the war.

and school-teachers, full of generous ideals and emotions . . . and boys, vaguely idealistic and largely thrilled by the desire for romantic enterprise and the hope of high happenings'.[56] Peter Hart's brilliant and meticulous investigation of County Cork confirms the youthfulness of the IRA's membership. A Volunteer over thirty, he records, 'was generally considered an "old man"'.[57]

Some nationalists appear to have joined the British army to gain if not experience, at least arms. We have seen how one of Tom Barry's motivations was 'to get a gun'. Late in 1917 a group of adventurous republicans joined the 11th Battalion Royal Dublin Fusiliers at Wellington (subsequently Griffith) Barracks. One evening they brought a boat along the Grand Canal and made off with all two hundred rifles in the barracks.[58] During the March retreat in 1918 the Scottish writer Eric Linklater found himself serving next to a sergeant of the South Irish Horse. The Irishman's opinion of the war was 'simple and instructive: it was useful training for the approaching conflict with England'. He urged Linklater to join him: 'Scotland and Ireland together: we'd knock the bloody English to hell.' Linklater said he had no quarrel with England. 'Ach', replied the Irishman, 'everybody has a quarrel with England, if they'd only the bloody sense to see it!'[59]

Undoubtedly the likelihood of Irishmen joining what became the IRA when the war was over increased over the period of the conflict. It is scarcely conceivable that Monk Gibbon's experience in the Tipperary town barracks at Christmas 1917 could have happened before the Rising. Late on Christmas night, after much champagne had been drunk, a Munster Fusilier rose to toast 'Ireland a Nation!', and 'went on to say that they were in this struggle against the Germans and would see it through, but that when that struggle had been decided there was another coming, and there was no doubt in his mind on which side he would be found then'.[60] Although in the end there was no huge flood of Great War veterans into the IRA, some did make that perilous passage, no doubt arguing to themselves that the fight for Ireland could as well, if not better, be carried on at home as on some foreign field.

Some of the republican volunteers were women; clearly the rebels were advanced in more than just nationalism. The most famous female rebel was Constance Markiewicz, who like some of the other thirty Irish Citizen Army volunteers out at Easter 1916, carried a firearm. Their sixty Cumann na mBan ('women's association') colleagues were not so privileged. None of them took an active part in the fighting; they were restricted to nursing, cooking and carrying despatches.[61] With this conventional allocation of gender roles Cumann na mBan reflected the situation on the opposing side much more closely than did the ICA. Although women did not serve in combat roles, the scale of the Great War for the first time in Ireland and Britain involved women in a wider social and economic network of

Figure 1.6 Women workers at the Lambkin Brothers factory, Cork, packing tobacco for troops on active service.

support for the war effort. As the nature of modern general war became more 'total', so too did the engagement of the civil population in the conflict. In Great Britain, after conscription was imposed from January 1916, and where an industrialised economy was largely directed to war production, this process was particularly intensified. One result was the increasing 'feminisation' of the workforce; so much so that images of female munitions workers, Women's Land Army volunteers, women bus and tram conductors, and so on have become the stock-in-trade of illustrated war histories.[62]

In Ireland, however, the absence of conscription reduced the pressure for women to take up occupations previously reserved for men, although some women secured war-related employment, especially in the industrialised north-east. But as in the rest of the United

Kingdom, great numbers of women participated in voluntary war work. As yet their efforts and their history are only scrappily recorded, if at all. Modern Ireland's amnesia regarding the First World War still extends to this civil mobilisation of support. While a handful of radical and unrepresentative women have been intensively studied, the huge numbers of Irish women engaged in undoubtedly less exciting, though still serious, wartime activities as yet constitute a kind of historically hidden Ireland.

To a certain extent the Great War was 'good for business' in Ireland.[63] This was especially true in the northeast where the shipbuilding, engineering and textile industries responded to the expanded wartime demand for their products. According to the company history, the great Belfast shipbuilders Harland and Wolff made a 'staggering' contribution to the war effort. With well over 20,000 workers, the company completed 201,070 gross tons of merchant vessels during 1918 alone, as well as substantial numbers of heavy bombers in an entirely new aircraft works.[64] The linen industry, which had been in recession in 1914, faced further difficulties with the interruption of flax supplies from Belgium and Russia. Although 50,000 of the 80,000 workers were female, the workforce was disrupted by military enlistment and a drift to higher-paid munitions work. Demand for aeroplane cloth, however, rose dramatically during the war and the Ministry of Munitions placed contracts valued at over £11,000,000 with Irish firms for some 50,000 miles of this material.[65]

Textile machinery and general engineering concerns secured munitions contracts. One such was James Mackie & Sons in Belfast, who produced an estimated seventy-five million shells. Mackies, indeed, took on a number of women for this work.[66] The Great Southern and Western Railway Company in Dublin produced nearly a million fuse bodies between February 1917 and the end of the war.[67] State-owned 'National Munitions Factories' were established in Dublin, Waterford, Cork and Galway, but they operated on quite a small scale, employing only 700 men and 1,400 women in all. There were a few existing Irish 'war industries', the most notable being Kynoch's high explosives plant at Arklow, County Wicklow, with a workforce of some two thousand and which produced over a hundred tons of cordite a week during the war. But there were attendant risks. On 21 September 1917 twenty-seven workers were killed in an explosion. An official report dismissed wild theories that a German submarine had shelled the factory and suggested that the explosion might have been deliberately caused, though it failed to present any evidence for sabotage, by Sinn Fein or anyone else.[68] The domestic security situation following the Rising, however, seems to have prompted the removal of Thomas Grubb's optical instrument factory (which manufactured all Britain's submarine periscopes) from Rathmines, County Dublin, to St Albans in England in 1917.[69]

Farmers did well during the war. By 1918 the value of agricultural produce was about double what it had been in 1913, although this was in the context of wartime inflation of both prices and wages. Farm labourer wages, for example, rose by between 60 and 70 per cent. Underpinned by compulsory tillage orders, there was a substantial increase (by 1.7 million acres during 1916–18) in the area of tillage, which in turn demanded more labour than did mere grazing. Writing in 1918, Edward Lysaght identified a 'revolution' in Irish farming which had become profitable and more self-supporting than it had been for the previous seventy years.[70] Rural prosperity in turn no doubt undermined the economic impulse for enlistment in the British army. The experience of the fishing industry also illustrates the ways in which the gains and losses of the war touched Irish people at home. Although the disruption of continental, especially Russian, markets affected the herring trade, the volume of whitefish landed increased two-thirds in weight and over four-fold in value between 1914 and 1918. Yet the costs could be high, as demonstrated in April 1918 when two Howth fishing boats were sunk by a German submarine with the loss of five lives.

The following month twelve vessels from the County
Down fishing fleet were also sunk by an enemy U-boat,
though happily no lives were lost.[71] Ships were sunk by
enemy action in Irish waters in every year of the war,
though, apart from the *Lusitania* in 1915, the most devastating incident was the torpedoing of the mail boat *Leinster*
off Dublin Bay on 10 October 1918 with the loss of five
hundred lives.[72]

For those women who secured war employment, the
rewards could be significant. Florence Ross, who got a job
in a shell factory established by the Dublin Dockyard
Company, earned an average of fifty shillings a week, compared to two shillings in her previous employment as an
apprentice dressmaker.[73] And the work could certainly be
fun, as seems to have been the case for the 'foundry girls' at
Mackies in Belfast, who even produced their own in-house
magazine, *The Turret Lathers*. Yet the shadows of the war
fell across them all. One woman's 'Thoughts in a
Munitions Factory' included the following: 'Midst the
laughter and the singing I often wonder why I am with
others engaged in this awful occupation . . . It is difficult to
think of women in the Twentieth Century engaged in such
an occupation, but then we must think of the havoc
wrought by our enemies.'[74] The war also provided opportunities for women in other sectors. Because of the short-
age of men, for the first time in its history the Royal
Victoria Hospital, Belfast, appointed a woman, Dr
Margaret Purce, to be house surgeon.[75] Across Ireland, 239
Voluntary Aid Detachments supplied over 4,500 women
for nursing and auxiliary service at home and abroad.[76] We
know, from a war memorial in St Anne's Church of Ireland
Cathedral in Belfast, that eighteen sisters and staff nurses
of Queen Alexandra's Imperial Military Nursing Service
lost their lives in the war, but the wider extent of enlistment
and engagement in this sphere awaits proper investigation.[77] As I have noted, there were nurses in the GPO in
Dublin at Easter 1916 and some female ICA Volunteers
elsewhere. Forty-six (or so[78]) civilian women were killed in

the Rising, including one nurse, Margaret Keogh, caught in crossfire (a metaphor for the experience of women in the Irish revolution?) as she went to help a fallen Volunteer at the South Dublin Union.[79]

Many thousands of women did voluntary work throughout the war. The Irish War Hospital Supply Depot had 6,000 registered women volunteers in eight subdepots across Ireland manufacturing surgical and other hospital equipment. At the 'Central Red Cross Workrooms' in Dublin, 300 women workers knitted over 20,000 pairs of socks and 10,000 mufflers for the troops. In the north the Ulster Women's Unionist Council established an Ulster Women's Gift Fund for servicemen's 'comforts' which by 1918 had raised over £100,000. They also funded an Ulster Volunteer Force hospital at Pau in southern France.[80] 'Tens of thousands' of women, affirmed one celebratory publication in 1919, 'in the quiet of their homes, worked incessantly for the men at the front'.[81] In the south-west, too, women provided the initiative for many charitable ventures associated with the war, like the Cork Women's Emergency Committee, the Soldiers and Sailors Refreshment Committee and a Tipperary club to help the families of servicemen.[82] As in other spheres, there was a parallel effort on the advanced nationalist side. After the Rising Kathleen Clarke, widow of the executed leader Tom Clarke, with other bereaved women set up what became the Irish National Aid and Volunteer Dependants' Fund. By April 1917 they had collected over £100,000.[83]

Considering the bereaved of the war brings us back to Henry Harris with whom we began. Part of his argument for the 'other half million' was based on the figure of 49,435 'known dead' listed in the eight volumes of *Ireland's Memorial Records*, 'being the names of Irishmen who fell in the Great European War, 1914–1918, compiled by the Committee of the Irish National War Memorial'.[84] Like his half million, this figure also looks inflated. Although the men and women listed were almost certainly dead,[85] their status as 'Irish' is less certain. Included in the

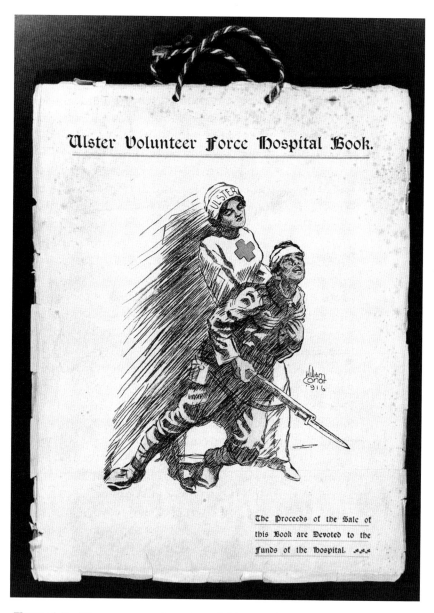

Figure 1.7   There are several versions of this 1916 drawing by the Belfast artist
William Conor, here used on the cover of a fund-raising booklet for
the Ulster Volunteer Force Hospital. Another version, published as
a print by the stationers McGowan & Ingram, was inscribed 'For
Us!'

painstakingly collated lists are men who served in Irish units, including those born outside Ireland, and others in dominion and colonial formations. Many, if not most, of these were part of the Irish diaspora, but the careful statistician may exclude any individuals not unequivocally Irish. Thus the total of 49,000 can be reduced. Kevin Myers has proposed 35,000,[86] as has Patrick Casey who, working from official records of British soldiers who died in the war, has found 29,779 men born in Ireland among the fallen. To this figure he has added a further estimate of 'approximately 5,000' to allow for Irishmen in the armies of British colonies and the USA.[87] In 1926 the registrar-general of the Irish Free State calculated that 27,405 soldiers had died on active service outside the British Isles.[88] David Fitzpatrick, using 'sample analysis', suggested that only about 25,000 of those recorded were both born and enlisted in Ireland.[89] Perhaps so, but these careful yet restrictive criteria may not themselves be completely satisfactory. In the absence of a proper investigation of all 49,000 entries, we may continue to speculate.

In the meantime, and so that among all these dry statistics we should not forget the individuals concerned, I offer one casualty: William Lumley Hackett, listed in *Ireland's Memorial Records* merely as 'Canadians; died of wounds, Casualty Clearing Station, November 5, 1918'. But Willie Hackett's next-of-kin were in Dublin. He came from a family of six girls and two boys, and had emigrated to Canada a couple of years before the war. His older brother, Robert ('Bert'), had followed him across the Atlantic early in 1914. In February 1915 (*not* August or September 1914) Bert joined up; a year later Willie followed him into the Canadian army. Both served (though not in the same battalions) in the Canadian Machine Gun Corps in France. Bert, who was commissioned lieutenant in August 1918, returned to Canada after the war was over.[90] On leave in 1917 both brothers got back to Dublin for one final family reunion, recorded for posterity at William McRea's photographic studio in Berkeley Road, Phibsborough. While

Figure 1.8 The family of William Lumley (Willie) Hackett, Dublin, August
1917. *Back row (left to right)*: Mabel, Willie, Muriel, Bert, Olive;
front row: Ethel, Isabella (his mother), Alice, Bella. Willie and Bert
are in Canadian army uniform. Bella's husband, Joe Richards, was
another casualty of the war. Serving with the Canadian infantry
attached to the Royal Air Force, he died on 1 April 1918.

Bert and Willie were serving in the forces, their three
unmarried sisters, Muriel, Olive and Mabel, were living in
Dublin. In 1916 Mabel, Willie's twin, was put out of her
job at Jacob's biscuit factory, one of the strong points occupied by the rebels during the Easter Rising. This one
family's history, therefore, encapsulates some of the main
themes of Ireland's response to the Great War, drawing
together as it does enlistment, bereavement, the 1916
Rising and the civilian experience of the war years.

2 Participation: Suvla Bay, the Somme and the Easter Rising

The military experience of the war, abroad and at home

Very near the end of Peter Weir's film *Gallipoli*, when the Australians are making a series of terribly costly attacks across open ground against entrenched Turks with machine guns, the following exchange takes place:

[AUSTRALIAN] RADIO OPERATOR: . . . the British are ashore at Suvla.

[GENERAL] GARDNER: Are they meeting heavy opposition?

RADIO OPERATOR: None sir . . . Apparently they're just sitting on the beach drinking cups of tea.[1]

This counterpointing of lives of brave and indomitable Australians being thrown away in wasteful charges during the Gallipoli campaign, which any Australian viewing the film will understand to have been itself a wholly futile enterprise, while the apparently imperturbable British drink tea on Suvla Beach, reflects one of the main themes of the film, which is that the flower of Australian youth misguidedly travelled halfway round the world to fight, at great cost, a British war which was essentially none of their concern. There is, too, a strong element, familiar to aficionados of *Oh! What a Lovely War*, or *Blackadder Goes Forth*, of the 'lions led by donkeys' school of Great War studies.[2]

Gallipoli, where the Australian and New Zealand Army Corps, Anzac, first went into battle during the Great War, has become part of the Australian nation's 'creation myth'. Australia had only united in a federation in 1901 and the 'Australian Imperial Force' which set off in late 1914 was the first specifically *Australian* military formation ever to go to war. Although the whole Dardanelles expedition was a disastrous failure, and although very many more Australians went on to serve and die on the Western Front than on the Gallipoli Peninsula,[3] it is the latter which resonates down the years, so much so that in commemorating the First World War Remembrance Day – which is still 11 November in Australia – is less important than 25 April, Anzac Day, a national holiday when well-attended dawn services mark the very moment when the first Australian set foot on the beach near Cape Helles. The beach itself, where annual services are also held, has become a poignant and powerful 'site of memory',[4] especially to young Australians, backpackers touring Europe, now some four generations on from the young men who fought there.[5]

What has this to do with Ireland? The soldiers who landed at Suvla Bay during the night of 6 August and the next morning were the British 11th Division and the 10th (Irish) Division. It may not have suited Peter Weir's dramatic requirements, nor one supposes any political subtext, for the radio operator to say 'the British *and Irish* are sitting on the beach drinking cups of tea',[6] but the fact remains that half of the troops landed at Suvla that night comprised the first of Ireland's three Kitchener 'New Army' volunteer divisions to see action in the Great War. Suvla itself was a failure; it was undoubtedly the least successful of the three amphibious landings made during the campaign. A parallel could perhaps be drawn with the Australian experience: a subordinate part of the empire loyally responds to the call of the 'Motherland', but sacrifices much to no great effect. Yet, while the Australian (and New Zealand) experience continues to find an echo (and much more than that) over eighty years later, of all the amnesiac aspects of Ireland's engagement with the Great War, the history of the 10th (Irish) Division is the most profoundly forgotten.

In exploring the participation of Irish soldiers in the Great War, I shall concentrate on three New Army divisions: the 10th (Irish) and 16th (Irish) Divisions, and the 36th (Ulster) Division. Although Irishmen served in many other formations, these three divisions were (and are) the most closely identified with Ireland's wartime mobilisation of military manpower. The 16th Irish Division has come to be seen as most nearly fulfilling the Redmondite 'project', but both it and the 10th Division have been regarded generally as representing nationalist Ireland. The creation of both these divisions, however, did not run absolutely smoothly. For both military and political reasons, Kitchener and the War Office were unwilling to allow Irish Volunteers *en bloc*, complete with officers, to be converted into units of the British army. There were disputes about the commissioning of officers for the divisions, and even over the design of a distinctively Irish divisional badge.[7]

The 10th Division was one of the first six New Army divisions authorised during August 1914. It did not fill up as quickly as the War Office hoped. Indeed, reflecting the problems with recruiting in rural areas, the only English division which similarly lagged behind was the 12th (Eastern) Division, drawing its men from agricultural East Anglia.[8] But political considerations held back the other 'Irish' division, which Redmond wanted to become a 'Nationalist and catholic "Irish Brigade"', achieving 'a political and confessional homogeneity' which mirrored 'that of the Ulster Division'.[9] The explicit establishment of the Ulster Division, moreover, as an unambiguously unionist and Protestant formation, drawing on the Ulster Volunteer Force, also looked as if it might delay the division's deployment on the battlefield. Both Cyril Falls (later the historian of the division) and his fifty-year-old father took commissions in the Ulster Division, but his younger brother, Leslie, enlisted in the 10th Division 'simply because it was the first formed and, having hurried home from Canada, he did not wait to join us'.[10]

Figure 2.1   *Off: the Ulster Division*, by William Conor (charcoal and red chalk on paper, 55 × 37.3 cms). Conor drew these cheery fellows before they left Ireland in July 1915 for England and the Western Front.

We might claim the 10th Division to be the 'purest' Irish response to the call of 1914. It was the least politicised of the three raised in Ireland and contained arguably the keenest, most willing Irish recruits, less concerned with maintaining the integrity of their pre-war Irish situation as with getting to the battlefront, for whatever reason, as quickly as possible. In this, of course, they were to be successful.

Despite the fact that some drafts from England were used to fill up the 10th Division, the unit's historian, Bryan Cooper, who served with the Connaught Rangers, calculated that 70 per cent of the men and 90 per cent of the officers were Irish.[11] The division began training in Ireland but at the end of May 1915 it left for England. Reporting on its valedictory march through Dublin, the *Irish Times* proudly observed that it had drawn men 'from all classes of the community . . . and from all quarters of the city, from the fashionable centres and from the slums'. The scenes of enthusiasm with which the division was sent off 'proved that the city pulsates with ardent enthusiasm for the cause of the Allies'.[12] John Redmond specifically welcomed the deployment of the division. It was, he said, 'the first definitely Irish Division that ever existed in the British Army', and its creation marked 'a turning point in the history of the relations between Ireland and the Empire'.[13] 'For the first time in history', he asserted, the Irish people had 'put a national army in the field'. They had done so 'for the express purpose of defending Ireland' from Prussian domination, 'and of doing their share in helping to rescue the unfortunate and heroic peoples who have already fallen under it'.[14]

One part of the division, 'D' Company of the 7th Battalion Royal Dublin Fusiliers, was an especially homogeneous 'pals' formation drawn from middle- and lower middle-class sporting and professional men. Originally instigated as a band of commercial volunteers by F. H. Browning, the 1914 president of the Irish Rugby Football Union, the company drew in some three hundred lawyers, students, clerks, businessmen and suchlike.

Another company of the 7th Dublins represented a rather different network and was composed of Dublin dockers, many of them 'Larkinites', after the charismatic trade union leader, James Larkin.[15] Inevitably, we know more about the white-collar volunteers of 'D' Company, commemorated in a memorial record painstakingly gathered together by the barrister Henry Hanna during 1916. This volume was his response to the grievous losses suffered by his compatriots at Gallipoli.

The Irish Division got ashore at Suvla relatively unscathed. Touchingly, Hanna found that 'D' Company likened parts of the Mediterranean landscape to that at home around Dublin. One beach was a 'pebbly white strand like that at Portmarnock'; another part was 'like Dollymount', while behind the foreshore were low clay cliffs 'rather like the shore at Killiney Bay'. But in the battle for Chocolate Hill, which overlooked the beaches, and where the men found themselves advancing over 'rocks and shrub, resembling the lower slopes of Ticknock' in the Wicklow Mountains, and, a week later, in attempting to seize the high Kiretch Tepe Sirt ridge to the north of the landing ground, the Irish formation took heavy casualties. 'D' Company, 'which had landed 239 strong', was now 'reduced to 108 all told'.[16] Bursting with the enthusiasm of youth, the poet Francis Ledwidge, who was with the Inniskilling Fusiliers at Kiretch Tepe Sirt, wrote that 'it was a horrible and a great day. I would not have missed it for worlds.'[17]

Other parts of the division suffered equally and Bryan Cooper reflected that 'the 10th Division had been shattered, the work of a year had been destroyed in a week, and nothing material had been gained. Yet', he added,

> all was not in vain. It is no new thing for the sons of Ireland to perish in a forlorn hope and a fruitless struggle; they go forth to battle only to fall, yet there springs from their graves a glorious memory for the example of future generations. Kiretch Tepe Sirt was a little-known fight in

Figure 2.2 Irish Guards in the trenches at Wytschaete, Belgium. A photograph taken by Corkman Father Frank Browne SJ, who served with the Guards as a chaplain from 1916 to 1919.

> an unlucky campaign, but if the young soldiers of the 10th Division who died there added a single leaf to Ireland's crown of cypress and laurel, their death was not in vain.[18]

We may not agree that dying gloriously in battle is in itself sufficient justification for the terrible human cost, but the sentiments expressed here in the middle of the war by Cooper, himself a sensitive and thoughtful man, precisely reflect the meaning drawn by republicans from the sacrifices of Easter 1916. They provide an unsettling echo of Patrick Pearse's own celebration of martial virtue and the 'dead generations' invoked in the 1916 Proclamation.

The losses of the 10th Division, the first, it should be remembered, from among the volunteers of autumn 1914, had an impact back home. It was a time, wrote Katharine

Tynan, 'when blow after blow fell day after day on one's heart'. No doubt reflecting the concentration of middle-class Dublin professionals involved, Tynan, a writer married to a magistrate who moved in these circles, recalled that 'so many of our friends had gone out in the 10th Division to perish at Suvla. For the first time came bitter-ness, for we felt that their lives had been thrown away and that their heroism had gone unrecognised.' She met mourners 'everywhere. One day at Ely House there were two new war-widows at the luncheon-table, and one girl whose brother had been killed.' She described Dublin as 'full of mourning', and observed many black-veiled figures – mothers and wives of the 10th Division – at morning masses in Newman's University Chapel 'follow-ing the horrible disaster of Suvla Bay'.[19] There was, more-over, a tragic local footnote to the history of the Dublin pals. F. H. Browning, who had done so much to raise 'D' Company, was mortally wounded when his party of Volunteer Corps 'Gorgeous Wrecks' – so-called for the royal title, Georgius Rex, on their arm-bands – was ambushed in Northumberland Road during the 1916 Rising.

In his semi-autobiographical novel, *Changing Winds*, much of which is set in Dublin during the war, St John Ervine suggested that the events of Gallipoli, together with wartime prosperity, undermined support for advanced nationalism. 'Dublin', he wrote, 'was full of men and women mourning for their sons who had died at Suvla Bay'; they 'were in no mood for rebellion'.[20] Army wives and mothers, like Sean O'Casey's Bessie Burgess in *The Plough and the Stars*, were not likely – to say the least – to be especially sympathetic to stay-at-home Irish Volunteers. On Whit Sunday 1915 (23 May), just a month after the regular 1st Battalion Royal Munster Fusiliers, along with the 1st Battalion of the Dublins, had suffered two-thirds casualties in the Gallipoli landings on 'V' Beach, a parade of Irish Volunteers over one thousand strong returned to Limerick station 'through the Irishtown quarter, where many soldiers' families lived'. Here 'they were furiously attacked by a crowd of women – mostly', reported the police, 'wives of the Munster Fusiliers'. The Volunteers 'had to be shepherded through the danger zone by an escort of constables'.[21]

The response to the Rising when it came in 1916 was clearly affected by the numbers of Irishmen serving in the war. One Anglo-Irish officer, by no means a fervent unionist, was home in Dublin on leave at the time. 'The sympathies of all parts of Dublin, including the slums', he recalled, favoured the government. 'There were far too many Dubliners fighting with Irish regiments, in France and elsewhere, for the population to feel that this was the right moment to embarrass England.'[22] Certainly there was resentment at the disruption and destruction occasioned by the Rising, which was widely compared to that in France and Flanders, though there was also some exploitation as locals looted city-centre shops. 'I have just returned from walking round the GPO and Sackville [O'Connell] Street', wrote one Dublin resident on 1 May, two days after the rebels had surrendered. 'If you look at pictures of Yprès or Louvain after the bombardment it will give you some idea of the scene.'[23] Parts of 'gallant little Belgium', it seems, had been recreated in Ireland.

By some accounts – and there is a sort of mythic quality to this, for these stories are more easily found than is reliable authority on which to base them – there was 'unpleasantness' at the very start of the affair. As one historian retells, 'queues of women lining up outside the GPO to collect their British army separation allowance' protested on being 'told that with the establishment of an Irish republic the allowances had ceased'.[24] Another narrative has an 'angry crowd' of workers and '"Separation Allowance" women' outside Jacob's biscuit factory on Easter Monday.[25] In Enniscorthy, County Wicklow, one of the few places outside Dublin where rebellion occurred, 'separation women' also complained about the post office being closed. Here the Volunteers were sympathetic and

Figure 2.3 The Grand Place, Iper/Ypres, showing the damage so often compared with that in Dublin after the Easter Rising. This is another photograph taken by Father Browne.

gave the women 'permits for provisions similar to those given to the families of our own men'. Shortly afterwards one of the Volunteers, Robert Brennan, 'overheard two of them talking as they came out of a provision shop carrying parcels. I expect that the allowance was more generous than they had been getting because one said to the other: "Glory be to God, Katie, isn't this a grand government."'[26]

At the end of the Rising, after the surrender, another Volunteer recalled as they were marched away being subjected at points along the way 'to abuse from women, dependants of British soldiers'.[27] Brighid Lyons Thornton remembered a large crowd of women' outside the gates of Kilmainham Gaol:

> Now we never had the Brits to protect us before, but luckily the soldiers guarded us very heavily because when the gates were opened and we were marched out there

were such shrieks of hatred. Never did I see such savage
women. A lot of them were getting the separation
allowance because their husbands were off fighting in
France and they thought their livelihood would be taken
away because of what we had done. A lot of it seemed to
be directed against the Countess's breeches and puttees.[28]

There is, of course, a political dimension to memories such
as these: opposition to the Rising exists, but in effect it
comes only from people who depended on the 'economic
conscription' which James Connolly so robustly excori-
ated.

The linkages between the circumstances of the Great
War and those of the Easter Rising, however, are much
greater, indeed more symbiotic, than these personal vig-
nettes may suggest. The First World War provided both
the opportunity and the timing for the Irish republican
rising of Easter 1916. It presented a suitably violent model
for political action and defined the moment when that
action was likely to occur. Like the war, the Easter Rising
was simply the 'continuation of politics by other means'.
For Irish separatists, the Great War offered both moment
and mode.

Even before Redmond's Woodenbridge speech and the
split in the Volunteers, a conference of revolutionary
leaders on 9 September 1914, including Pearse and other
members of the militant and clandestine IRB, along with
James Connolly, the socialist leader of the 200-strong Irish
Citizen Army (ICA), agreed that the European war would
provide the opportunity for an Irish insurrection. It was
decided to begin planning for an uprising and also to get in
touch with Germany for support. The Irish-American
Clan na Gael organisation asked the German ambassador
at Washington for help and sent Sir Roger Casement to
Berlin to negotiate the practical details. Not only was
Germany, as England's enemy, seen as an ally for separatist
Irish republicans (and, of course, it had been a source of
weapons for both unionist and nationalist paramilitaries

before war broke out), but the more internationalist republicans argued that the war could enhance freedom generally
by destroying the British Empire and British imperial
domination of the world. 'Once the chief factor governing
the conflict is perceived', declared Casement in an anonymously published pamphlet, 'namely the British claim to
own the seas and to dominate the commercial intercourse
of the world, then the cause of Germany becomes the cause
of European civilisation at large. Germany is fighting the
battle of Europe, the battle of free trade, the fight to open
the seas of the world.' Here were more Big Words – civilisation and freedom – rhetorically marshalled by Casement
in a mirror image of those employed by John Redmond,
Tom Kettle and others in support of the Allied war effort.
Casement also noted the significance of the war in advancing the likelihood of armed insurrection at home. The war,
he wrote, had 'come sooner than was expected. The rest of
the writer's task must be essayed not with the author's pen,
but with the rifle of the Irish Volunteer.'[29]

James Connolly thought that Irish working-class rebellion, especially against so great an imperial power as
England, might, happily, precipitate the general toppling
of capitalism. 'Starting thus', he wrote just after the outbreak of the war, 'Ireland may yet set the torch to a
European conflagration that will not burn out until the last
throne and the last capitalist bond and debenture will be
shrivelled on the funeral pyre of the last war lord.'[30]

The Volunteers' split over the issue of participation in
the war in the autumn of 1914 increased the likelihood of
an insurrection in Ireland. Naturally the most militant
republicans were among the leaders of the new Irish
Volunteers. The split, moreover, released Pearse and his
colleagues from the tedious necessity of having to argue
their case with moderate and, from their point of view,
gravely misguided constitutional nationalists. Declaring in
October 1914 that since the anti-Redmond Volunteers
'may be depended upon to act vigorously, courageously,
promptly, and unitedly if the opportunity comes', Pearse

believed that 'we are at the moment in an immensely stronger position than ever before'. Airily calculating that the support of 10,000 to 15,000 men might be forthcoming, he asserted with superb confidence that 'this small, compact, perfectly disciplined *separatist* force is infinitely more valuable than the unwieldy, loosely-held-together mixum-gatherum force we had before the split'.[31]

In the early summer of 1915 planning for a rising began in earnest and by the new year the coming Easter had been decided upon for its launch. The tactics adopted were those of an orthodox military operation. Although Bulmer Hobson in the Volunteers and Sean O'Casey in the ICA (among others) argued in favour of guerrilla operations, Pearse was determined to challenge the might of the British Empire openly in the field of battle. As Charles Townshend has observed, Pearse required violence 'to have not just a moral basis but a moral mode of expression'.[32] With uniformed and disciplined troops the republican leaders sought to secure proper belligerent status, legitimately representing, as the 1916 Proclamation had it, 'a Sovereign Independent State'. Thus the symbolic nature of the Rising, though reflecting the mode of conflict simultaneously being conducted in France, Flanders and elsewhere, far outweighed military effectiveness. In fact, the same could actually be said (though for different reasons) of the situation along the Western Front, where the military effectiveness of symbolically important mass frontal assaults might also be called into question.

When the Rising finally came, in the context of the wider European war, it was a very small-scale affair and was not immediately either very popular or very successful. It was perceived as a mainly German-inspired rising, not least because of the pro-German sentiments expressed by the Volunteers. A month before the Rising, Mrs Hamilton Norway, wife of the secretary to the GPO, observed a parade down Grafton Street in Dublin singing 'Die Wacht am Rhein'.[33] Pearse and his colleagues had sought and been promised some help from Berlin. A German ship, the

Aud, arrived off the west coast of Ireland with a cargo of arms, but it was intercepted by the Royal Navy and scuttled on Good Friday. The same day Sir Roger Casement was landed in County Kerry from a German submarine – ironically his mission was to try to prevent the planned rising on the grounds that insufficient German assistance was being provided – but he was quickly captured and later executed for treason. The proclamation which Pearse himself read at the start of the Rising (but not from the *steps* of the GPO[34]) recorded the support of 'gallant allies in Europe'. But in the end the Irish were left to act alone.

Following Pearse's wishes the tactics adopted were those of an orthodox military operation. This was reflected in the plan to seize and hold prominent public buildings in Dublin, including the General Post Office, which became the insurgents' headquarters. Desmond Ryan, Pearse's secretary who served in the GPO, afterwards reported Michael Boland, an ex-British soldier who had fought in the 1899–1901 South African War, complaining about Pearse's static strategy. He dismissed it as 'a mad business. Shut in here with our leaders, and the flags over our heads to tell the enemy just where to find us when they want us. We should have taken to the hills like the Boers, but we're here now and we'll just have to stick it.'[35] Like the Western Front it became a war of attrition, and the lessons of the Western Front were taught again on the streets of Dublin. Cavalry was no use whatsoever, as those unfortunate Lancers who came down O'Connell Street on the first day discovered, and artillery, which eventually brought the rebels to surrender, was essential. And, as Charles Townshend has observed, the fierce fighting at Mount Street Bridge on Wednesday 26 April saw raw British conscripts 'as inexperienced as the Volunteers themselves' suffering dreadful casualties 'in New Army-style shoulder-to-shoulder attacks that prefigured the Somme in miniature'.[36] Dublin folk-memory has it that the unfortunate British reinforcements initially believed that they actually were in France.[37] For many of the soldiers in the care of

Vivienne Smyly, a volunteer nurse, working in Dublin
Castle, it made little difference. 'We're in Hell again', they
said, 'we might as well go back to France.'[38]

Five days into the Rising, in a morale-boosting despatch
to the GPO garrison, James Connolly over-optimistically
drew an explicit comparison between the British Army's
apparent performance in Dublin and that in the wider
conflict:

> For the first time in 700 years the flag of a free Ireland
> floats triumphantly in Dublin City. The British Army,
> whose exploits we are for ever having dinned into our ears,
> which boasts of having stormed the Dardanelles and the
> German lines on the Marne, behind their artillery and
> machine-guns are afraid to advance to the attack or storm
> any positions held by our forces. The slaughter they
> suffered in the first few days has totally unnerved them
> and they dare not attempt again an infantry attack on our
> positions.[39]

In fact the rebels themselves were close to surrender at this
point. Some 1,800 insurgents occupied a number of strong
points, though some were stronger than others. The decision to hold St Stephen's Green, and dig *trenches* there,
without seizing all the buildings overlooking the park,
closely matched, with less justification, the situation at
Suvla where the Turks were able to fire down into the 10th
(Irish) Division positions. The rebels held out for a week
before overwhelming force obliged them to surrender. In
all 500 people were killed and 2,500 wounded, the majority
of whom were civilians caught in crossfire. Sixty insurgents and 132 troops and police died. During the same
week, at Hulluch on the Western Front units of the 16th
Division suffered 570 men killed and over 1,400 wounded
in a gas and artillery attack.[40]

Constantly in contemporary accounts we find the Rising
subsumed within the wider conflict. One soldier, who had
seen a comrade die at his side during the attack on the City
Hall, said that 'the only thing which made it possible to

Figure 2.4   'Ypres on the Liffey': looking from O'Connell Street down North
Earl Street towards Talbot Street. A souvenir picture postcard of
the destruction in Dublin, published by W. & G. Baird of Belfast in
1916.

bear was the certainty they were fighting Germany as truly
as if they were in France. In his opinion, the Rebellion was
Germany's last trump card, and would prove the turning-
point of the war.'[41] Oliver St John Gogarty's typically sar-
donic view was that the Rising 'could do nothing but good
for the British army, as it would redeem their credit in
Europe, bringing them their sole current victory'.[42] In the
context of the war in 1916, despite the drama of the rebellion, Irish affairs were of only subsidiary importance. The
Battle of Verdun was raging on the Western Front. On the
day the Easter Rising began there was a Zeppelin raid on
East Anglia and five days later General Townshend surrendered at Kut in Mesopotamia where 9,000 British and
Indian troops were taken prisoner. The pressures of
wartime policymaking in general undoubtedly contributed
to the somewhat haphazard approach to Irish matters
taken by the government.[43]

The government's response to the Rising inevitably
reflected the wartime circumstances. Martial law was

imposed almost immediately and a military governor, General Sir John 'Conky' Maxwell, was appointed. He was not Lord Kitchener's initial choice for the job. Kitchener had suggested Sir Ian Hamilton, who had commanded at Gallipoli but was currently unemployed following the evacuation of the peninsula at the beginning of the year. Sir William Robertson, the chief of the Imperial General Staff, thought Hamilton an unwise choice. 'There is', he wrote on 26 April, 'a good deal of bitterness in Ireland about Suvla &c . . . It is very desirable to send a competent man, who so far as Ireland is concerned has no past record.'[44] Maxwell, who had been GOC in Egypt and partly implicated in the Gallipoli disaster, 'never had any appetite for the . . . enterprise',[45] and seemed to fit the bill. He had some relevant experience, having served briefly as military governor at Pretoria in South Africa in 1900–1. His chief qualifications for the Dublin job, nevertheless, were that he was *not* Sir Ian Hamilton and that he was available. He was not a general of the first rank. If he had been, considering that there was a war on, he would hardly have been unemployed.

But, if Maxwell had no past record so far as Ireland was concerned, he surely had a future one. His security policy was initially quite stringent. After the surrender, the leading rebels were quickly put before courts-martial and charged 'that they had taken part in an armed rebellion and in the waging of war against His Majesty the King, such act being of such a nature as to be calculated to be prejudicial to the defence of the realm and being done with the intention of and purpose of assisting the German enemy'.[46] Ninety death sentences were imposed, of which fifteen were carried out over a ten-day period. The adjutant-general at the War Office, Sir Nevil Macready, who had experience of Irish affairs, eight years later still commended Maxwell's 'energy and determination' in quelling the rebellion and punishing the rebels; 'rebels, let it be remembered, not only against their own country, but against all the Allies who were fighting to free Europe from

Prussian domination'.[47] The rather long drawn-out (but was it?) series of executions is widely blamed for both exacerbating a growing public alienation from the administration in Ireland and boosting support for Sinn Fein. There is a case, though not I think a very strong one, for arguing that, without the ostentatious linking of the Irish cause with Germany, the leaders of the Rising might have been treated in a less draconian manner, and this might in turn have had less of an impact on public opinion. J. J. Lee has argued, moreover, that much criticism of the Rising was based not so much on a fundamental antipathy to its objectives as a concern with the methods adopted, and that the ambiguous public response helps explain the undoubted shift in opinion towards the republican separatists in the aftermath of Easter 1916.[48] To this we might add that the 'ambiguous public response' to the war – favouring its (apparent) aims, but becoming increasingly disenchanted with its methods and its human cost – may equally help to explain the falling away of support in Ireland for the war effort.

The impact of the Rising on serving Irish soldiers in the British army was much less apparent than its impact on popular opinion. On 26 April General Sir Henry Wilson, a Protestant unionist brought up in the south of Ireland, noted in his diary that rebels in Dublin had occupied the Post Office and other buildings. 'A marvellous state of affairs', he noted, '& I should think almost equal to the capture of Verdun from the Boche point of view.'[49] Willie Redmond (John Redmond's brother) was 'devastated' especially by Pearse's appeal to 'the gallant German allies'.[50] Francis Ledwidge was deeply troubled by the events in Dublin. 'Yes, poor Ireland is always in trouble', he wrote to an Ulster Protestant friend on the day the first leaders were executed. 'Though I am not a Sinn Feiner and you are a Carsonite, do our sympathies not go to *Cathleen ni Houlihan*? Poor MacDonagh and Pearse were two of my best friends.'[51] Stephen Gwynn, a Nationalist MP serving with the Connaught Rangers, recalled that the men were indignant about the Rising: 'they felt they had been stabbed in the back'.[52] During May 1916 the 8th (Service) Battalion of the Royal Munster Fusiliers, which had been raised as part of the 16th Division at Buttevant, County Cork, in September 1914, found themselves faced by two German placards. One read 'Irishmen! Heavy uproar in Ireland. English guns are firing at your wifes [*sic*] and children.' The other announced the fall of Kut to Turkish forces. According to the regimental history (not an entirely unbiased source) the men responded by singing 'God Save the King' and captured the placards which were later presented to King George V.[53] Terence Denman has concluded that 'from the magnificent achievements of the 16th Division on the Somme just a few months after the Rising it is clear that whatever disquiet the events in Ireland produced they did not damage its fighting performance'.[54]

Unionists, too, felt that they had been stabbed in the back by the Rising,[55] but on the whole they were less deeply affected by it than were nationalists. In a sense, a violent uprising was no more than they might have expected from their political opponents. Despite the pious hopes of John Redmond and Tom Kettle, common service in the British war effort actually did little to reconcile Ulster unionists even to constitutional nationalists. Unlike nationalists, it was not so much their *methods* they objected to (both unionists and nationalists had, after all, resorted to threatening armed paramilitary action in pursuit of their political objectives) as their *aims*. Ulstermen were, however, not averse to assuming a rebellious demeanour when it suited them. Recalling the first day of the Somme, one soldier wrote: 'Every time the Huns attacked we sent them reeling back with something to remind them that they were fighting Irishmen. We couldn't help taunting them a lot. "Would you like some Irish rebellion?" we called out to them, and they didn't like it.'[56]

The exploits of the Ulster Division at the Battle of the Somme – its first major engagement – rapidly achieved legendary status. Going over the top on 1 July, the division suffered terrible casualties during the assault on Thiepval Ridge and the supposedly impregnable Schwaben Redoubt. The Redoubt was taken but, being unsupported by the formations on either side, the division had to withdraw from the very hard-won position. On the first two days of the Somme the division lost 5,500 all ranks, killed, wounded or missing out of a total of about 15,000 men. The date of the battle was especially significant for the Ulstermen as it was the actual date (by the defunct Julian calendar) of the Battle of the Boyne in 1690,[57] which marked the crucial victory of the Protestant King William III over the Catholic King James II. On the eve of the Somme battle Sir Oliver Nugent, commanding the Ulster Division, wrote to Sir George Richardson, the commander of the UVF back home: 'We could hardly have a date better calculated to inspire national traditions amongst our men of the North.'[58] For the attack some men wore their Orange sashes or orange lilies, traditionally worn for the Boyne commemoration.[59] There is a very famous account from a correspondent of *The Times* which is often quoted, and which lyrically describes the Ulster Division advance: 'I am not an Ulsterman, but yesterday as I followed their amazing attack I felt I would rather be an Ulsterman than anything else in the world.' They 'charged over the two front lines of the enemy's trenches, shouting "No Surrender, boys!"'[60]

The Ulster Volunteers had encountered much less difficulty than Redmond's National Volunteers in transforming themselves into an army division. Unlike their nationalist compatriots, virtually all the UVF officers had previous military experience and thus were deemed suitable by the War Office for direct commissions. Being formed 'on perhaps the most strictly territorial basis of any Division of the New Armies', the 36th exemplified on a grand scale the 'pals' battalions of some other divisions. 'The company, the platoon', wrote the division historian, 'was a close community, an enlarged family. In after days, in the trenches and in billets behind the lines, the talk, not only of men from Belfast and the larger towns, but of those from the country villages, would be of streets and, in the latter case, of farms and lanes of which those present had known every detail from childhood.'[61] The particularly concentrated nature of the Ulster Division, not just socially but also in terms of its religion and politics, meant that its losses on the first day of the Somme, grievous enough in themselves, had a disproportionately great impact back home.

The news of the division's successful advance – though not its brevity – travelled home faster than the casualty returns (this was usually the case), so the initial reports in the local press were of triumph and brilliant achievement. Soon enough the catastrophic level of losses became known and struck deep in the close-knit community that had sustained the formation. As A. T. Q. Stewart memorably, if somewhat impressionistically, wrote: 'In the long streets of Belfast mothers looked out in dread for the red bicycles of the telegram boys. In house after house blinds were drawn down, until it seemed that every family in the city had been bereaved. The casualty lists were full of familiar names, and always after them in brackets appeared the UVF unit to which they had belonged.'[62] For the first time in its history the Orange Order abandoned its Boyne commemoration processions on 12 July and, at the suggestion of the Lord Mayor, five minutes' silence was observed at noon on that day.[63]

Once the full, terrible story of the battle got back home it began to be stitched permanently into Ulster's Protestant loyalist tradition. Three lines from a verse published in the *Londonderry Sentinel*, purportedly written in hospital on 2 July by a dying soldier, demonstrate how the smallest local communities were associated with the battle:

> With the war-cry 'No Surrender' they quickly found the foe,
> And onward dashed, from trench to trench, as streams the running tide,

The Fountain, Dark Lane, Rosemount, and the lads from
    Waterside.[64]

On 19 July 1916 the *Belfast News-Letter* published 'The
Charge of the Ulster Division at Thiepval' by Major
Samuel K. Cowan, MA:

Was ever a Charge in the world like this?
Shall ever a son of Ulster miss
A fame that is wholly and solely his –
    A fame of sublimest splendour?
The lads who laughed in the face of Death!
Above the roar of the cannon's breath
Singing their sacred shibboleth
    Of 'The Boyne!' and 'No Surrender!'[65]

Although these ditties, and other forces, sustained the
story of the Somme through the post-war years, there is
also a sense in which history stopped on 1 July 1916. Like
Suvla Bay for the 10th Division, it was a moment for the
36th Division after which nothing would ever be the same
again. A. J. P. Taylor remarked that the 'zest and idealism'
of Kitchener's army perished on the Somme.[66] Sixty years
on, reflecting on 1 July 1916, one veteran, Jim Donaghy of
the 10th Royal Inniskilling Fusiliers, said: 'The close bond
of the Battalion as a whole would never be the same. Just as
part of the Battalion died that day and it would never be the
same, so part of Ulster died.'[67] A more contemporaneous
account, of the 11th Royal Irish Rifles from south Antrim,
completed just after the war, closes with the Ulster
Division on the Somme. 'To many in Ulster', wrote the
author, 'this great event marks in reality the passing of the
glorious Division recruited during the first six months of
the war.' While the formation went on to fight famously in
more battles, 'the Division was never again quite the same
as before that memorable day'. It was hoped that the
memoirs being published would be

of interest to Ulster people as describing the everyday life
of a unit of their Division during its first eight months in

France before the novelty of the life in billets and in trenches had worn off, and become merely monotonous, and while the point of view was still that of the native Ulsterman rather than the British soldier.[68]

When the full extent of the losses at the start of the Somme battle became apparent, Belfast Corporation passed a special resolution of congratulation, explicitly linking the division's sacrifice with the 'freedom of small nations' and paying homage to the heroic dead who had 'laid down their lives and resigned the bright hopes of youth, and love, and ambition to save their country from the fate of Belgium, Servia and Poland'.[69] It is possible that some of the Belfast councillors and aldermen knew that direct, though not very effective, assistance was being given to Serbia by the 10th (Irish) Division which included one brigade (the 31st) more or less drawn from the north of Ireland.[70] The 10th Division had been withdrawn from Gallipoli at the end of September 1915 and deposited at Salonika in Greece, the most futile theatre of the Great War, by the middle of the following month. During November they moved up to the front just over the Serbian frontier in what is today Macedonia.

Francis Ledwidge, serving with the Inniskillings, drew a parallel between Serbia and Ireland. Home on leave in May 1916 he remarked that 'the Serbians impressed me very much. I consider Serbia, poetically, like Ireland – a poor old woman wandering the roads of the world.'[71] In appalling winter weather towards the end of 1915 – nearly 2,000 men collapsed with exposure and frostbite – the division delayed but did not prevent a Bulgarian advance before withdrawing back to Greece, having suffered some 1,350 additional casualties.[72] The division, becoming progressively less 'Irish' as replacements from home dried up, remained in Salonika for a year and then finished the war in the Egyptian Expeditionary Force, fighting at Gaza and participating in the capture of Jerusalem in December 1917.

Figure 2.5 Memorial crosses which Sir William Hickie arranged to be erected
in the 1920s. *Top and middle:* 16th (Irish) Division cross at
Guillemont on the Somme, France. *Bottom:* 10th (Irish) Division
cross at Rabrova, Macedonia. A similar 16th Division cross stands at
Wytschaete in Belgium.

And what of that other band of 'Ireland's unknown soldiers', as Terry Denman has put it, the 16th (Irish) Division, caught in a historical and political no man's land?[73] They, too, fought in the Battle of the Somme though, fortunately for them, not on its opening day. They were involved in the comparatively successful engagements of Guillemont and Guinchy from 5 to 9 September 1916. The fate of those serving in the division is exemplified by that of Tom Kettle who was killed on 9 September. For him the Rising was 'a terrible experience'. Although he had no sympathy with the rebellion itself – 'he used to say bitterly [recorded his wife] that they had spoiled it all – spoiled his dream of a free united Ireland in a free Europe' (a striking prediction)[74] – he correctly anticipated how posterity would view him vis-à-vis the 1916 leaders. 'These men', he wrote, 'will go down in history as heroes and martyrs; and I will go down – if I go down at all – as a bloody British officer.'[75]

Eight months later, up the line in Belgium, the 16th and 36th Divisions were deployed alongside each other at the Battle of Messines. It was the closest the army came to creating John Redmond's dearest hope of a fully fledged Irish Army Corps, analogous to Anzac or the Canadian Corps. Here, on 7 June 1917, after a great series of mines were blown, the two divisions captured their objective of Wytschaete – 'Whitesheet' – a village strong point on the summit of the Messines Ridge, three hours and forty minutes after 'zero'. It was the 'first completely successful single operation on the British front since the outbreak of the war',[76] and the casualties were 'incredibly light', a mere 1,400 killed and wounded for both divisions.[77]

Among those who fell, however, was Willie Redmond, Nationalist MP and younger brother of John, representative of the more radical tendency within what was socially and politically a rather conservative grouping. He was an attractive character, full of energy and (mostly) cheerful enthusiasm, 'the Irish d'Artagnan', as Shane Leslie described him.[78] Redmond was acutely sensitive to the

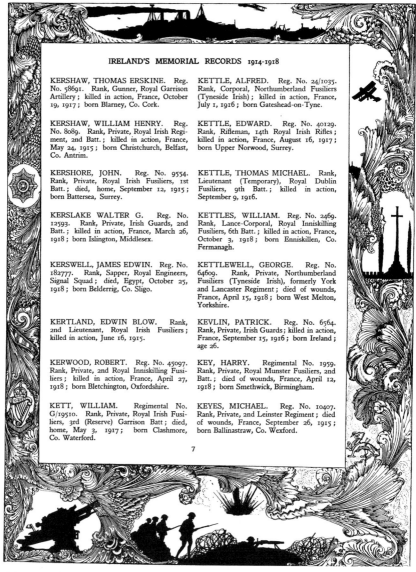

KERSHAW, THOMAS ERSKINE. Reg. No. 58691. Rank, Gunner, Royal Garrison Artillery; killed in action, France, October 19, 1917; born Blarney, Co. Cork.

KERSHAW, WILLIAM HENRY. Reg. No. 8089. Rank, Private, Royal Irish Regiment, 2nd Batt.; killed in action, France, May 24, 1915; born Christchurch, Belfast, Co. Antrim.

KERSHORE, JOHN. Reg. No. 9554. Rank, Private, Royal Irish Fusiliers, 1st Batt.; died, home, September 12, 1915; born Battersea, Surrey.

KERSLAKE WALTER G. Reg. No. 12593. Rank, Private, Irish Guards, 2nd Batt.; killed in action, France, March 26, 1918; born Islington, Middlesex.

KERSWELL, JAMES EDWIN. Reg. No. 182777. Rank, Sapper, Royal Engineers, Signal Squad; died, Egypt, October 25, 1918; born Belderrig, Co. Sligo.

KERTLAND, EDWIN BLOW. Rank, 2nd Lieutenant, Royal Irish Fusiliers; killed in action, June 16, 1915.

KERWOOD, ROBERT. Reg. No. 45097. Rank, Private, 2nd Royal Inniskilling Fusiliers; killed in action, France, April 27, 1918; born Bletchington, Oxfordshire.

KETT, WILLIAM. Regimental No. G/19510. Rank, Private, Royal Irish Fusiliers, 3rd (Reserve) Garrison Batt.; died, home, May 3, 1917; born Clashmore, Co. Waterford.

KETTLE, ALFRED. Reg. No. 24/1035. Rank, Corporal, Northumberland Fusiliers (Tyneside Irish); killed in action, France, July 1, 1916; born Gateshead-on-Tyne.

KETTLE, EDWARD. Reg. No. 40129. Rank, Rifleman, 14th Royal Irish Rifles; killed in action, France, August 16, 1917; born Upper Norwood, Surrey.

KETTLE, THOMAS MICHAEL. Rank, Lieutenant (Temporary), Royal Dublin Fusiliers, 9th Batt.; killed in action, September 9, 1916.

KETTLES, WILLIAM. Reg. No. 2469. Rank, Lance-Corporal, Royal Inniskilling Fusiliers, 6th Batt.; killed in action, France, October 3, 1918; born Enniskillen, Co. Fermanagh.

KETTLEWELL, GEORGE. Reg. No. 64609. Rank, Private, Northumberland Fusiliers (Tyneside Irish), formerly York and Lancaster Regiment; died of wounds, France, April 15, 1918; born West Melton, Yorkshire.

KEVLIN, PATRICK. Reg. No. 6564. Rank, Private, Irish Guards; killed in action, France, September 15, 1916; born Ireland; age 26.

KEY, HARRY. Regimental No. 1959. Rank, Private, Royal Munster Fusiliers, 2nd Batt.; died of wounds, France, April 12, 1918; born Smethwick, Birmingham.

KEYES, MICHAEL. Reg. No. 10407. Rank, Private, 2nd Leinster Regiment; died of wounds, France, September 26, 1915; born Ballinastraw, Co. Wexford.

7

Figure 2.6 A sample page from *Ireland's Memorial Records* (Dublin, 1923) containing the entry for Thomas Kettle and showing one of Harry Clarke's marvellous decorative borders.

allegation that Nationalist MPs were mere recruiting
agents for the British government. As one satire, written
by a Volunteer who had served in the GPO in Dublin,
went:

> Fly to France and Belgium,
>   That's where Ireland needs you;
> Fight for Russia's gentle Czar,
>   Who with his flour feeds you;
> Help the yellow Jap to be
>   Your future lord and master;
> Rush to aid your foreign friends,
>   Faster, boys, and faster!
> And in case there's no one left
>   To give you half a cheer,
> When your heads and legs come home –
>   I'll stay here.[79]

For Willie Redmond it was rather different. 'I can't
stand asking fellows to go and not offer myself', he wrote at
Christmas 1914.[80] Although over fifty years old, he was
determined to join up and serve in the front line with the
16th Division. It was an endearing, if pathetic, desire.
Clearly physically unfit, his presence in the trenches was as
likely to endanger his concerned fellow countrymen as to
encourage them. It is tempting to portray this quixotic
venture as reflecting the ultimately futile Redmondite
response to changing political circumstances in Ireland.
Willie Redmond had his wish to join in the fighting, and he
fell during the Messines battle. Fatally injured, he was
brought into an Ulster Division field ambulance post, a
circumstance which encouraged those who thought and
hoped that common service in the war might help to over-
come the rift between Irish nationalists and Irish unionists.
'The story of his death in action side by side with the
Ulster Division', wrote the Dublin correspondent of *The
Times*, 'has impressed North and South with a feeling of
their essential unity.'[81] These hopes, however, were not to
be fulfilled, though Willie Redmond remains an iconic

figure for those who still profess faith in the reconciling power of war service.

Two months later – Denman calls it 'triumph and disaster'[82] – the two divisions again fought alongside each other, but on this occasion they were 'broken to bits'[83] at Langemarck during the Third Battle of Ypres, that series of engagements frequently named after the most bloody one, Passchendaele. Between 2 and 18 August, in really dreadful conditions, the 16th Division suffered 4,200 casualties, including the legendary chaplain, Father Willie Doyle, who was recommended for the Victoria Cross but failed to be awarded it as 'the triple disqualification of being an Irishman, a Catholic and a Jesuit proved insuperable'.[84] The 16th of August, the day Doyle was killed, was the worst day. That evening General Nugent reflected on the experience of the Ulster Division: 'It has been a truly terrible day', he wrote to his wife. 'Worse than 1 July I am afraid.'[85] The previous year the division had gone down gloriously, having been let down by others. On this occasion they themselves had failed and let others down. There are no jaunty ditties about the 'Boyne' and 'No Surrender' at Langemarck.

As for 'friendship and esteem' between 'Orange and Green factions', as one historian puts it,[86] there was not always, alas, much of that either. Jim Donaghy from the Derrys was captured during the German spring offensive of 1918 and in the prisoner-of-war camp found the 'old enmity' springing up: 'The men of the 16th and 36th Divisions didn't sleep in the same accommodation, so as the men of the 36th Division were in the minority, myself and three others had to bivouac outdoors. We moved well away to a separate area.'[87]

From time to time, usually in the more popular military histories, it is observed that Irish soldiers were involved at the very beginning and very end of the Great War. At 7.00 a.m. on 22 August 1914, Corporal E. Thomas (a fine Irish name) of the 4th Royal Irish Dragoon Guards is said to have fired the first shots of the war, while a soldier of the

5th Royal Irish Lancers is alleged to have been the last British serviceman killed on Armistice Day. This is not of any great moment – perhaps of some antiquarian interest – but noting a terminus to the war provides the opportunity to observe that Irish participation in military activity did not cease when the whistle blew on the Western Front in November 1918. Veterans of the British forces, and of the Easter Rising, fought alongside each other and against each other in that congeries of conflicts which afflicted Ireland between 1919 and 1923.

Some 'Irishmen in khaki' went on to join the IRA when they came home after the war. Two examples are the assassins in June 1922 of another Irish soldier, the Longford-born Field Marshal Sir Henry Wilson, recently retired Chief of the Imperial General Staff. Both Joseph O'Sullivan and Reggie Dunne had served on the Western Front during the war. Neither had joined up in the first flush of wartime excitement. O'Sullivan, from Bantry, County Cork, enlisted in the Munster Fusiliers in January 1915, and Dunne, an expatriate from a British army family, enlisted in the Irish Guards in June 1916. In a statement which he was prohibited from reading at his trial, Dunne, who had become the commandant of the London brigade of the IRA, asserted a common purpose for their British and Irish military service:

> We both joined voluntarily for the purpose of taking
> human life, in order that the principles for which this
> country stood should be upheld and preserved. These
> principles, we were told, were Self-Determination and
> Freedom for Small Nations ... We came back from
> France to find that Self-Determination had been given to
> some Nations we had never heard of, but that it had been
> denied to Ireland.[88]

Whether O'Sullivan and Dunne, and those like them, joined the republican cause out of patriotic loyalty, peer pressure, unemployment, sheer boredom or whatever – no doubt the motives for enlistment in the IRA were (and are)

Figure 2.7   Rudyard Kipling with the Irish Guards at Warley Barracks, Essex,
1919, when Kipling was writing the war history of the regiment,
partly as a memorial to his only son, John.

as diverse as those for taking the king's (or queen's) shilling
– whatever the reason, in the first instance they frequently
found themselves fighting against fellow ex-soldiers in the
Black and Tans and the Auxiliary Division of the Royal
Irish Constabulary, not to mention, of course, regular soldiers as well.[89] Many of these men, on both sides, were,
perhaps, war-damaged goods, and possibly otherwise
unemployable.[90] Thus the shadow of Suvla, Salonika and
the Somme fell across the hostilities of Ireland's post-war
'Troubles' as surely as it darkened the lives of individuals
more directly involved with those battles, whether as casualties, survivors or the bereaved.

One – unlikely – Irish victim of the Great War will carry
us on to the cultural resonances of the conflict. This is John

Kipling, Rudyard Kipling's only son, who is included in *Ireland's Memorial Records* by virtue of having fallen serving as a subaltern in the 2nd Battalion Irish Guards.

At the outbreak of the war, John, not quite seventeen years old, had tried to join up, but was turned down on the grounds of age and also poor eyesight.[91] He then proposed to enlist in the ranks, but with the help of his father's old friend Lord Roberts, an Irishman, he secured a commission in the Irish Guards. After nearly a year in training, he landed in France on 17 August 1915, his eighteenth birthday. He first went into action about 4.00 in the afternoon of 27 September, during the Battle of Loos. Within forty minutes '2nd Lieutenant Kipling was wounded and missing'. Thus Rudyard Kipling bleakly recorded his son's fall, in the war history of the Irish Guards which he wrote in part as a tribute to 'my boy Jack'. Two other officers died in the engagement and some twenty-five men. 'It does not seem to have occurred to anyone', commented Kipling, 'to suggest that direct Infantry attacks, after ninety-minute bombardments, on works begotten out of a generation of thought and prevision, scientifically built up by immense labour and applied science, and developed against all contingencies through nine months, are not likely to find a fortunate issue.'[92] ('Issue', let us recall, is the term used in genealogies for children and so, for Kipling, the *issue* was doubly unfortunate.)

Before the war, Kipling had been one of the most articulate, leading English supporters of the Ulster Unionist cause. Despite his jocular celebration of the Irish soldier in India, his tendency was to dismiss the Irish Catholic nationalist as a sort of 'lesser breed without the law'. But in writing his history of the Irish Guards he came to modify his passionate, and sometimes bitter, exclusive allegiance to Ulster loyalism. Although the Irish Guards, while 'young on the Army List', were a sort of paradigm of the old order – Ascendancy Anglo-Irish officers with a smattering of loyal 'Castle Catholics' leading decent, honest Catholic farm boys – Kipling was nevertheless so moved by the deeds of the regiment that he modified his opinion of Catholic Ireland from antagonism to admiration. And, maybe here, in the creative imagination of Rudyard Kipling, if not actually in the ranks of soldiers themselves, is a reconciliation of two contending narratives of Irish history. Kipling's creative, imaginative writing (though his regimental history is deliberately loaded down with prosaic details of what happened to the Guards during the war, and especially of what happened to individual junior officers) epitomises one literary, cultural response to the war, and an attempt to make sense of, or at least just to lend some coherence to, the events of 1914–18.

3 Imagination: onlookers in France

Irish cultural responses to the war

Lennox Robinson's play *The Big House: Four Scenes in Its Life* was first produced in Dublin in September 1926. It is set at Ballydonal House in County Cork, the home of St Leger Alcock and his family: Protestant, Anglo-Irish, Ascendancy people, not unlike Robinson himself, though his politics were nationalist. He was a strong adherent of the Irish literary revival, and managed the Abbey Theatre in Dublin from 1909 to 1914. The play opens at 'about ten-thirty on a November morning 1918'. In fact it is 11 November and the first scene begins with a discussion about how the yard bell is to be rung, for the first time in twenty years, in celebration of the peace. We learn that the Alcocks' elder son, Reginald, a wild, attractive, but potentially rather dissipated fellow, had died a hero's death in France. The younger boy, Ulick, a steadier 'born farmer', and devoted to Ballydonal, is serving in France, but is expected to come home to take over the property. As the clock strikes eleven and the yard bell begins to ring, a telegram arrives. It is, of course, the news of Ulick's death, from wounds, three days earlier.[1]

Beyond the tragic conjunction of Armistice and bereavement,[2] the play is a kind of template or paradigm for the classic Irish Big House narrative, for example as expounded subsequently by Elizabeth Bowen or Jennifer Johnston. The second scene is set in June 1921 during the Anglo-Irish War, when an embittered Black and Tan, who had served with Reginald in France, challenges the Alcocks' loyalty. Then the action moves on to the civil war, in February 1923, when, inevitably one supposes, Ballydonal is burnt down as a reprisal. The Alcocks, decent, honourable, loyal people, contemplate their home and their life destroyed by the Great War and the Irish revolution. At the end, the passionate daughter Kate, while mourning the loss of her beloved Ulick and recognising that she is neither fully Irish nor English, resolves to settle in the new Ireland, unlike her parents who are leaving for England.

Here we have not only an epitaph for the old-style Big House, but also an indication of how the Anglo-Irish could yet legitimately play a part in the independent state. Robinson's linking of the Great War – and the poignant melodrama of Armistice Day – with the passing of the old order recurs in his biography, written five years later, of Bryan Cooper, the historian of the 10th (Irish) Division, who served at Suvla and Salonika. 'Almost without exception', he wrote, 'the big houses were emptied of all men of a fighting age.' The Great War witnessed 'the last chapter in the history of many families'.[3] For the declining Ascendancy class the Great War was the last in a series of blows, beginning in the 1870s, which left them utterly demoralised: the land had gone, their political role – both local and national – had passed away, and now, most grievously, their sons had suffered disproportionately heavy casualties in comparison to the losses of any other Irish social group, except perhaps the Belfast Protestant working class. One might hazard that the notion of a 'lost generation', so powerful in post-war Britain,[4] applies most forcefully to this single segment of Irish society. In November 1932 in Great St Mary's Church, Cambridge, the Reverend Frederick Simpson declared that 'a generation was not decimated but decapitated . . . *Our Born leaders are dead.*'[5] With their self-image as the natural leaders of Irish politics and society, this is precisely what happened to the Anglo-Irish community.

For those who survived, however, like Bryan Cooper and Robinson's fictional Kate Alcock, there was a chance to participate in the new Ireland. We have seen how Cooper in his account of the slaughter at Suvla expressed the hope that the young soldiers of the 10th Division would not have died in vain. In a lyrical passage towards the end of his history he amplified this theme, later taken up by others in the wake of Willie Redmond's death in Flanders. Within the 10th Division, wrote Cooper, 'the old quarrels, the inherited animosities were forgotten, and men who would have scowled at one another without speaking became comrades and friends. Only those who know Ireland can realise how difficult this was.' It was to be hoped, he added, 'that the willingness to forget old wrongs and injustices, and to combine for a common purpose, that existed in the 10th Division, may be a good augury for the future'.[6]

Cooper wrote this in 1917, after the Rising, but before the advance of militant separatism had fully emerged and before the events of 1919–23 had exacerbated divisions in Ireland and added new 'wrongs and injustices' to the collective Irish arsenal of animosity. Yet, in the aftermath of all this Cooper himself channelled his optimistic and inclusive vision of Ireland into active politics. A former unionist politician, even briefly MP for South Dublin in 1910, he stood successfully for the Dáil – Yeats spoke for him on the hustings – and, unlike most of his coreligionists other than a few notables in the Senate, participated in the public political life of the Irish Free State. His sudden death in 1930 at the early age of forty-six brought this experiment to an untimely conclusion.

In his biography of Cooper, Lennox Robinson remarks on the wonderful peacefulness of Ireland in 1919. The start of the 'Anglo-Irish War' is conventionally dated to the Soloheadbeg ambush on 21 January 1919, but hostilities did not seriously get going until the following year. Thus a sort of peaceful interlude followed the Armistice. This is reflected in a visual cultural response to the end of the Great War, a painting by the 21-year-old Mainie Jellett

Figure 3.1   *Peace*, by Mainie Jellett (oil on canvas, 61.5 × 81.5 cms). This painting was begun at Fintragh House, Donegal, in the summer of 1919.
It is also known by the title *The Bathing Pool*.

which in 1920 won the annual Royal Dublin Society
Taylor Art Prize, a substantial scholarship of fifty pounds.
The subjects specified for the competition that year were
Peace for figure painting and *The Bathers' Pool* for land-
scape. Jellett submitted a picture of her two younger sisters
and two other girls by a sunny beach for the figure painting
category. The artist came from a prominent Protestant
Ascendancy family. Her grandfather had been provost of
Trinity College, Dublin, and her father, William Morgan
Jellett, was a leading Dublin barrister. At about the time
Mainie began her picture, in July 1919, her father was
being elected an MP for Trinity College, the last ever
Unionist from southern Ireland to be returned to the
United Kingdom parliament at Westminster.

Jellett's painting encapsulates the last peaceful summer
of Ascendancy Ireland: a unionist (and female) vision of

tranquillity and a souvenir of 'the family's first real holiday in five years'.[7] But its existence as a response to the end of the Great War was quickly forgotten. Epitomising the amnesiac tendency of southern Ireland to the war, even in the relatively rarefied realm of fine art, the painting, originally entitled *Peace*, subsequently became known as *The Bathers' Pool*. Not until 1991, when a major exhibition of Jellett's work was held in Dublin, were we reminded of its real provenance.[8] Jellett spent her prize money on travelling to Paris where she largely abandoned this kind of old-fashioned figurative work and became a pioneer Irish modernist. Perhaps her artistic trajectory therefore supports the argument that the Great War provided an enormous boost for cultural modernism, the 'shock of the new' and so on.[9] There is some evidence for this in the work of another Irish artist, William Orpen (to whom we shall return), yet none at all in that of the socially most distinguished Irish painter of the day, John Lavery.

Lavery, a Catholic, was the son of a not-very-successful Belfast wine merchant. He had been brought to Glasgow as a youth, grew up there and made his early name as one of the 'Glasgow School'. In the years immediately before the First World War he had gained a European reputation as a very highly regarded – and successful – painter of portraits and landscapes.[10] On 4 August 1914 Lavery was in Dublin on holiday but returned to London immediately on hearing the news of war. In his memoirs he said he found himself 'in a very awkward corner'. Albeit an Irishman, he loved London and 'was honoured by Englishmen'. He regarded himself as a pacifist, though 'without the moral courage of a Bernard Shaw [another Irishman] or a Ramsay MacDonald', the Labour politician. Lavery had, moreover, 'German sympathies, since there I had been looked on as one of the greatest painters and overwhelmed with commissions'.[11]

In the event Lavery decided 'to run with the hare and hunt with the hounds',[12] and, although he was fifty-eight years old, he enlisted in the 28th County of London

Territorial Regiment – the 'Artists' Rifles' – which eventually included such other artists as John and Paul Nash and Charles Sergeant Jagger, as well as the Irish music critic and composer, Herbert Hughes.[13] Together they drilled in the quadrangle of Burlington House: 'rather a scrubby lot of painters, sculptors, actors, musicians, hairdressers, scene-shifters, etc., of all ages'. Arriving late one day for drill, Lavery overheard the bemused spectators discussing this motley crowd. 'Who are they?', one asked. 'Don't you know? Why they're German prisoners. Aren't they awful?' Physically, Lavery was not up to soldiering and his doctor ordered him to stick to his paint-pots: 'You will do more for your country with your brush than with your rifle', and so 'in the end they went to the trenches and I went to bed'.[14] Lavery still wanted to get to France and was making arrangements to go out as part of the new British propaganda branch – Wellington House – run by Charles F. G. Masterman, when both he and his wife, Hazel, were injured in a car accident in Park Lane. Hazel was particularly badly affected and for a year Lavery was unable to leave her for any significant length of time.

William Orpen, the next most famous Irish artist of the day, was also on holiday in Ireland, at Howth, just north of Dublin, on 4 August 1914. A much younger man than Lavery – he was thirty-six in 1914 – Orpen had a brilliant reputation, especially (though not entirely) as a portrait painter. He was a Dublin Protestant who, although he had effectively settled in London before the First World War, regularly returned to Dublin to teach at the Metropolitan School of Art and to show at the Royal Hibernian Academy.[15] There was an air of radical chic about him. In September 1913 he joined other writers and artists, organised by George Russell (who used the pseudonym 'AE'), in helping the trade union leader James Larkin during the bitter Dublin lock-out. Although he certainly evinced a warm sympathy for the underdog in any given situation, Orpen was not a particularly political animal. Yet, along with his immensely successful society portraits, he occasionally painted 'fantasy' or 'parable' pictures, which demonstrate a harder, satirical edge to his work.

One of the earliest of these was entitled *Sowing the Seed for the Board of Agriculture and Technical Instruction in Ireland*. In this 'whimsical allegorical composition', the 'nude figures of a young woman of classic proportions and two putti-like children, male and female', are contrasted with an older, fully clothed man and woman. The male figure, thought by some to be a clergyman, is dressed in his best 'Sunday black'. One of Orpen's explanations (there are a number) of this obscure work was that he intended it to symbolise 'the new Sinn Fein movement: the girl', he asserted, 'represents the spirit of Sinn Fein in 1913', when the picture was painted, 'sowing the seed. You see the crop springing from it while the older ones look on.' 'Be that as it may', remarked one critic, 'the beautiful quality of the painting is beyond dispute.'[16] Two other striking and important Irish pictures, painted in 1914–16, *The Western Wedding* and *The Holy Well*, confirm Orpen's taste for the political and allegorical, a feature which was to emerge in some 'equally startling images' in his war paintings. As Kenneth McConkey put it, '*The Western Wedding* became the Western Front.'[17]

The outbreak of the war did not immediately affect Orpen very greatly, though at some personal inconvenience he lent his Rolls Royce to the Red Cross, and the death of his friend Hugh Lane, director of the National Gallery of Ireland, on the *Lusitania* when it was torpedoed by a German U-boat in May 1915 was a sharp personal loss. In London during the early part of the war his studio assistant was Seán Keating, a brilliant young artist and a committed Irish nationalist. When conscription in Britain became inevitable in 1916, Keating decided to go back home to Ireland (like Michael Collins and others). He pressed Orpen to return with him:

> I said to him before I went: 'Come back with me to
> Ireland. This war may never end. All that we know of

civilisation is done for. It is the beginning of the end. I am
going to Aran. There is endless painting to be done. Leave
all this. *You* don't believe in it.' But he said: 'No.
Everything I have I owe to England. I am unknown in
Ireland. It was the English who gave me appreciation and
money. This is their war, and I have enlisted. I won't fight,
but I'll do what I can.'[18]

While Keating went off to Ireland to paint *Men of the West*
and, later, *Men of the South* (themselves both 'war' paintings of a sort, depicting the citizen soldiers of Irish separatism), Orpen in March 1916 secured a commission in the
Army Service Corps and went off to paint, for example,
Dead Germans in a Trench and *The Thinker on the Butte de
Warlencourt*.

There is no direct evidence that the Easter Rising affected
Orpen greatly, though the change in atmosphere in Dublin
which followed may have dismayed him. During the Rising
the Royal Hibernian Academy building in Lower Abbey
Street, near the GPO, was destroyed, along with several of
his paintings. But the last of Orpen's annual family holidays
in Ireland had occurred in August 1915, and the artist
visited his homeland again for only one day in 1918.[19]

Lavery, meanwhile, was becoming more involved with
Irish affairs. In 1916 Mr Justice Darling invited him to
record the trial of Sir Roger Casement and, working
covertly in the jury box, produced a portrait of the doomed
Irishman in the dock.[20] According to his memoirs, at some
point during the war, possibly after the Rising, Lavery's
Irish-American wife Hazel urged him to 'do something'
for his country.[21] Lavery responded by painting a triptych
with Hazel as the Madonna, a role she had taken in London
society *tableaux vivants*, fund-raising for war charities.[22]
The centrepiece, *The Madonna of the Lakes*, was exhibited
in the 1917 Royal Academy show. Lavery got Sir Edwin
Lutyens to design a frame specially 'using celtic spiral
motifs', and the finished work was presented as an altar
piece to St Patrick's Church, Donegall Street, Belfast,

Figure 3.2   *Men of the West* (oil on canvas, 102 × 127 cms). These 'citizen
soldiers' were painted by Seán Keating in 1916 after he returned
home to Ireland from London. Keating is the figure on the left of
the picture, which was painted for the Irish National Aid and
Volunteer Dependants' Fund.

where the artist had been baptised.[23] With this work
Lavery, though he was no bigot, clearly identified himself
with Irish Catholicism.

About this time, in the spring of 1917, a new Department
of Information, headed by the writer John Buchan, took
over the British government's main war propaganda effort.
The department set up an 'artists' establishment', the first
two of whom were William Orpen and John Lavery. The
choice of two Irish artists was seen by some 'as a propaganda move in itself, designed to demonstrate Anglo-Irish
solidarity in the face of the German menace and counter the
very different impression left by the Easter Rising'.[24]

From mid-April 1917 Orpen worked on the Western Front, though, like all the official war artists (and Church of England chaplains) he was prohibited from going to the front line. Thus he remained officially detached from the conflict. Unlike most other war artists, who spent much shorter terms in France, refreshed by trips home, Orpen, apart from May–July 1918, remained in France continuously until September 1919. After the war he published an account of his time as a war artist as *An Onlooker in France*. Here he expressed his intense sympathy for the common soldier and gave 'sincere thanks for the wonderful opportunity that was given me to look on and see the fighting man, to learn to revere and worship him'.[25] In a poem, 'Myself, Hate and Love', Orpen asserted that there was only 'one man alone' whom he could truly admire:

> I mean the simple soldier man,
> Who, when the Great War first began,
> Just died, stone dead
> From lumps of lead,
> In mire.[26]

Here we sense the fascination and admiration of the observer – the 'mere looker on'[27] – for the men of action who were fully (and tragically) engaged in the conflict. The war, too, seems to have stimulated the subversive streak in Orpen's work which emerges in his more allegorical paintings, a tendency sharpened, no doubt, by the inevitable contrast between his smooth society portraiture and the cruel realities of the Western Front. One friend of his, the journalist Sidney Dark, wrote that the war forced Orpen 'into the great world. His blinds were pulled up. He was taken by the scruff of his neck and forced to look out of his window and what he saw hurt him, appalled him, disgusted him.' There is a marked contrast between Orpen's brilliantly coloured battlefield landscapes, mostly painted during his first year in France, and the 'darker vision' which followed. The simplicity of the earlier paintings, observes Bruce Arnold, 'vanished into a more complex, more frightening series of pictures'.[28] Throughout his time as a 'war artist', Orpen's depictions of people vividly reflect his humane sympathy, and in some cases they also convey a distinctly unsettling message, not necessarily one which his propaganda masters may have had in mind when he was originally appointed. Writing in 1937, Seán Keating asserted that these works constituted 'an austere and piti-less statement, a crushing reply to the pronouncements of the Biological Necessitarians, the disciples of the late Mr Kipling, the chauvinist, and the apologists for war'.[29]

In an essay on Irish cultural responses to the Great War published in 1993 I identified two main themes in both the literary and the visual representations of the conflict. The first was the utter degradation and demoralisation of the war, which sprang from the artists' concern with the human costs involved. The second was one of distance, disengagement or detachment from the war.[30] There is nothing particularly *Irish* about the first; it is a common theme which draws together such people as Wilfred Owen, Henri Barbusse and Erich Maria Remarque. But for the second, the combination of Irishness, with the sometimes ambiguous and qualified enlistment in the war effort, and the natural detachment of the artist, especially the visual one, enhances that distance, a fact which is especially apparent in the works of William Orpen.

This can be illustrated by two particular paintings from the one hundred and fifty or so images Orpen pro-duced as a war artist. The first is *The Thinker on the Butte de Warlencourt*, an artificial mound near the village of Le Sars on the road between Albert and Bapaume. Orpen visited the area, which had been devastated during the Battle of the Somme, in the summer of 1917. Coincidentally, at about the same time units of the 36th (Ulster) Division passed through the site of Le Sars on their way up to the front.[31] Orpen painted a landscape of the Butte, as well as a pen and water-colour picture of a sol-itary pensive soldier seated on the mound. He included reproductions of both in his war memoir, entitling the

Figure 3.3 *The Thinker on the Butte de Warlencourt* by Sir William Orpen (oil
on canvas, 91.5 × 76 cms), in which the artist quotes the French
sculptor Auguste Rodin's celebrated *Thinker*. The original, water-
colour version of this painting was completed in 1917, the year
Rodin died.

latter *A Man Thinking, on the Butte de Warlencourt*.[32] This now rests in the Imperial War Museum, which records the picture as *The Thinker on the Butte de Warlencourt*, the title by which a later oil version is also known.[33] The first, more resonant, title, *A* Man *Thinking*, takes us beyond the superficial uniformity of the soldier to the individual human beneath, reflecting on the repulsive circumstances of the battlefront. This vivid image was widely reproduced and 'became something of a visual metaphor for war'.[34] It is Orpen's 'simple soldier man', from his verse already quoted, who 'just died', or, as perhaps in this case:

> Lived through hell,
> Words cannot tell,
> For four long years
> And more
> Of misery
> Until the war
> Was ended.

The second picture, *Armistice Night, Amiens*, sardonically commemorates the end of the war in a wild, decadent, drunken burlesque, posed, as it were, on a stage set of destruction, with the searchlight beams providing hints of the mechanical abstraction of modern, industrialised war. At the time Orpen was quite ill with severe blood poisoning, which confined him to Amiens for almost three months from November 1918. He did not much care for the town, a 'rest and recreation' centre just behind the British lines on the Somme. He had been billeted there in 1917 and described it in his memoir as

> a danger trap for the young officer from the line, also for the men . . . The drink the Tommies got in the little cafés was terrible stuff, and often doped.
>
> Then, when darkness came on, strange women [Orpen was no prude or misogynist, far from it] – the riffraff from Paris, the expelled from Rouen, in fact the badly diseased from all parts of France – hovered about in the

Figure 3.4 *Armistice Night, Amiens* (oil on canvas, 91.5 × 71 cms), by Sir William Orpen. This is a bleak view of the triumphant end to the war, painted when the artist was exhausted and ill with severe blood poisoning. A companion picture, *The Official Entry of the Kaiser*, mockingly shows the German emperor as a crude effigy being escorted in by various grotesque figures (see Arnold, *Orpen*, p. 356).

blackness with their electric torches and led the
unknowing away to blackened side-streets and up dim
stairways – to what?[35]

And there, in a bacchanalian triumph, they are, celebrating
victory at the end of the war.

Although Orpen himself invited Lavery to join him in
the war-zone, Lavery did not get to France until after the
Armistice, when he was sent to record women's work in
hospitals and base camps. During the war, from 1917, he
was attached to the navy at home as an official war artist and
he produced a fair body of work which he later dismissed –
specifically in comparison with Orpen's paintings – as
'totally uninspired and dull as ditch-water . . . Instead of
the grim harshness and horror of the scenes', he had 'given
charming colour versions, as if painting a bank holiday on
Hampstead Heath'. Even painting North Sea convoys
from an airship, he 'felt nothing of the stark reality of my
fellow-men being blown to pieces in submarines or slowly
choking to death in mud. I saw only new beauties of colour
and design as seen from above.'[36] Some critics agreed.
When Lavery's naval canvases were exhibited at the end of
1918 the *Manchester Guardian* remarked that 'the trend of
modern art has made one look for something more than
this, something more mental and memorable; but Sir John
Lavery stands faithfully to his charming impressionism
and carries on gallantly'.[37]

One in particular of Lavery's wartime paintings confirms
and expresses this sense of detachment from the conflict: of
the artist as a 'mere looker on'. It is *The Studio Window, 7
July 1917*.[38] The painting shows a daylight aerial bombing
raid on London and we see the painter's wife kneeling on a
chaise longue apparently looking at the aircraft. But she is
not. Hazel Lavery, the smart, confident, superb society
hostess, was terrified by the war, and was especially
unnerved by the threat of bombing from Zeppelins or other
aircraft. Her indisposition after the Park Lane accident
seems to have been as much a sort of nervous breakdown as

Figure 3.5 *Daylight Raid from My Studio Window, 7 July 1917*, by Sir John
Lavery (oil on canvas, 141.5 × 89.9 cms). The attack on London by
twenty-one German Gotha biplanes was clearly visible from
Lavery's Cromwell Place studio. In the original version, Hazel
Lavery was kneeling before a statuette of the Madonna.

a direct result of concussion. As originally painted, this picture showed Hazel kneeling before a statuette of the Madonna, praying for comfort and release from the awful threat represented by the distant aircraft. Lavery kept the painting until 1929, when he gave it along with a very substantial collection of other works to the Belfast Municipal Museum and Art Gallery (now the Ulster Museum). Before he donated the picture, however, he painted out the Madonna 'and with it, all reference to his wife's fretfulness'.[39] This is the only significant Great War painting in a public collection in Ireland, and it provides a strikingly civilian and detached vision of the war, which is reduced to a distant pattern of aircraft in conflict. Orpen's painting, *German Planes Visiting Cassel*,[40] presents a similar battlefield vision of distant conflict. Together they are visual reflections of Yeats's detached expression of involvement in the Great War contained in his famous poem 'An Irish Airman Foresees His Death', where 'A lonely impulse of delight/Drove to this tumult in the clouds'.

Orpen's exhibition 'War' at Agnew's (London) in May 1918, where he exhibited 125 pictures, caught the attention of Langton Douglas, director of the National Gallery of Ireland. He was, he told the artist, 'very anxious' for the exhibition to go to Dublin. 'Irishmen', he wrote, 'are proud of Sir William Orpen and his pictures would help to lift some of them out of their parochialism.'[41] But in the end both the costs of bringing the pictures to Dublin, which the National Gallery of Ireland was unable to meet, and, possibly, the political situation, with the threat of conscription exciting Irish passions, combined to deny Irish people in Ireland a sight of the war art of the greatest Irish painter of the day. The exhibition instead went to the United States. The one main gap in the National Gallery's collection of Orpens remains his war art. Even if the will to acquire an example had existed, the gallery was not permitted to hang works by living artists.[42] Besides, the purchase grant of £1,000 per annum had been cut as a war economy measure, so no funds were available.

In 1919 the newly established Imperial War Museum in London commissioned Orpen to produce three paintings of the peace conference for a total fee of £6,000. In the first two, *A Peace Conference at the Quai d'Orsay* and *The Signing of the Peace in the Hall of Mirrors, Versailles, 28 June 1919*, the statesmen are dwarfed by the overwhelming size of the state rooms they occupy, their situation, it appears, reflecting the magnitude of the international problems being tackled. Orpen's design was widely interpreted as satirical. Reflecting specifically on these two pictures, John Lavery observed that 'no British painter since Hogarth has ridiculed people in power so effectively as Orpen'.[43] The third painting was originally intended to show some forty 'politicians and generals and admirals who had won the war' and Orpen conceived another monumental setting in the 'Hall of Peace' on the way into the Hall of Mirrors. But, having begun work on the painting, he changed his mind. 'And then, you know', he later told the London *Evening Standard*, 'I couldn't go on. It all seemed so unimportant somehow beside the reality as I had seen it and felt it when I was working with the armies. In spite of all these eminent men, I kept thinking of the soldiers who remain in France for ever . . . So I painted all the statesmen and commanders out.'[44]

Orpen replaced this picture with *To the Unknown British Soldier in France*. The Hall of Peace was retained, but now it held a single coffin draped in a Union Jack,[45] flanked by two 'gaunt wraiths from the trenches',[46] rather like armorial supporters, modelled on an actual individual Orpen had encountered wandering shell-shocked behind the lines in France and sketched as *Blown Up: Mad*.[47] Above the coffin floated two putti holding green and gold garlands. One description of the picture, apparently approved by Orpen himself, noted that 'the gilded pomp of the Palace of Versailles' was 'imaginatively contrasted with the ragged misery of the ghostly boy-soldiers who watch over the coffin of their comrade. Festooned Cupids and the Cross shining in the distance are symbols of the "Greater Love"

Figure 3.6 *To the Unknown British Soldier in France,* by Sir William Orpen (original version). This was voted 'Picture of the Year' at the Royal Academy's 1923 summer exhibition.

of those who have laid down their lives.'[48] The picture reflected Orpen's own view that 'after all the negotiations and discussions, the Armistice and Peace, the only tangible result is the ragged unemployed soldier and the Dead'.[49]

Many critics did not like the painting, although the public did, voting it 'Picture of the Year' at the Royal Academy's 1923 summer exhibition. The Imperial War Museum refused to accept it. Opinions tended to divide on political lines. The left-wing *Daily Herald* welcomed it as 'a magnificent allegorical tribute to the men who really won the war'.[50] The Liberal *Liverpool Echo* responded equally sympathetically. Sir William Orpen, it reported, had declined 'to paint the floors of hell with the colours of paradise, [or] to pander to the pompous heroics of the red tab brigade. The Imperial War Museum may reject the picture, but the shadow legions of the dead sleeping out and far will applaud it with Homeric hush.'[51] By contrast, the right-wing *Patriot*, taking the opportunity also to criticise John Lavery for his public sympathy with Irish nationalism, disagreed and called it

> a joke – and a bad joke at that. Sir William Orpen, by the way, is an Irishman, like his brother artist Sir John Lavery . . .
>
> The English people are very patient and very indulgent. But perhaps they are not quite so stupid as some of the Irish who live amongst us suppose. When an Irishman who accepts the hospitality of this country and profits by its wealth and its culture espouses the cause of Sinn Fein like Sir John Lavery, or takes liberties with our feelings of reverence like Sir William Orpen, there is an obvious comment which rises to the lips, but is not usually uttered. If these are their feelings, why do they not go and live in their own country? Certainly to artists who have a turn for the grotesque and the fantastic desolation of war, there are excellent subjects ready to hand in Southern Ireland.[52]

Five years later Orpen painted out the soldiers, cherubs and garlands and gave the picture to the Imperial War

Figure 3.7 *To the Unknown British Soldier in France*, by Sir William Orpen (final version: oil on canvas, 152.5 × 128 cms). Presented to the Imperial War Museum in 1928 as a memorial to Earl Haig.

Museum as a memorial to Earl Haig (who had just died), 'one of the best friends I ever had', he said. 'I would like to do my tiny bit to his memory.'[53]

This apparent volte-face, from commemorating the ordinary soldier – now in his turn painted out – to the commander-in-chief himself, presents a conundrum to our jaundiced – or is it more perceptive? – eyes, when disenchantment with the Great War inevitably, especially perhaps, encompasses the generals – the 'butchers and bunglers' of the high command, as a recent book title has it.[54] Haig, however, was also identified with the welfare of the rank and file, for example through the Royal British Legion and the Earl Haig Fund. In one sense Haig might stand with the 'lions', while the 'donkeys', the politicians or 'frocks' (from their frock-coats), are yet further from the battlefield. Nevertheless it is difficult when a refreshingly perceptive observer like Orpen (that is to say, one whose views generally coincide with one's own) turns out to be unreconstructed in some respects. We must, therefore, pause and reflect – as with the rationality of enlistment – that they 'do things differently' in that foreign country which is the past.

Like both Orpen and Lavery, Ireland's leading composers at this time, Charles Villiers Stanford and Hamilton Harty, straddled the Irish Sea. They were, indeed, if anything, more 'English' than either of the two artists. Both were firmly located in the mainstream of English musical life. Yet they were also clearly and identifiably Irish, if only because both produced 'Irish' compositions – symphonies, rhapsodies and tone poems – albeit primarily for the English market. Stanford, professor of music at Cambridge University and professor of composition at the Royal College of Music, was one of the leading *English* composers of the day. Aged sixty-two in 1914, he was at the summit of his profession. As a recent, fascinating discussion of the musical politics of the time put it: he had a 'dual identity as an Irishman *and* an Englishman',[55] reflecting in cultural terms the political dilemma progressively faced during the war years of the Irish Home Rulers who heeded Redmond's call to enlist.

In the role of 'public intellectual', Stanford wrote several articles about music and the war. In 1916 he asserted that 'at no time has a great country failed to produce great composers when its resources have been put to the supreme test of war', adding the significant qualifications that the 'ideals of the nation' should be high, its principles of action 'just' and 'that it possesses a sound incentive to call forth a genuinely patriotic effort'.[56] It is clear that 'Britain' or 'England' – they are in Stanford's view the same: he uses the terms 'British' and 'English' quite indiscriminately – is one of the 'great countries' he has in mind. 'Ireland' is not mentioned (is it not a 'great country'?), though was undoubtedly subsumed within 'Britain' in Stanford's understanding. Ironically, at a time when patriotism was at a premium (and perhaps because this was so) such a sweeping conflation of separate national identities became increasingly untenable during the war and its aftermath. But it was precisely some of the strains unleashed by the conflict, of which the Easter Rising was one result, which 'finally shattered the notion of the inviolable unity of Britain'.[57]

Stanford did not compose much during the war. Apart from that curiosity, 'The Aviator's Hymn', of 1917, there are organ sonatas, number two of which, 'Sonata Eroica', is dedicated to 'Charles Marie Widor and the great Country to which he belongs'. The second movement is entitled 'Verdun – Solemn March', recalling the heroic French defence of the fortress during 1916. Sandford's Irish Rhapsody No. 5, completed on St Patrick's Day 1917, is dedicated to the Irish Guards, the senior regiment of Irish infantry in the British army.[58] The Easter Rising had an indirect effect on his work. After the outbreak, Stanford (a convinced unionist) refused permission for his opera *Shamus O'Brien* to be staged. As it dealt with the 1798 rebellion – O'Brien is a flamboyant Irish rebel – the composer (needlessly, one feels) feared that it might exacerbate the political situation. It understandably did not occur to Stanford that the patronising stage-Irish Paddywackery of the opera might itself evoke a hostile response.[59] A choral piece, 'The Last Post' (words by W. E. Henley), which he had written in 1900 during the Boer War, was revived in 1916 and performed by the Belfast Philharmonic Society that October.

While considering what was performed in Ireland during the war, we can dismiss any suggestion that German or Austrian music was boycotted. In March 1915 Richard Strauss's 'Tod und Verklärung' ('Death and Transfiguration'), an especially apt choice for wartime, was performed in Belfast. In October the same year the Belfast Philharmonic Society paired Brahms's 'Songs of Love' with Sir Alexander Mackenzie's rather less enduring 'Empire Song'. An organ recital in Dublin a fortnight later concluded with the *Tannhäuser* overture, and in February 1918 a Belfast concert heard Elgar's war cantata 'The Fourth of August' performed with Wagner's overture to *Der Meistersinger von Nürnberg*.[60]

The Ulster-born Hamilton Harty, thirty-five years old at the beginning of the war, spent two years on 'hydrophone duties' in the North Sea, perhaps an especially suitable posting for a musician.[61] He did not write any specifically 'war' music, but the conflict undoubtedly influenced public perceptions of his work. In November 1919 he conducted a performance of his own cantata, 'The Mystic Trumpeter', in Belfast. This was a setting of words by the American Quaker and pacifist poet Walt Whitman which Harty had completed in 1913. The text tells of how the trumpeter's music evokes not only the chivalry and martial spirit of crusaders, but also the power of love and the triumph of joy in the future. The scheduling of the work for November 1919 was hardly coincidental and the music critic of the *Belfast News-Letter* interpreted it explicitly in the light of the war just ended. The composer, he wrote, 'has made his music eloquently expressive of the passion and pathos which were felt by Whitman as he thought of the horrors of war and proclaimed the power of love'.[62]

One musical miniature from the post-war years picks up the unifying and liberating impulse with which Irishmen marched off to the war, and also presents an unexpected vision of their return. This is a song, 'With the Dublin Fusiliers', published in 1924, two years after the 'Dubs', along with the other Irish infantry regiments raised in what was by now independent Ireland, had been disbanded. The piece comprises an arrangement of an Irish air by Stanford to fit words by his long-time collaborator, Alfred Perceval Graves, a more unambiguously Irish poet than his more famous son Robert.[63] With an echo of 'gallant little Belgium', the verses celebrate the time

> When Irishmen together band
> In arms to aid a Sister Land,
> And free her from a tyrant's hand.

The song ends reassuringly:

> Then Peace returned and from the war
> By land and sea we homeward bore
> Till all along old Dublin's shore
> Rang out a shout of welcome.[64]

From a modern perspective this vision of great cheering crowds welcoming back the returning soldiers seems so dramatically out of kilter with what we believe to have been the case of Dublin opinion – radicalised and alienated from the trappings of British rule – as to be literally fantastic. Yet perhaps it was not so very far from the truth, and Messrs J. B. Cramer's commercial risk in publishing the song not so very great, for on Armistice Day 1924, 20,000 veterans paraded in College Green, Dublin, in front of an estimated 50,000-strong crowd. That year, moreover, the British Legion announced that nearly half a million poppies had been sold in the Dublin area.[65]

The cultural traffic was by no means all one way, nor was the interplay of music and politics necessarily very straightforward. It will be remembered, for example, that Edward Elgar composed incidental music for Yeats's play *Dairmuid and Grania*, and also, although a Catholic, signed the British version of the Ulster Covenant, pledging support for the Ulster Unionist cause.[66] Before the Great War the young English composer Arnold Bax, who had fallen under the spell of Celticism and the Gaelic revival, came to live in Dublin between 1911 and 1914. In 1916, in a volume co-authored by Stanford, he was described as 'the musical counterpart of the "Celtic Twilight" school of poetry'.[67] Bax, for his part, trenchantly asserted that Stanford was 'not Irish enough'. Albeit 'an Irishman by birth, he belonged to that class, abominated in Irish Ireland, the "West Briton"'.[68] Bax learned Irish and under the pseudonym of Dermot O'Byrne he published stories, plays and poems, some of which were regarded by the government censor in 1918 as subversively supporting the Irish republican cause, still, at this stage, identified as in league with Germany. Bax also wrote ostentatiously Irish nationalist music. In 1916 there was an orchestral tone-poem 'In Memoriam Pádraig Pearse', and in 1920 a Phantasy for viola and orchestra, incorporating Irish folk-tunes and culminating 'in a triumphal intonement of "A Soldier's Song"'.[69]

Although Ireland remained Bax's 'spiritual home', during the inter-war years he lost some of his greener tinges. In 1937, as Arnold Bax and not as Dermot O'Byrne, he accepted a knighthood and in 1941 he became Master of the King's Music. Perhaps the most ironic and touching manifestation of Bax's voyage back from Tir na Nog and his youthful Celtic radicalism was his re-use of material from the unpublished and unperformed (until the late 1990s) 'In Memoriam Pádraig Pearse' in a score for David Lean's quintessentially English film of *Oliver Twist* in 1948. A 'beautiful elegiac tune' from the earlier piece was reworked into 'Mr Brownlow's tune' for the film.[70] It was a long way indeed from the 'steps of the GPO'.

While the ironies of Bax's creative and public life are both interesting and entertaining, they also illustrate the extent to which events during the period in question, including the Great War and the Easter Rising, clearly stimulated a cultural response. Composers, like artists and writers (whatever they themselves may think or hope), do not operate in a political vacuum, though occasionally they may work in a kind of no man's land between the barbed-wire entrenchments of true believers.

An apt example of the potential political difficulties attending any Irish cultural representation of the Great War is Sean O'Casey's play *The Silver Tassie*, which was controversially turned down by Yeats for the Abbey Theatre in 1928. The following year it played for a few weeks in London. It was not staged in Dublin until August 1935, when it provoked strident clerical criticism for blasphemy and bad language. In fact, the work had already offended the Lord Chamberlain's office in London whose permission was required before any public performance was staged. Among the changes required was the substitution of 'Oh look out!' for 'God Almighty', 'drenching' for 'pissing' and 'mother's' for 'bitch's'.[71] The play, which O'Casey intended to express 'the horror of war and its aftermath',[72] tells the story of three footballing pals who return much changed from the war: one is blinded, one terribly crippled and one is a hero with a Victoria Cross. The experimental second act is set 'somewhere in France'. One of Yeats's objections to the piece was that this was 'written out of opinions' rather than actual experience. Yet, whatever literary criticism might be offered against what is undoubtedly an uneven play, there was an underlying political difficulty in putting sympathetically portrayed British soldiers on the stage of the Abbey Theatre in the late 1920s.

Of the small number of Irish plays on Great War themes only one was written by a soldier who actually served on the Western Front, Patrick MacGill. Anticipating Sebastian Faulks's novel *Birdsong* by some sixty years, MacGill's play *Suspense* draws on the work of tunnelling miners for its tension. A group of British soldiers (including one who was played as an Irishman in the first London production) hear enemy sappers mining beneath their trench. The tension mounts unbearably until, to the soldiers' intense relief, they are stood down. But as they withdraw the mine goes off and they turn back to their fate at the Front. 'Murder! War is always murder!', are the despairing final words of the piece.[73]

Apart from this play, MacGill left a considerable body of war literature, including poetry, reportage and four novels.[74] He was born into very humble circumstances and aged fourteen migrated from Donegal to work in the Scottish potato fields. Later he became a navvy for the Caledonian Railway. In 1911, after the success of his *Gleanings for a Navvy's Scrap Book*, he secured a job as a journalist on the *Daily Express*. A very successful autobiographical novel, *Children of the Dead End*, followed in 1914, by which time MacGill had been taken up by Canon John Dalton of St George's Chapel, Windsor, and employed editing ancient manuscripts in the Chapter Library of Windsor Castle. He had travelled a long way from his cabin in Glenties. He has, nevertheless, been regarded as a characteristic 'working-class novelist'.[75] And yet his wartime work, while starkly realistic and described as 'bitter' and 'scathing', was not in any fundamental way subversive. *The Red Horizon*, indeed, attracted a foreword by Lord Esher, president of the County of London Territorial Association and deputy governor of Windsor Castle. Esher's contribution to the book (which he privately described as 'harmless'[76]) was apparently solicited in order to forestall court-martial proceedings against MacGill for being too revealing in his writing.[77]

The Red Horizon follows MacGill's own unit, the London Irish, from their landing in France in the spring of 1915 through to their time in the front line later that year. It is clear from the start that the unit is both Irish and British. Cheerful Cockneys and Cumbrians mix with the Irish recruits. When the battalion parades to the local church, their pipers arrive at mass playing 'The Wearing of the Green', and at the end of the service 'we sang the national anthem, ours, "God Save the King"'. The Irish, though, are everywhere. Coming across a unit of the Scots Guards, the unnamed narrator hears 'the brogue that could be cut with a knife . . . and the kindliness that sprang from the cabins of Corrymeela and the moors of Derrynane . . .

"Irish?" I asked. "Sure," was the answer. "We're everywhere. Ye'll find us in a Gurkha regiment if you scratch the
beggars' skins.'"[78] Nor does MacGill, who served as a
medical orderly, pull his punches in graphic descriptions of
terrible wounds, rotting corpses, shell-shocked comrades
and the penetrating, nauseating smell of the trenches.
(Orpen said 'one could not paint the smell'.[79]) But the tale
is not one of unrelieved horror, which no doubt explains
why the censor eventually passed it, Lord Esher endorsed
it and it sold 37,000 copies by 1918.[80]

The war in *The Red Horizon* exists as an immutable fact
of life and MacGill's characters accept it as such. They
may not like the conflict – no sane man would – but theirs is
'not to reason why'. They respond to their shocking
circumstances with resilience and a matter-of-fact accep-
tance of death. In a curious way the book celebrates the *joie
de vivre* of the Irish and British soldiers, irreverent, cheerful and fiercely loyal to each other. Whatever might have
been the case at the time of enlistment, the crucial factor
holding the army together in the face of death at the battlefront is not patriotism or commitment to some abstract
high war aim, but *esprit de corps*. Army morale was evidently safe enough in the hands of Patrick MacGill.
Indeed his reassuring portrait of the Expeditionary Force
as fundamentally 'sound' reflects the historical truth. The
British army (unlike the French) was not riven with muti-
nies or widespread disaffection. Perhaps, then, MacGill's
soldiers were as typical as he himself was not. Authorship
clearly set him apart from the run-of-the-mill soldier, and
his semi-autobiographical narrator in *The Red Horizon* was
a cultured fellow, who found that 'Old Montaigne in a dug-
out is a true friend and a fine companion.' One of
MacGill's strengths as a writer is that he tempers the reassuring qualities of his narrative with the unsettling and
frightening realities of the war, two sides of the soldier's
experience which he combined in a quatrain at the head of
The Red Horizon's final chapter, entitled, with a hint of
irony, 'Romance':

The young recruit is apt to think
Of war as a romance;
But he'll find its boots and bayonets
When he's somewhere out in France.[81]

There is no 'romance of war' at all in MacGill's sombre and neglected 1921 novel *Fear!*. In an unsigned introduction (though possibly written by MacGill himself) it is explained that 'the blue pencil of the Censor was too busy during the War to allow a realist such as Patrick MacGill a chance of exposing the truth'. And it is a book with a message. 'Unconstrained by the thought of blue-pencil', MacGill 'has been able to write about war as war actually is'. The terrible realism of the story 'will bring home to all the conviction that such things must never be allowed to happen again'.[82] The novel is narrated by Henry Arthur Ryder, a conscript, and it charts his progressive moral degeneration. On a trench raid Ryder finds himself in a virtually psychopathic frenzy when it comes to using his bayonet: 'filled with a wild and wicked joy, I lunged the steel forward and caught the man on the face, shoving the bayonet through his gas-mask and through his head'. He loses any belief he may have had in God; as a stretcher-bearer (like MacGill) he has to step on bodies, living and dead; a colleague graphically describes the bungled execution of his mate for cowardice in the face in the enemy; he visits a prostitute (for the first time) but staggers off apparently before completing the job. 'I was', he writes, 'now a ship that had lost its anchor and was at the mercy of every buffeting wave.'[83] At the last – and surely very near the end of the war – he is killed in yet another pointless attack. The book is a very early example of a genre of grimly realistic writing which was to become quite widespread later in the decade. One critic has remarked that 'had *Fear!* been published in 1929 it might have achieved minor fame; coming as it did in 1921, it has been decently forgotten'.[84] All the same, the novel still sold quite well, achieving 16,179 copies by the fourth printing.[85]

The only other 'Irish' novel set wholly on the Western Front, Liam O'Flaherty's *Return of the Brute, was* published in 1929, but it, too, was 'decently forgotten' until a facsimile reprint was issued in 1998. Studies of O'Flaherty's writing do not tend to dwell on the work. Patrick Sheeran has described it as 'one of the worst [novels] ever published'.[86] The book presumably draws on O'Flaherty's own experience. Born on the Aran Islands and educated at Rockwell College, Blackrock College, the Holy Cross Seminary at Clonliffe and (briefly) University College, Dublin, he joined the Irish Guards in 1915 (not, it might be noted in August 1914, when he had turned eighteen). He spent six months on the Western Front, culminating with his being shell-shocked at Langemarck in September 1917, and was later discharged from the army. *Return of the Brute* is set in the mud of Arras in March 1917 and describes the events of a few hours during which all but one of a section of nine soldiers perishes. The chief theme in the novel is the utter degradation and demoralisation of the war and the (perhaps intended) effect of the work is to anaesthetise the reader to the horrors of the front. But it is gratuitous horror, as one critic observed, 'like *All Quiet [on the Western Front]* without the sensitivity'.[87] Although individual scenes have a certain 'monstrous vigour',[88] there is no narrative development, and Gunn's rising madness is particularly unconvincing. As the *Times Literary Supplement* reviewer wanly remarked: 'there is hardly a soul in that bombing section less revolting than Gunn and the Corporal themselves. These people hardly require the war to make them repulsive.'[89]

O'Flaherty's novel was published ten years after the end of the war, at a time when quite a few other such bleakly disillusioned works were being produced. Nothing of quite such power was published during the war, although there are elements of verismo in Patrick MacGill's writing. When considering the domestic impact of the war, the question which naturally arises is: what did people in Ireland think was going on in France? What did they *imagine* the war was like?[90] Apart from such literature as might have been available, there were also newspaper reports and letters home. Yet all three of these sources of information were subject to censorship, a factor which evidently constrained MacGill. Among the most intimidating and unsettling manifestations of the war were the daily casualty lists which dominated the newspapers. Clearly, while they may have been spared some of the gruesome details, people at home soon came to appreciate the war's human cost. But this, too, had a brutalising effect mirroring that which afflicted the soldiers at the front. In St John Ervine's novel *Changing Winds* the mother of one of Henry Quinn's friends remarks on 'how indifferent one becomes to the death lists'. 'And everywhere', muses Quinn, 'it seemed to him, that coarsening process was going on, a persistent blunting of the feelings, an itching desire for more and grimmer and bloodier details'.[91]

A similar point is made in Pamela Hinkson's *The Ladies' Road*,[92] first published in 1932 and one of the most impressive novels of the home front during 1914–18. The book is dedicated to Hinkson's mother, Katharine Tynan. Hinkson was in her mid-teens at the start of the war and spent much of the following years at Brookhill House, near Claremorris (County Mayo). The action of the novel moves between two family homes: 'Cappagh' in Ireland, modelled on Brookhill, and 'Winds' in England, idyllically sited on the Downs. The main character, Stella Mannering, is at school during the war. There she 'almost carelessly' turns to the casualty lists 'wondering if there was anyone she knew. There was a certain excitement about seeing the name of someone one knew.' But on this occasion she finds the name of her beloved cousin Philip, and 'she never turned to it [the casualty list] carelessly again'.[93]

There is a clear echo of the impact of these lists in the writing of a strongly republican author a couple of years after Hinkson's book. In her semi-autobiographical novel, *The Marriage of Nurse Harding*, Annie M. P. Smithson significantly has one of her characters learn of the fifteen

executions of rebel leaders after the Rising as if they were
Western Front casualties:

> But more bitter still was the news brought to Ballafagh
> during the following days. Execution after execution;
> wounded men taken out to be killed; courtmartial after
> courtmartial, and the great pit at Arbour Hill being filled
> with the bodies of those who died for their fatherland . . .
>   Aileen, reading those terrible lists in the newspapers –
> that superb Roll of Honour which will be enshrined
> forever on Irish hearts – was glad when at last the tears
> came, and she could weep.[94]

At one level the clear evocation of Great War casualty lists
in relation to the comparative handful of fatalities associated with the Easter Rising may seem grotesque. But in
truth it merely reflects the emblematic importance of these
martyrs to the construction of the new state, which was
itself born in revolutionary violence, and the concomitant
irrelevance of those who fell fighting in the war. Another –
rhetorical – conflation of the Easter Rising with the Great
War is to be found in an inscription by the author, Mrs
Hamilton Norway, in a copy of her memoir, *The Sinn Fein
Rebellion As I Saw It*.[95] Dedicating the book to Mr T. G. V.
Orpen in November 1916, Mrs Norway wrote 'Lest We
Forget', a phrase which after the war became indelibly
associated with Remembrance, but one which in this
context anticipated future Novembers and connects it with
the events of Dublin 1916.

The melancholy theme of Pamela Hinkson's novel is
that the women are victims too. Stella, her sister, sister-in-
law and aunt suffer terrible losses: both brothers and her
uncle are killed. In the face of the family's sacrifice Stella
worries about being unable to contribute to the war effort,
about being 'a useless mouth'.[96] Hinkson's mother makes
the same point in her memoirs. In Mayo she and Pamela
felt their 'alienation' and detachment from the war. Pamela
'envied even those who were under air-raids. Anything,
anything, except the immunity (in a sense) which had been

forced upon us.'[97] In Katharine Tynan's novel, *The Golden Rose*, set in the west of Ireland where the author herself lived during the war, her character Carmel O'Reilly wants 'to be somewhere where people were feeling the stress and suffering of the war. The poor people about them were hardly aware of the war except in so far as it affected prices.'[98]

One category of Irish writer remains to be considered: the poets, sometimes regarded as the most characteristic single group of literary participants in the conflict. There is a (perhaps apocryphal) story of a *Punch* cartoon of two soldiers 'going over the top' on the Western Front. One remarks to the other: 'I shouldn't really be here at all. I have never written a line of poetry in my life.' Wisely perhaps, military historians have traditionally been a little bit suspicious of poets and other such literary folk in general. In a bibliographical essay on the 'Home Front' in the Great War, the distinguished military historian David Woodward, for example, categorically stated that 'the literary response to the war, *of course*, should *never* be used as documentary evidence'.[99] Perhaps Paul Fussell is to blame, for in his hugely influential book, *The Great War and Modern Memory*, he did just that, using poetry – from a smallish sample of writers – as 'documentary evidence'. The book itself as literary criticism is admirable; as history rather less so.[100] I am, however, already guilty of the same general sin, and I do not think that historians should refuse to use poetry as evidence, simply *because* it is poetry, though it should always perhaps be employed with some caution. In Ireland, in any case, we tend to conflate poetry with history – and politics – more readily than our more reticent English neighbours.

Although there are a number of Irish Great War poets and versifiers (that is to say, who used the war in some sense as their subject matter), soldier and civilian, unionist, nationalist and republican,[101] I want to concentrate here on just one, Francis Ledwidge, who was not only the best Irish poet of the war, but is an especially exemplary figure for the

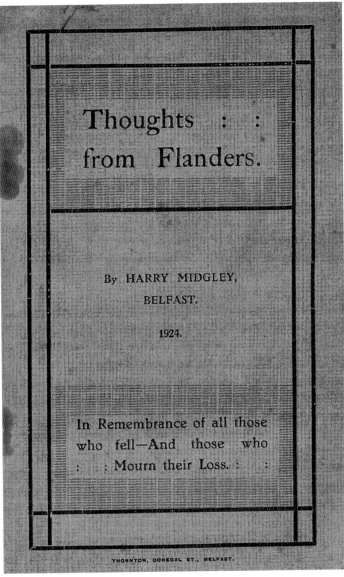

Figure 3.8 The front cover of *Thoughts from Flanders* by Harry Midgley (1892–1957). One of the many ephemeral cultural responses to the war, this volume of sentimental Christian socialist verse draws in part on Midgley's service with the Ulster Division. Midgley was later leader of the Northern Ireland Labour Party, but ended up as a Unionist cabinet minister.

whole range of Irish experience in the conflict, used, for example, in recent years in a marvellously resonant poem by Seamus Heaney.[102]

Born in 1887 near Slane, in the Boyne valley, Ledwidge came from a poor, rural background. He worked for the local council as a road-mender, and having socialist leanings became a trade-union organiser. As a young poet with literary ambitions, he was encouraged, and supported financially, by Lord Dunsany, a literary man more famous then than now. Thus, into the equation comes a relationship between Protestant Ascendancy Ireland, the second oldest title in the Irish peerage, Eton, Sandhurst and the Guards, and a representative of the dispossessed Catholic majority.[103]

Ledwidge was an activist. He was a founder member of the Slane Branch of the County Meath Labour Union and in 1914 he was elected to Navan Rural District Council. He was also one of the original members of the Slane corps of the Irish Volunteers, and although he went with the minority which broke away after Redmond's Woodenbridge speech, towards the end of October 1914 he decided to enlist. 'I joined the British Army', he explained, 'because she stood between Ireland and an enemy common to our civilisation and I would not have her say that she defended us while we did nothing at home but pass resolutions.'[104] 'We but war', he wrote, 'when war/Serves Liberty and Keeps a world at peace'.[105]

With the 10th (Irish) Division he went to Suvla Bay and Salonika, fell ill in Serbia and was invalided home. The Rising hit him hard, especially the execution of his friend Thomas MacDonagh, another poet, who had been in command at Jacob's biscuit factory. MacDonagh had translated a classic Gaelic Irish poem, 'The Yellow Bittern', and Ledwidge wrote a touching short poem in MacDonagh's memory, including the wonderful lines:

> He shall not hear the bittern cry
> In the wild sky, where he is lain.[106]

Ledwidge recovered and was posted to Belgium to serve with the 16th (Irish) Division near Ypres, when it was deployed alongside the Ulster Division.

Ledwidge is sometimes characterised as a 'pastoral' poet, and he certainly wrote movingly of the countryside, especially that of his beloved Boyne valley. But he also wrote of the war and his place in it. His biographer, writing in the early 1970s, was at pains to stress his 'allegiance to nature' and repulsion from the conflict. In a strikingly mistaken reading of Ledwidge's work, she asserted that 'he never saw anything in war but waste and futility. He tended to recoil from it even in his verse.'[107] The truth is more complex. A late poem, 'Soliloquy', begins with a celebration of summer and autumn at home in Ireland. Then it moves on to Ledwidge's present situation at the battlefront:

> And now I'm drinking wine in France,
> The helpless child of circumstance.[108]
> To-morrow will be loud with war,
> How will I be accounted for?
>
> It is too late now to retrieve
> A fallen dream, too late to grieve
> A name unmade, but not too late
> To thank the gods for what is great;
> A keen-edged sword, a soldier's heart,
> Is greater than a poet's art.
> And greater than a poet's fame
> A little grave that has no name.[109]

So, it is not so straightforward. Ledwidge, who both celebrated and deplored the war and soldiering, challenges us with the contradictions and ambiguities of his own engagement with the conflict, his own response to it, and our response to him. For Seamus Heaney he is 'our dead enigma'.[110] His experience also reflects that of his friends Thomas MacDonagh and Patrick Pearse who, by opting for physical force rather than poetry at Easter 1916, demonstrated a shared belief that 'a keen-edged sword' and 'a soldier's heart' were 'greater than a poet's art'. Ledwidge is important because we can find in him echoes of Ireland's predicament then, and resonances for its situation now.

Francis Ledwidge got his 'little grave' soon enough. Killed by an artillery shell on 31 July 1917, he was, ironically, back mending roads behind the front line. He is buried in Artillery Wood Cemetery at Boesinghe, close to Iper. In the graveyard register he is listed as '16138 Lance Corporal F. E. Ledwidge', to which is added a comment, presumably provided by one of his superior officers: 'Ledwidge was a poet who wrote mostly about Ireland and fairies.' Suitably, perhaps, 'a poet's fame' remains with him in that now peaceful place. In 1997, marking the eightieth anniversary of his death, a memorial was erected as close as possible to the exact location of his death. On it is quoted a verse from the Thomas MacDonagh poem, 'He shall not hear the bittern cry', and all of 'Soliloquy'. It is not so very far from where Willie Redmond is buried, and from where on 11 November 1998 a new Irish First World War memorial was dedicated by the heads of state of Belgium, Ireland and the United Kingdom, reminding us that the *imagination* and the *commemoration* of the war continue to exercise a strong and meaningful hold even three generations on from the end of the conflict.

4 Commemoration: 'turning the 11th November into the 12th July'

Irish politics and the collective memory of the war

The history of one of the largest and earliest Irish Great War memorials, that of the 36th (Ulster) Division at Thiepval on the Somme, demonstrates some characteristics of Irish war memorials and, indeed, of Irish commemoration of the First World War in general. There was a problem with money, in this case a careful attitude to the spending of scarce funds, a suspicion of professional advice and a distinct aesthetic conservatism and lack of artistic imagination.

At a meeting in Belfast called on 17 November 1919 to consider the matter of a memorial in France to the Ulster Division, the Ulster Unionist leader, Sir James Craig, reported that he had gone with Colonel Wilfrid Spender to the Royal Academy exhibition of war memorials, which had been arranged in part to raise the artistic standards of proposed monuments. Spender, like Craig, had served in the division itself, and later became secretary to the Northern Ireland cabinet when Craig was prime minister of the province. Neither of the men 'had been greatly struck by any of the suggestions, and they came to the conclusion that when they enlarged a cross or a cenotaph or anything of that sort beyond a certain scale, it lost its reality, and did not impress the view at all'. Craig had also obtained a copy of the Royal Institute of British Architects' rules with regard to architectural

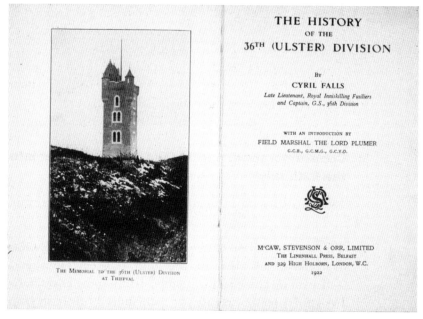

Figure 4.1 The title page and frontispiece of Cyril Falls's *History of the 36th (Ulster) Division*. The 'Ulster Tower' and the history are both war memorials, the history being dedicated 'to the men of the Ulster Division, returned from the War, and to those who have not come back'.

competitions, and had discovered the 'harsh' regulation that an independent referee with the final power of decision had to be appointed. But the memorial committee 'felt that there was no architect they knew of to whom they could give such an open cheque, and who might decide upon a design which they as a committee did not think reflected the spirit of Ulster. The expense [of a competition] would also have been very great, and he thought it would be better to keep the money in their pockets.'[1] In the end Craig proposed that the committee should commission a replica of 'Helen's Tower', a Scottish baronial affair erected in 1861 as a memorial to his mother by the marquess of Dufferin and Ava in the grounds of the Clandeboye estate where the Ulster volunteers had trained in 1914 and 1915.

The chosen design did not meet with universal approval. The *Irish Builder*, always quick to champion modern architecture, deplored it as 'a replica, . . . always an unsatisfactory thing, for while the original may be apt enough in the expression of an ideal, the copy is usually poor, tame and uninteresting'.[2] The 'Battle Exploit Memorials Committee' in London worried lest the rather ecclesiastical look of the proposed design might offend the anticlerical party in France.[3] But the required permissions were secured and the monument erected in a remarkably short time. It was formally dedicated by Field Marshal Sir Henry Wilson (who thought it 'a beautiful building') on 18 November 1921.[4]

Few other Irish war memorials were completed quite so expeditiously. It was almost twenty years before the Irish National War Memorial in Dublin, the grandest of all the Irish memorials, was ready to be dedicated, and even then it was not complete. But the somewhat tortuous history of its planning and construction is instructive, because it raises a number of issues about Irish Great War commemoration. In July 1919 at a meeting in the Viceregal Lodge summoned by the viceroy, Lord French, whose full title, 'Viscount French of Ypres and High Lake (County Roscommon)' neatly linked Ireland and 'gallant little Belgium', it was agreed to erect in Dublin a Great War Memorial Home, to be used by current and ex-servicemen. Almost immediately the scheme fell into difficulties. The military authorities bluntly announced that the memorial trustees 'could not put up a thing of that kind, because they did not approve of men in the service being in a Club with ex-soldiers who were not under discipline or control'.[5] The Anglo-Irish conflict compounded the difficulties and the memorial home scheme was dropped. But the trustees were fully resolved to have some memorial which would 'stand in the capital of Ireland' and 'keep alive in the hearts of the Irish people for ever the glorious memory of their heroic dead, who in the world's greatest struggle for freedom died for the honour of Ireland'. Contributions to the fund were received from all parts of Ireland and totalled some £42,000.

A wide range of possible schemes were canvassed as befitting the national war memorial. This echoed similar debates going on in Ireland, Great Britain and other parts of the empire.[6] In the first place a decision had to be made on the fundamental consideration as to whether a memorial should, on the one hand, be practical or utilitarian, or, on the other, purely ornamental or symbolic. In most cases following the First World War, the decision went to the symbolic. (It was markedly different after the Second World War.) There was nothing, it seemed, more enduring than bronze itself.

The original Irish proposal, in fact, had been to *combine* utility – a club 'to provide board and lodging and recreation for men who fought in the war and those serving in the Imperial Forces of the Crown' – with some degree of architectural monumentality. In contrast to James Craig's Ulstermen, the Irish National War Memorial committee had decided to hold 'an open competition amongst Irish architects for the design' and invited the Royal Institute of Architects in Ireland to nominate a member to advise them.[7]

This still-born plan was followed by a plethora of proposals, including 'a monument or cenotaph to be erected in some conspicuous place in Dublin'; a memorial hall to contain records of fallen soldiers 'with or without suitable decorations, trophies or paintings by Irish artists'; model villages and workshops for disabled ex-servicemen; and 'schemes for memorial charitable funds for the benefit of ex-soldiers'. A suggestion in 1919 that a replica of Sir Edwin Lutyens's Cenotaph in Whitehall be erected in Dublin got short shrift from the *Irish Builder*.[8] The cenotaph, it remarked, is 'simple and dignified and therefore free from objection', but it was 'certainly not an architectural triumph . . . For a permanent memorial [at this stage the London cenotaph was still only a temporary structure] something more ornate and imposing, and enriched with appropriate sculpture is desirable.'[9] The journal concluded, moreover, that 'a memorial to Irish soldiers erected in the capital of their native country ought to be the product of Irish talent, Irish hands, and be of Irish materials',[10] a admirable aspiration which, in the end, was over two-thirds fulfilled.

In the early 1920s about £5,000 of the National War Memorial funds were spent collecting the records of all the fallen and publishing them in *Ireland's Memorial Records*. One hundred copies of the eight-volume set were printed 'for distribution through the principal libraries of the country'. The printing, decoration and binding of the volumes was 'carried out by Irish artists and workers of the highest reputation and efficiency'. The most remarkable feature of the volumes are the 'beautiful symbolical borders' designed by the artist Harry Clarke, best-known for his work in stained glass. Clarke provided a title page and seven page borders, repeated throughout the volumes, which 'incorporate Celtic and Art Deco motifs, battle scenes in silhouette, medals, insignia and religious and mythological scenes, all drawn in pen and ink'.[11] A further £1,500 was spent building stone crosses to replace wooden ones erected on the battlefields to the Irish divisions. Two commemorated the 16th Division: at Guinchy on the Somme, and at Wytschaete, near Iper, where it had fought alongside the Ulster Division. The other cross marked where the 10th Division had fought in the Salonika theatre, in what had then been Serbia, by 1923 was Yugoslavia and is now Macedonia. In addition to a more specific inscription, each cross carries the words, 'Do cum Glóire Dé agus Onóra na hÉireann' ('For the glory of God and honour of Ireland').

The opinion of the main Irish veterans' association, the Legion of Irish Ex-Servicemen (which later became the 'British Legion (Irish Free State Area)'), tended towards a purely ornamental memorial. They felt that the war memorial should be 'a statue, obelisk or cenotaph of exceptional beauty and grandeur, sited in some central part of the City of Dublin'. The memorial trustees, still striving to include some practical benefit, then proposed purchasing the private gardens in Merrion Square (directly in front of Leinster House, the seat of the new Irish legislature) and building a monument there before presenting the whole property to the City of Dublin for use as a public park.

The proposed transfer of property underpinning the scheme required private legislation which came before the Oireachtas (legislature) in 1927, and here it came unstuck. There was quite a lively debate in the Senate, with opposition coming from unexpected quarters. General Sir William Hickie, a member of the council of the Irish National War Memorial and representative of the British Legion, felt that the scheme could not meet the 'exceptional beauty' requirement of the legion. He also worried about the problems that would arise from the thousands of people who would assemble in the square on Remembrance Day. This also concerned Sir Bryan Mahon (who had commanded the 10th Division during the war), who added that a mere public park was not enough. Rehearsing the classic case for an ornamental memorial, he said it 'ought to be an impressive and lasting structure whether in the form of a Celtic cross, cairn, a triumphal arch or anything else, standing by itself, unenclosed, where everyone can see it, everyone approach it and know what it represents'. Phoenix Park, he said, the largest urban park in Europe, where the 1926 remembrance ceremonies had satisfactorily been held, was the ideal location.[12]

Oliver St John Gogarty, wit, surgeon, poet and James Joyce's 'stately plump Buck Mulligan', was lukewarm about the whole project, as, indeed, he had been about the war. 'A war memorial', he declared, 'is a comfortless thing.' He pointedly added that 'in Greece there is no war memorial to the Persians'. In any case, he thought that the money should be spent on housing for ex-servicemen.[13] Andrew Jameson, from the Dublin distilling family, who chaired the war memorial finance committee, spoke at length on the history of the memorial and pressed the *utility* of the Merrion Square scheme on his fellow senators. He thought, moreover, it 'quite possible' that there would be enough money left over to erect 'in the Phoenix Park a monument that might rightly and reasonably be comparable to the London Cenotaph in answering all the requirements of the military authorities' in providing a venue for well-attended Remembrance ceremonies.

The most interesting contribution to the debate came from Senator W. B. Yeats, a resident of Merrion Square. He was not greatly concerned about the problems of large demonstrations. 'Armistice Day', he predicted, 'will recede. These men will not live for ever. I hope it is not going to become a permanent political demonstration in this country, to be carried on by the children of ex-servicemen. It will grow less and less every year.' Yeats rather favoured the erection of 'a dignified monument . . . with the names of the men who served in the Great War . . . Their great grandchildren, perhaps a century hence', he fancied, could go into the square 'and point out the names of their ancestors upon that monument'. All in all he supported the scheme 'for the health of the Dublin children and the delight of all the citizens'.

Yeats's support did not sway all his colleagues and the Senate divided 19–19 on the issue. The bill passed with the casting vote of the cathaoirleach (speaker), Lord Glenavy, a unionist. 'Without pronouncing any opinion whatever' on its merits, Glenavy thought the measure should have the opportunity of 'running the Gauntlet' in a joint committee of the Senate and Dáil.[14]

The government, however, was implacably opposed to the plan. A year before it came to the legislature, William Cosgrave, the president of the Executive Council, had told James MacNeill, the Irish Free State representative in London, that 'a large section of nationalist opinion regards the scheme as part of a political movement of an imperialist nature and view it with the same resentment as they view the exploitation of Poppy Day in Dublin by the most

hostile elements of the old Unionist class'. There seemed
to him to be few practical benefits for ex-servicemen and,
besides, 'the presence of a memorial distasteful to a large
body of citizens directly facing the seat of Government is
clearly undesirable'.[15]

When the issue was debated in the Dáil in March 1927,
Kevin O'Higgins, Cosgrave's vice-president, forcefully
outlined the government's position. 'To devote Merrion
Square to this purpose', he declared, 'would be to give a
wrong twist, as it were, a wrong suggestion to the origins of
this State.' But O'Higgins wanted it clearly understood
that he spoke 'in no spirit of hostility to ex-servicemen'.
Reflecting the frequently opposing tensions between personal and public loyalties, he reminded deputies that two of
his own brothers had served in the war: Michael was killed
in Flanders and Jack had served as a surgeon-commander
on Admiral Beatty's flagship.[16] 'No one', he said, 'denies
the sacrifice, and no one denies the patriotic motives which
induced the vast majority of those men to join the British
Army to take part in the Great War, and yet it is not on *their*
sacrifice that this State is based, and I have no desire to see
it suggested that it is.' Picking up a concern that the admirable Sir William Hickie had expressed the previous
September, O'Higgins said he deprecated 'profoundly the
mentality of either side that would like to make of the 11th
November a Twelfth of July'. He hoped there would
'always be respectful admiration . . . for the men who went
out to France and fought there and died there, believing
that by so doing they were serving the best interests of their
country'.[17]

Captain William Archer Redmond, carrying a torch for
his late father, John, and uncle, Willie, was strongly in
favour of the scheme. 'What is needed most today', he
argued, 'is a policy of appeasement and reconciliation.'
The best means of bringing this about was 'on the basis of
agreement amongst all who in different spheres and in
different circumstances fought for Ireland in different
fields of battle and on different occasions, to tolerate and

facilitate the commemoration, without offence to either side, of their respective dead'. He dismissed O'Higgins's argument about the location of the memorial as having 'no force or gravity'. He asked one question: 'Are the surviving British ex-servicemen [he had served with the Irish Guards] to be regarded as citizens of this State with equal rights with any other citizens, or are they not?' Refusing to allow the scheme, he concluded, would 'leave a very bad impression indeed on our fellow-countrymen in the North and also on the people of Great Britain'.[18] But the government's opposition was decisive, the legislation was defeated and the scheme was abandoned.

Although Fitzwilliam Square, on the south of the city centre, and Parnell Square, on the north – both rather smaller than Merrion Square – had been suggested by O'Higgins as possible locations for the memorial, Andrew Jameson rejected both as 'utterly unfitted'.[19] The trustees of the war memorial then turned to Phoenix Park which, although not very central, had in the mid-1920s become the venue for the annual Remembrance commemorations. While sizeable demonstrations had been held in Dublin on both the official Peace Day in July 1919 and the first anniversary of the Armistice, the civil and political commotions of the next few years greatly limited the scope for public commemoration.[20] In 1919 these events had been accompanied by 'rowdy scenes in Dublin', with clashes between unionist and nationalist supporters. Up to the two minutes' silence, as one unionist newspaper reported, 'nothing had occurred to mar the impressive nature of the celebration in any part of the city, but hardly had the Trinity students concluded the singing of "God Save the King", when a crowd of young men, mostly students from the National University, appeared in College Green, shouting rebel cries and singing the "Soldier's Song" . . . A scene of wild disorder followed.'[21]

In 1923 and 1924 a temporary cenotaph was erected in College Green, outside Trinity College, on 11 November and great crowds gathered to mark the anniversary, but sporadic fighting between nationalists, unionists, ex-servicemen and, of course, students of both political persuasions also occurred. In 1925 the police commissioner, with the government's approval, refused permission ('for traffic reasons'[22]) for College Green to be used and the event moved to St Stephen's Green. The following year it moved to Phoenix Park, further from the centre of Dublin, though undoubtedly a more spacious location. There it stayed for ten years or so.

In the meantime the trustees of the Irish National War Memorial commissioned Frank Scarlett, a young English architect working in the University College Dublin School of Architecture, to design a stone 'monumental arch' to stand at the front gate of Phoenix Park. The commissioners of public works, who were responsible for the park, saw 'no architectural or aesthetic reason' why permission should be refused, but in July 1928 the Executive Council turned this proposal down.[23] The design of an arch in a prominent public position – analogous to the Royal Dublin Fusiliers' Boer War memorial ('Traitors' Gate') at the Grafton Street corner of St Stephen's Green – was, one assumes, thought to be too triumphal in character. It is also clear that the government favoured some more practical memorial, which would be of direct benefit to ex-servicemen or their families. In this, moreover, they were certainly following the original conception of the whole war memorial scheme.

In the spring of 1929 Cosgrave took a straw poll of his colleagues on a number of proposals. Not surprisingly the two suggestions most widely favoured – a scheme of apprenticeships and a children's educational fund – involved no physical memorial whatsoever. 'A Home with grounds' and 'a housing scheme' came next in preference. Further down the list were playgrounds, industries for the unemployed and 'a ship to tour around Ireland with reduced fares for ex-servicemen's families'. A memorial park came eighth out of twelve, and a pure monument was the least popular option of all.[24]

As it happened, one of the more favoured suggestions, a 'housing scheme', was already well in hand from quite another source. In 1919 the British government, concerned about the prospects for ex-servicemen in what was clearly becoming a hostile nationalist Ireland, provided with the Irish Land (Provision for Sailors and Soldiers) Act a housing and land settlement scheme including up to 7,600 dwellings.[25] The vice-president of the Irish Local Government Board, Sir Henry Robinson, thought it would be 'a good object-lesson' for 'disloyal people' in nationalist districts 'to note that the Government had not forgotten the patriotic Irishmen who stood by the Empire in times of stress'. As violent opposition to the government built up in 1920–1 there was also a worry that ex-servicemen might join the rebels. 'Ex-servicemen as a class in Ireland can be a great political asset or the reverse', wrote Sir John Anderson of the Irish Office. 'They are just the sort of people the rebels would like to entice into the ranks of the Irish Republican Army.' The were criticisms from Sinn Fein that the scheme represented a new 'Plantation', but there is no evidence that the nearly 4,000 houses eventually completed (70 per cent of which were in the Free State) constituted centres of unrepentant loyalty to the *ancien régime*. The dwellings were built to a deliberately high standard – fit homes, indeed, for heroes to live in – and the largest development, 247 houses at Killester, north of Dublin, was planned on notably up-to-date garden-suburb lines. Some of the names used in the housing estates commemorate the war: Messines Park in Derry City, Earl Haig Park in Cregagh, Belfast, and a 'soldiers' colony' nearby, which includes Hamel Drive, Somme Drive and Thiepval Avenue. Little pockets of 'soldiers' cottages' still survive across Ireland, although the Irish Sailors' and Soldiers' Land Trust, which was established to administer the scheme after partition, was wound up in 1987.

By the late 1920s the war memorial trustees were becoming increasingly anxious about their lack of progress and even contemplated the unhappy possibility of having to return subscriptions. In 1927 Andrew Jameson had told the Senate of one man who wanted his £500 back so that he could 'erect his own memorial in his own church to the memory of his son'. Although on the same occasion Jameson had said that 'to put up in the Phoenix Park a monument costing £45,000, where only few people would see it, would be, to my mind, an extreme waste of money',[26] by 1929 this is exactly what he had come to accept. Presented with the government's preferences for a war memorial, Jameson told Cosgrave that Phoenix Park was, in the opinion of his committee, the 'only suitable site'. The Board of Works was instructed to investigate the possibilities of the park and its vicinity, and in December 1929 they came up with an 150-acre site, already publicly owned, at Islandbridge just across the River Liffey from Phoenix Park.[27] Although the site, as the *Sunday Times* complained, was 'a distant backwater', it was also 'the nearest site that is considered politically expedient, and the protection of which can be reasonably assured'.[28] Since the finished project would be a public park, Cosgrave told Jameson that the government would be prepared to contribute to the cost. The construction work, moreover, could be given to unemployed ex-servicemen, providing that needy group with a direct benefit.[29] Thus the Islandbridge proposal combined the desirable qualities of monumentality, utility and, for the perceived public good of the independent Irish state, a certain degree of invisibility.

The war memorial committee were delighted at last to have secured a site. It was a great relief, as Jameson told Cosgrave, since they had been 'wandering in the wilderness for so many years'.[30] Jameson at once engaged Sir Edwin Lutyens to draw up a design. Lutyens was widely regarded as the foremost British architect of the day, with a striking gift for great public schemes: New Delhi, the Cenotaph, Western Front battlefield monuments and the great Catholic cathedral in Liverpool (which, however, never got beyond the crypt). Lutyens's mother was Irish, the sister of a brother officer whom Lutyens's soldier father had married in Canada. According to his (English) biographer, Lutyens inherited from her an 'Irish gift for fantasy and laughter'. He had done a little work in Ireland before the war: Lambay Castle (completed 1912) for Cecil Baring and some restoration at Howth Castle. His other main commission was controversial and unbuilt, being Sir Hugh Lane's scheme for a Dublin municipal art gallery, which Lutyens in 1913 proposed to accommodate on a bridge over the River Liffey. This fantastic scheme – already widely criticised – perished with Lane on the *Lusitania* in May 1915.[31]

Lutyens had quite a wide Irish acquaintance – Orpen and Lavery were friends, as was Oliver Gogarty. He spent an enjoyable weekend, staying with Andrew Jameson, in Dublin in August 1924 during the Tailteann Games.[32] Jameson seems to have had no difficulty in persuading Lutyens to take the commission. By October 1930 plans had been drawn up. The design, wrote T. J. Byrne, chief architect of the Office of Public Works, was 'admirable for the purpose and worthy of the strongest recommendation'. It would, he noted, rely 'more upon gardening and arbori-culture than upon building work; it will derive its effect not from the presence of an overpowering monumental struc-ture but from the beauties of a "Garden of Remembrance" set amid . . . simple and appropriate surroundings'.[33]

The memorial itself was to include a great central lawn with a 'Stone of Remembrance', identical to that adopted for use in Imperial War Graves Commission battlefield cemeteries, and a thirty-foot high cross, similar to one which Lutyens had designed also for battlefield sites, but which had been rejected in favour of Sir Reginald Bloomfield's 'Cross of Sacrifice'.[34] Flanking the stone are fountains and four pavilions or 'book rooms', intended to house copies of *Ireland's Memorial Records* and 'connected by pergolas which open out into circular and terraced gardens'. Beyond this central Memorial Plot, which was to be planted with trees and shrubs, Lutyens planned a

Figure 4.2 Irish National War Memorial, Islandbridge, shortly after completion in 1938. Looking north-east, across the valley of the River Liffey, Phoenix Park and the Wellington Monument can be seen in the distance. The 'Stone of Remembrance' is in the centre, flanked by the four pavilions, or 'book rooms'.

circular shelter, 'described as the Temple', at the far end of one of the avenues leading to the memorial. Also among the proposed 'ancillary' works was a three-arched bridge across the River Liffey to connect the war memorial with Phoenix Park.[35] T. J. Byrne estimated the total cost of the scheme at £167,000. Of this £56,000 was due to the Memorial Plot, £58,000 to the ancillary works and the remainder to professional fees, roads, fencing and the development of the park as a whole.

Apart from the ancillary works, it was agreed that the costs would be shared between the war memorial trustees and the state. The trustees' assets had been accruing interest throughout the 1920s and at this stage amounted to some £54,000. The government earmarked £50,000 from

funds authorised by the 1931 Unemployment Relief Act, a
very considerable commitment at a time of widespread
economic depression and when the national finances were
in a particularly parlous state. It was further agreed that the
labour force for the scheme would be composed half of ex-
British army men and half of National (Free State) ex-servicemen.[36] So it was that the project took on both a
practical and an ecumenical aspect.

Work began at the end of December 1931 and was completed in the spring of 1938, although the buildings and
hard landscaping had been finished by March 1936. Irish
stone (mostly granite) was used exclusively throughout,
and to make the scheme especially labour-intensive the
stone was cut and moved by hand where possible.[37]
Lutyens was responsible only for the design and working
drawings. The work itself was admirably directed by T. J.
Byrne, who said that working under Lutyens had been 'the
best experience of his life'.[38] Lutyens travelled to Ireland
on several occasions while work was in progress. He was
particularly impressed with the quality of the workers. In
August 1935 when the memorial was 'nearly finished' he
purchased a sixteen-shilling bottle of whiskey to share
with the masons. These included one 'communistic'
fellow, a father many times over, who when the first bottle
was finished bought another himself. 'Communists',
wrote Lutyens to his wife, 'may be fearsome with other
people's money, but they are certainly generous with their
own. I could do nothing but had to submit – to a man with
21 children spending on me 16/– out of his 50 shilling
wage.'[39]

There were hopes in 1939 that the ancillary works might
be completed, but when Lutyens's estimate of costs for the
River Liffey bridge came in at between £34,000 and
£44,000, depending on the materials used, the trustees
abandoned this plan. A revised scheme for permanent rail-
ings enclosing the Memorial Plot, costing £10,000, was put
to the government for state assistance. But by the time it
came to be considered by the taoiseach, Eamon de Valera,

Figure 4.3   Irish National War Memorial, Islandbridge, looking east towards
the central lawn from one of the circular sunken rose gardens.

in October 1940, he considered 'in view of the war
conditions' that the question could not 'usefully be
pursued at present'.[40]

The international situation had already affected plans
for the formal opening of the war memorial. De Valera, a
veteran of the 1916 Rising, had been quite well disposed
towards the memorial. When his government took power
in 1932 the work of the memorial had been continued 'in
the same spirit of toleration, co-operation and mutual
goodwill in which it had been inaugurated'.[41] In December
1938 representatives of the 'British Legion Ireland
(Southern) Area' were told that it was de Valera's intention
to be present at the opening ceremony, though this was
'conditional on the absence of anything which might tend
to create ill feeling or resentment or to embarrass the
Government in the slightest degree', no doubt a warning to
avoid singing 'God Save the King' or promiscuously

displaying Union Jacks. In turn, Major J. J. Tynan, for the Legion, noted that it 'would be virtually impossible to exclude Northern Ireland in view of the fact that the memorial is an all-Ireland one'. The Legion, indeed, might 'consider it desirable . . . to invite the Governor General and the Prime Minister of Northern Ireland', but he promised to consult further with the government before issuing any invitations. On 4 April 1939 the taoiseach's secretary indicated to the Legion that 30 July would be a convenient date for the opening, but three weeks later the whole plan collapsed.

On 25 April de Valera himself saw Captain A. P. Connolly and Major Ryan, respectively chairman and secretary of the Legion, to tell them that circumstances had now changed. He had hoped that the planned ceremonial opening 'would have a good effect by signifying that Irishmen who took different views in regard to the war of 1914–18 appreciated and respected each other's views'. But the 'tenseness of the international situation' (Germany had just completed its occupation of Czechoslovakia, and on 7 April Italy had invaded Albania) and the 'consequent ferment' in Ireland had changed the situation. The British, moreover, had announced that conscription was to be introduced, and there was a possibility that it might be applied 'to our fellow countrymen in the Six Counties'. In these circumstances the planned ceremonial opening 'might evoke hostility and give rise to misunderstanding'.[42] The formal dedication was postponed indefinitely, though from 1940 the annual Armistice Day ceremony was held at Islandbridge. Thus de Valera's generous-spirited and inclusive intention to participate in the commemoration of Ireland's Great War dead was undermined by Irish *realpolitik* and the possibility of some Irish participation at Britain's side, willing or otherwise, in a new conflict.

At least by 1939 substantial progress had been made in constructing a permanent memorial to that group of Irish war dead who had fought with the British army in 1914–18. By contrast, those who had fought *against* the British were

Figure 4.4   Irish cavalry passing the cenotaph erected to the memory of
Michael Collins and Arthur Griffith. This temporary structure was
placed on the lawn of Leinster House, next to the National Gallery
of Ireland which can be seen here.

less adequately commemorated. Shortly after independence William Cosgrave's government commissioned Professor George Atkinson of the Dublin Art College to design a memorial to Arthur Griffith and Michael Collins. Atkinson produced a tall, stylised Celtic cross, with relief medallions of Griffith and Collins by the sculptor Albert Power and a Gaelic inscription, repeating that on the Irish battlefield memorial crosses in France, Flanders and Salonika: 'Do cum Glóire Dé agus Onóra na hÉireann'. It was placed on the lawn of Leinster House, overlooking Merrion Square where the Irish National War Memorial trustees had proposed to build. Like Lutyens's cenotaph in London, Atkinson's monument was first erected as a temporary structure of wood and plaster. Unlike Lutyens's monument, however, it was never replaced in permanent materials and was removed a decade after its installation in

1923.[43] De Valera, who came to power in 1932, approved designs for a replacement, first, in 1940, another Celtic cross and then, in 1947, an obelisk, by Raymond McGrath, which was eventually dedicated in 1950. One commentator has noted that the obelisk's 'extreme slenderness, it relatively discreet height and proximity to attention-absorbing buildings, and its position behind an elaborate railing make it almost invisible'.[44] So, in a curious way, this national monument reflects the public invisibility of Lutyens's garden in distant Islandbridge.

There is also a nationalist Garden of Remembrance. In 1935 a proposal was made in the Dáil for 'a national memorial for all who had died fighting for Ireland', to be located in the Rotunda Gardens in Parnell Square (also one of the locations considered for the Irish National War Memorial). The government accepted the proposal in 1938 and a competition was organised in 1946. A design was agreed, but the whole scheme was deferred until the impending fiftieth anniversary of the Easter Rising prompted its construction and the garden was formally dedicated on Easter Monday 1966.[45]

If de Valera had been present at an official opening of the Islandbridge memorial in 1939 he would have been the first Irish head of government to attend a public Great War commemoration. In 1926, just as an imperial conference was about to open, Stanley Baldwin, the British prime minister, invited William Cosgrave to the unveiling of a memorial tablet in Westminster Abbey 'to the memory of the One Million Dead of the British Empire who fell in the great War'. Cosgrave declined the invitation in an exceptionally sensitive letter:

> It is well known throughout Ireland that I and at least one other member of the Executive Council[46] were actively engaged in the hostilities which occurred in Dublin in April of 1916 while the Great War was in progress, and in which a number of casualties occurred on both sides . . . Amongst our citizens we number not a few who lost near

relatives during the fighting then. So far as those who
were killed amongst my companions are concerned, time
and subsequent happy developments have almost
completely cicatrised the wounds. But I know that there
are citizens of ours who on that occasion lost brothers and
sons who were serving in the British Army, and there still
remains amongst them – and not unnaturally – a feeling
of, I shall not say, bitterness, but rather of pain. For these
I fear lest the personal presence at this ceremonial, in
memory of their beloved ones, of one to whom they
attribute responsibility for their bereavement should re-
open wounds that are not yet quite healed. It is so easy to
hurt and so difficult to heal.

Cosgrave sent Kevin O'Higgins in his stead. On the urging
of Leopold Amery, the British secretary of state for both
the colonies and the dominions, Cosgrave's letter was
released to the press and attracted much favourable
comment.[47] For Cosgrave the chief impediment to his
presence in the abbey arose from the fact of *Irish* casualties
serving in the British Army during the 1916 Rising. With
this in mind, the Easter Rising looks less like a clear-cut
Irish challenge to British imperial rule than a kind of civil
war, with Irishman pitted against Irishman, brother
against brother, bearing all the peculiar bitterness of such
conflicts, as Cosgrave himself knew only too well.

Cosgrave's letter also serves to remind us of the place of
the bereaved in these rituals. I have so far concentrated on
the public and political dimension of Great War commemoration. By and large, narratives of these ceremonies
in Ireland have concentrated on the rowdy margins of
events: the student demonstrators, republican or unionist,
the flag-wavers and the flag-burners, the aggressive poppy-
sellers and the poppy-snatchers, and those who fitted razor
blades behind their poppies to discourage the same. But
these are marginal people. The great majority of the estimated seventy thousand out in Dublin in 1924, and the
many tens of thousands in subsequent years, did not do

these things and, I wonder, should we not shift our focus from the margins to the mass? Many people – who knows, perhaps most – were there for more private reasons. Like the Irish soldiers who enlisted – voluntarily – during the war, the range of motives bringing people out into the streets on Armistice Day and Remembrance Day must have varied from the Big Words – patriotism, or some other public political rationale – to more intimate and private impulses: group solidarity, family motives, friendship and comradeship. Since the British practice was (and is) to bury war dead on the battlefield, or as close as possible to the place of death, the bereaved have no local grave to visit. Few were able to go from Ireland to Flanders or France, let alone Gallipoli, Salonika or Palestine. So war memorials served as surrogate graves, and the Remembrance ceremony became an occasion for the bereaved to grieve and try to make sense of, or at least come to terms with, their loss.[48] There is a private narrative here as well as a public one, and who is to say which is the more important?

The 1916 casualties to which Cosgrave alluded in his letter also contributed to an Irish difficulty with the Imperial War Graves Commission, which was established in 1917 to mark and maintain the graves of all the empire's war dead. It was calculated that there were about two thousand war graves in Ireland, and in 1924 the British government proposed that the Commission should take charge of them, subject to the Irish Free State participating in the Commission, along with the other dominions and India. But the Irish government thought it politically undesirable to do so and 'accordingly undertook entire responsibility for all the work and expenditure'. The headstones, however, were (and remain) the standard Imperial War Graves Commission type, two feet eight inches high, - normally carrying unit insignia, the individual's service number, a religious emblem and in many cases a personal inscription of up to sixty letters chosen by the next-of-kin. Two Irish local authorities, Clare County Council and Sligo Corporation, objected to British imperial iconography such as 'regimental badges or other equivalent insignia' being engraved on the headstones. Though the Sligo objection was later withdrawn, the headstones in County Clare were erected without badges.[49]

A similar sensitivity affected the commemorative bust of Tom Kettle which a memorial committee planned to put up in St Stephen's Green, Dublin, in 1927. The commissioners of public works, fearing possible political repercussions, refused to permit the words 'Killed in France' to be included in the inscription. This, and other difficulties, held up the erection of the sculpture until 1937. Like the Islandbridge memorial, there was no official unveiling. The inscription finally approved included 'Killed at Guinchy 9 September 1916', but, in keeping with prevailing official attitudes to Ireland's engagement with the war, no indication is given of where Guinchy is, or what Kettle was doing there.[50]

The troubled history of the Irish National War Memorial was reflected in that of more local monuments. In the 1927 Senate debate Andrew Jameson had raised the possibility of having to return subscriptions because of the delays accompanying the scheme. In two cases this actually happened. In Cookstown, County Tyrone, a design for a statue was commissioned, but a strong lobby held out for the construction of a hospital. By the autumn of 1920, however, only just over £1,000 had been raised, not enough for either proposal, and the subscriptions were returned. In 1925 the scheme was revived, a fresh subscription list opened and, after £800 had been raised, a rather crude replica of the London Cenotaph was erected. Although Lurgan, County Armagh, began with grandiose practical ideas – a technical school, a cottage hospital and a public baths were all suggested – a monument was eventually decided upon, but no agreement could be reached on the design. The whole project was abandoned in March 1921 and, again, the subscriptions were returned. A fresh effort commenced in September 1923 and, eventually, a 'modest temple', surmounted by a bronze figure representing 'the

spirit of Victorious Peace' was unveiled in May 1928.[51]
Sometimes there was an embarrassing shortfall in subscriptions. An appeal for £25,000 launched in November
1918 for a County Antrim memorial had collected just over
£3,000 by 1936 when the county council took over the
scheme and completed it on a rather smaller scale than was
originally planned.[52]

As demonstrated in Cookstown and Lurgan, the debate
between practical and ornamental memorials went on in
the localities as well as Dublin and, although ornamental
memorials are by far the most common, a number of utilitarian projects were completed. There are several war
memorial halls, including one at Moneymore, County
Londonderry, and in Cavan a new operating theatre was
built for the County Infirmary. The greatest practical
memorial was the Presbyterian War Memorial Hostel built
in Belfast to house two hundred young persons and protect
them from the terrors and temptations of the big city. It
cost £86,000, of which over two-thirds had been raised by
the time it was completed in 1926. At the formal opening,
H. M. Pollock, the Northern Ireland minister of finance,
declared that 'much was said of memorials in marble and
stone and of statues, but the object of the hostel memorial
was to carry out a noble purpose, the combating of evil
influences and the attacks of the microbes of evil'. No
doubt to ensure this important function, the two sexes were
segregated into different floors, two for men and three for
'girls', 'there being separate entrances, with an elevator at
each'.[53]

The case of Cork is instructive in considering the sym-
bolism of ornamental memorials, both in their design and
inscription, as well as the ceremonies which go on around
them. Before 1925 there were two separate Remembrance
Sunday parades in the city, one organised by the Legion
and the other by the Cork Independent Ex-Servicemen's
Club. The former was a more Protestant body, while the
latter was almost entirely Catholic and nationalist. Both
parades went to the Boer War memorial at Gilabbey Rock

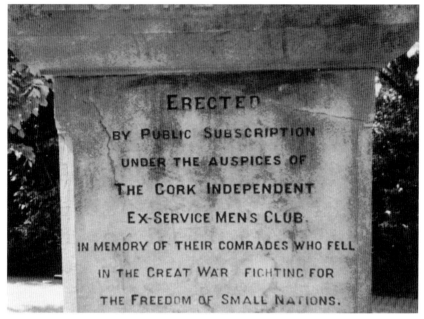

Figure 4.5   Cork war memorial (detail). Above the inscribed plinth is an obelisk with a bas-relief figure of a Royal Munster Fusilier.

to the west of the city centre. This monument is a Celtic cross, an unambiguously Irish design, but it commemorates an equally unambiguously *imperial* war. The inscription dedicates it to those 'who lost their lives in the service of the Empire'. The memorial itself was a target for anti-imperialists. On 28 December 1918 it was seriously damaged by a bomb and in November 1925 it suffered slight damage in another attack.[54]

But on St Patrick's Day 1925 the Independent Ex-Servicemen's Club unveiled a new memorial on the South Mall in the city centre, in a ceremony celebrated by both groups together. Reflecting a Redmondite nationalist tradition, the new monument commemorated those 'who fell in the Great War fighting for the Freedom of Small Nations'. Despite the initiative coming from a nationalist ex-servicemen's group, the memorial was shrouded in a Union Jack before the unveiling, as was the new Longford memorial, dedicated on 27 August 1925. No wonder, perhaps, in November that year that the republican Seán Lemass should excoriate the forthcoming Armistice Day celebrations as 'attempts to seduce the Irish nation and win support for the British connection . . . Though Irishmen might have differences', he declared, 'they stood when the Union Jack was waved in their faces as uncompromisingly against British rule as they ever did.' His fellow country-men 'meant no disrespect to the Irish survivors of the Great War, who wished to honour their dead comrades', but the Armistice Day display was simply 'an endeavour to use Ireland in the interests of the Empire'.[55]

There is a 'parallel text' to these monuments, especially the Celtic crosses in such places as Bray, Drogheda, Longford and Virginia. They were, according to one com-mentator, 'a mirror image of the nationalist monuments'.[56] At the same time as Great War memorials were being erected, Irish War of Independence and even Civil War memorials were being commissioned. On Sunday 11 November 1928, while a Celtic cross was being unveiled in Nenagh, County Tipperary, to the memory of those 'who fell in the Great War',[57] elsewhere in the town the leading republican Seán MacBride was laying the foundation stone of a memorial to the men of North Tipperary 'who gave their lives in the fight for freedom'. That day, said MacBride, 'some unfortunate people are mourning the death of their relatives killed during the European War fighting for England . . . We do not want to see other Irishmen fighting for British Imperialism on some foreign shore. Let Irishmen fight against England.'[58]

Not surprisingly, there are fewer nationalist monuments in Northern Ireland than in the South (though there has been a proliferation of republican memorials stimulated by the bitter conflict of recent decades). In the North the commemoration of the war became overwhelmingly an opportunity to confirm loyalty to the British link and affirm Ulster's *Protestant* heritage. The 'all-Ulster' memorial 'to the men of Ulster who fell in the Great War' – the home equivalent of the Thiepval tower, I suppose – comprises

Figure 4.6 Unveiling of Longford war memorial, 27 August 1925, caught here
in a still taken from a contemporary British Pathe newsreel film.

the west portals of St Anne's Church of Ireland Cathedral
in Belfast. Some district memorials, such as the one at
Kilkeel, County Down, stand within the grounds of
Protestant churches, fenced off from their fellow country-
men: a clear public statement indeed. The unveiling of the
Belfast Cenotaph on 11 November 1929 was almost exclusively a Protestant affair. The Belfast rabbi participated,
but the 16th (Irish) Division veterans – including many
west Belfast Catholics – were not even invited. Left off the
official list of wreath-layers (though the Ulster Women's
units of the British Fascists and the Italian Fascist Party
were included), the 16th Division Ex-Servicemen's
Association did lay a wreath, but only after the end of the
formal ceremony. The following year, however, they were
included quite high up the order of service. Their initial
exclusion may just have been a sin of omission, but a
revealing one all the same.

There were more inclusive ceremonies at other places. At Portadown, County Armagh, a town with a grand old (and continuing) reputation for sectarian strife, the Catholic Archbishop of Armagh, Dr O'Donnell, was invited to the dedication of the war memorial in November 1925. So too was the Protestant archbishop, together with the prime minister of Northern Ireland, Sir James Craig. The latter two attended, but in the event Dr O'Donnell did not. Perhaps the organisers' scheduling of him to pronounce the benediction immediately before the singing of 'God Save the King' was too much to take, for he sent the local parish priest to represent him. Yet both the Orange Order and the Ancient Order of Hibernians laid wreaths. Speeches were made by Major D. G. Shillington, a Unionist MP, a Methodist and formerly a captain in the Royal Irish Fusiliers, and Mr R. M. Cullen, a Catholic ex-NCO of the Connaught Rangers. Cullen said that their joint participation 'was emblematic of the brotherhood that was born in the gullies of Gallipoli and cemented on the firing steps of Flanders. (Applause.)'[59] Thus the reconciling potential of war service was asserted even in the 'Black North'.

The losses of the Ulster Division on the Somme came specifically to be associated with the freedom of Ulster Unionists to run their own polity – or 'statelet' as nationalists called it – in what emerged as Northern Ireland. For them the 'blood sacrifice' of the Somme was equal and opposite to that of Easter 1916. 'Somme Memorial' Orange lodges were formed and 1 July came to be marked by Orange processions. The most fraught and disputed of such 'traditional' marches in recent years has been that at Drumcree, near Portadown, along the Garvaghy Road. This is not a Twelfth of July Battle of the Boyne event but a First of July Somme commemoration. The mythic power of the sacrifice is further illustrated by the 'typical' Protestant family interviewed by a British journalist in the early 1980s who asserted that Ulster alone 'lost 50,000 men in the battle of the Somme'.[60] Murals depicting scenes from the Somme are painted and repainted on gable ends in

Figure 4.7 Somme memorial mural, Monkstown, County Antrim, painted in
1996 for the eightieth anniversary of the battle. Behind the soldiers
is the 'Ulster Tower' at Thiepval. Note the iconography and
inscription: an Irish shamrock, but a dedication purely to Ulster.

Protestant districts of Belfast and Northern Ireland.[61] In
one instance the Somme has literally been stitched into the
fabric of the Ulster loyalist tradition. Among the souvenirs
being sold to mark the seventy-fifth anniversary of the
Somme at the 1991 Belfast Twelfth of July parade was a tea
towel reproducing James Prinsep Beadle's imaginative
painting *Charge of the 36th (Ulster) Division, Somme, 1st
July 1916*. The artefact and its availability in effect turned
12 July into 11 November.

The Second World War marked a critical watershed in
the commemoration of the Great War in nationalist
Ireland. While independent Ireland remained neutral
during 1939–45, the First World War memorials through-

out the island and their accompanying ceremonies could become identified with support for the renewed British war effort. Indeed, for unionists, this was precisely the case. In these circumstances (and especially from a nationalist perspective) the rituals, flags, medals and anthems of Remembrance apparently became explicit manifestations of *Britishness*, so much so that Armistice Day parades in Dublin were prohibited during the war. After 1945, as Yeats had predicted (and perhaps hoped) in 1927, Remembrance ceremonies began to decline in the South. They became much more marginalised than had been the case before 1939. Old loyalties, however, were still being affirmed, and 'God Save the Queen' was sung at Islandbridge as late as 1956.[62]

Ten years later the fiftieth anniversary of the Easter Rising provided an opportunity for some re-evaluation of Ireland's engagement with the Great War. In February 1966 Seán Lemass, no stranger to criticising Remembrance ceremonies but now taoiseach, affirmed that the men who had enlisted in the British army 'were motivated by the highest purpose, and died in their tens of thousands in Flanders and Gallipoli, believing they were giving their lives in the cause of human liberty everywhere, not excluding Ireland'.[63] The chairman of the Office of Public Works, Harry Mundow, suggested 'as a symbolic gesture of recognition that these ex-British soldiers were part of the historic tradition of the Irish nation', that Lutyens's scheme for the Irish National War Memorial be completed and the planned bridge across the River Liffey be built.[64] In this case, Lemass turned down the proposal, and the memorial remains incomplete. During the post-war years, and especially in the 1970s, the Islandbridge memorial garden fell into considerable disrepair, but it was restored in the 1980s and formally dedicated some fifty years after its original completion. In 1994 Lutyens's little 'temple' was built and the whole park declared 'open and complete' (though it was not) by the minister of finance, Bertie Ahern, later taoiseach.[65]

One part of the Irish government-sponsored celebrations for the fiftieth anniversary of the Easter Rising unexpectedly brought together the two military traditions of the Great War years. The Irish composer Brian Boydell, professor of music at Trinity College, Dublin, was commissioned by the state broadcasting service, Radio Telefís Éireann, to write a piece for the anniversary. He responded with 'A Terrible Beauty Is Born', a cantata for three soloists (soprano, contralto and baritone), choir, narrator and orchestra. The libretto was prepared by Tomás Ó Súlleabháin, who drew on poems, not only by Yeats, whose powerful meditation 'Easter 1916' formed the core of the piece, and Thomas MacDonagh, a republican 'martyr' of the Rising, but also by Francis Ledwidge and Thomas Kettle, who were both killed on the Western Front. Ledwidge's poignant lament for MacDonagh ('He shall not hear the bittern cry'), which we have already noticed, was set for contralto solo, while the climax of the piece comprised a setting for baritone and chorus of Kettle's poem 'Cancel the Past' which envisioned the reconciliation of opposing Irish soldiers in a free Ireland ('Bond, from the toil of hate we may not cease/Free, we are free to be your friend').[66]

During 1966 unionists in Northern Ireland commemorated the fiftieth anniversary of the Somme. Coincidentally this also involved a bridge, in this case a new road crossing which was being built over the River Lagan in Belfast. It was proposed to name it the 'Somme Bridge', but Protestant extremists in the Belfast City Council succeeded in proposing 'Carson Bridge', after the Unionist hero. Fearing that this might prove inflammatory, especially at a moment when Northern nationalists were themselves celebrating the 1916 anniversary, and exploiting the fact that a royal visit was planned, wiser counsels prevailed and the Belfast unionists were finally persuaded to accept the 'Queen Elizabeth II Bridge'. The queen formally named it on 4 July (and escaped injury after a concrete block was hurled on to the bonnet of her car).

Sectarian passions had indeed been raised by the conflicting anniversaries.[67] Thus this bridge in Belfast joined Lutyens's unbuilt bridge in Dublin as Irish Great War memorials that 'never were'.

In more recent years, as has already been noted, there has been something of a revival of interest in the Great War and also the commemoration thereof. Part of this is manifest in the growing historical scholarship devoted to the period, but also in more popular historical societies and activities, such as the Western Front Association (1980), which now has branches in both Dublin and Belfast. The Royal Dublin Fusiliers Association was established in 1997 with the purpose of remembering 'those who have been forgotten for a long time, particularly the tens of thousands of Irishmen and indeed many women, who fell in the First World War'.[68] In Northern Ireland, the Somme Association was formed in 1990 'to ensure that the efforts of Irishmen to preserve world peace between 1914 and 1919 are remembered and understood'. There is an explicit cross-community dimension, a clear political agenda, 'to co-ordinate research into Ireland's part in the First World War and to provide a basis for the two communities in Northern Ireland to come together to learn of their common heritage'.[69] The association has restored the 'Ulster Tower' at Thiepval and built a Somme Heritage Centre near Newtownards, County Down, complete with archives, historical displays and a facsimile trench. When you join the association you become a 'Friend of the Somme', which is an odd thing, really, when you think about it: a *friend* of the Somme.

There has also been a cultural response with poems by Seamus Heaney and Michael Longley,[70] Frank McGuinness's magnificent play *Observe the Sons of Ulster Marching Towards the Somme* (first produced in 1985)[71] and Jennifer Johnston's novel, *How Many Miles to Babylon?* (also adapted for the stage and television). In a suggestive inaugural lecture entitled 'The Sure Confusing Drum' (a quotation from Heaney's 'In memoriam, Francis

Ledwidge'), George Boyce has proposed that this cultural flowering is a response to the Northern Irish 'Troubles' since the late 1960s.[72] But it also reflects a wider phenomenon: we can add Pat Barker and Sebastian Faulks to our Irish writers.[73] European developments, too, like the Historial de la Grande Guerre, at Péronne in the Department of the Somme, established in 1989, and the 'In Flanders Fields' Museum opened at Iper in Belgium in 1998, testify to an enlarged interest in the Great War, beyond Ireland. But if George Boyce is correct, then the tortuous Irish peace process might also have an impact on our engagement with the war and might underlie recent reaffirmations, in an Irish context, of the reconciling power of war service, or at least Ireland's Great War experience.

The renewed Irish interest in the Great War and its memory may have reached its apotheosis (though only time will tell) in the late autumn of 1998 with the dedication on 11 November of the 'Island of Ireland Peace Tower' on Messines Ridge in Belgium. Messines itself is a peculiar place in that, when you actually get there, it has disappeared and what you find is a place called Mesen, for you are in Flanders, in Flemish-speaking Belgium where French-language signs are scarce. This is disputed territory and the Flemish/French placenames tell their own story of communal competition. There is a resonance here with Northern Ireland's own so-called Stroke City − 'Derry/Londonderry' − to wit, Mesen/Messines, Iper/Ypres, Passendale/Passchendaele. On these grounds Mesen/Messines is probably a suitable place to locate an Irish war memorial, though we ought not to forget that the 10th (Irish) Division also fought over disputed territory in former Yugoslavia − Macedonia − and in Palestine/Israel − Gaza and Jerusalem. These would also be appropriate locations, if rather less accessible from Ireland.

Why Mesen? In the Battle of Messines (the official British terminology sticks to the French name) the 16th (Irish) Division and the 36th (Ulster) Division fought alongside each other in what was a sort of victory in June

1917. The divisions' objectives were taken with (in the standards of 1914–18) relatively low casualties. But am I alone in feeling a little uneasy about locating a 'peace tower' on the site of a *victory*? As we have already seen, the two divisions fought together on a second occasion, in August 1917, at Langemark (the French spelling is Langemarck), not far from Mesen. There they were 'broken to bits' – a defeat, surely, and in some respects a more suitable site for contemplative commemoration. Reflecting on Gallipoli and its place in the 'civil theology' of Australia, one writer has observed that Gallipoli's strong mythic potential depends on the campaign having been unsuccessful. 'Had it been a victory . . . the glorification of war could never have been kept at bay.'[74] Victory might appeal to only a part of the community, while defeat can evoke a ready response across the whole spectrum of political and ethical opinion.

Perhaps we need not worry too much about this point. Despite the best efforts of revisionist military historians, the First World War is still popularly regarded as a wholly futile exercise, and even an apparent victory like Messines will be subsumed within this broad conception. Visitors to the site, knowing nothing about the actual battle, will naturally assume that what happened there conformed to the stereotype of Western Front conflict familiar to us all: British soldiers (in this case Irish) climb out of the trenches and are mown down by machine guns. Many Irishmen did suffer in this fashion at Messines. The fact that many more did not, and that yet greater numbers of Germans fell in the battle need not disturb us.

What of the precise location of the tower? Terence Denman wrote of the 16th (Irish) Division being located in a 'historical no man's land',[75] and, in a way, the Messines tower is similarly situated between the entrenchments of opposing Irish political forces. It is, of course, not in Ireland, but, like the Islandbridge memorial, it has been placed at some distance (physical and also, perhaps, emotional) from the centre of Irish affairs. This may be no bad thing. It stands about three miles from the point where the two divisions actually fought together and advanced to capture the village of Wytschaete/Wijtschate – 'Whitesheet' to the Tommies. At that place there is a battlefield cross by the road into the village, erected by Sir William Hickie and the Irish National War Memorial in August 1926. The Messines Peace Tower is where the New Zealanders came up the hill. Indeed, it is just adjacent to a New Zealand memorial – an obelisk identical to other New Zealand monuments in France and Gallipoli. On each is the same painful inscription: 'From the uttermost ends of the earth'. The New Zealanders came further, geographically, than anyone else, and yet we might fancy that the nationalist Irish also came a long way, at least in political terms, and found it even further going home. The fact that it has taken eighty years to recover the journey serves to emphasise the distance. So perhaps it is not inappropriate to be beside the Kiwis, another island race, after all.

What of the structure itself? It is a traditional Irish round tower, a design selected specifically because it dated from before the Reformation. It was thus hoped to avoid any sectarian connotations. The tower is finished with limestone blocks taken from the infirmary of Mullingar Workhouse. In July 1998 this historic listed building was illegally demolished and the stones, like the men of the 16th and 36th Divisions, were exported willy-nilly to the Western Front. In order to regularise the situation Westmeath County Council were left to apply for planning permission 'to retain a demolished building': an Irish solution to an Irish problem.[76] In January 1919 Lord Castlemaine called a meeting in Mullingar to begin planning a County Westmeath war memorial.[77] Like quite a number of other schemes in what became independent Ireland, this came to nothing, but now, eighty years on, there is at last a Mullingar war memorial, though not in Mullingar. As a *symbolic* war memorial there is some irony in the fact that a substantial portion of the funding for the project came from surplus funds generated by the Irish

Figure 4.8 Island of Ireland Peace Tower, Mesen/Messines, Belgium, dedicated on 11 November 1998 by King Albert of Belgium, Queen
Elizabeth II of the United Kingdom and President Mary McAleese
of Ireland, who said that the occasion should be seen as a 'redeeming
of the memory' of the Irish who had died in the First World War
(*Independent*, 12 Nov. 1998).

Sailors' and Soldiers' Land Trust, the body originally charged with providing a *practical* memorial for veterans who had served in the Great War.[78]

A number of the reports about the Peace Tower asserted that this was the 'first official recognition' by the Irish state of the role played by nationalist Irishmen in the Great War.[79] Of course, it was not, although the *scale* of the recognition was greater and more unequivocal than ever before. William Cosgrave may not have gone to Westminster Abbey, or the Cenotaph, in 1926, but his deputy, Kevin O'Higgins, did, and a wreath on behalf of independent Ireland was laid at the Cenotaph annually throughout the inter-war years and beyond. Sporadically the Irish government was also represented at ceremonies in Dublin, and eventually at the interdenominational Remembrance service at St Patrick's Cathedral. The state, too, helped fund the Irish National War Memorial (more than the Northern Ireland government did), though creative accounting enabled it to claim that the subsidy was for unemployment relief and the creation of a public park. The greatest difference between this and the 1998 Peace Tower lies in the explicitness of the Irish state's unilateral recognition of the Tower. It is, as it were, a Sinn Fein – 'ourselves alone' – Irish acknowledgement of the Great War. Writing about these events, the former taoiseach, Garrett FitzGerald, has argued that 'nationalist Ireland now has the capacity to understand and accept the points of view of both the majority and the minority of nationalists in August 1914'. There is, he said, no longer any need to take sides, 'to identify with either Redmond or Pearse. Both played valid roles and can now be accepted side by side in our Irish Pantheon.' The Irish state, he concluded, has 'reached maturity'.[80]

The impulse behind the Peace Tower has been the wholly admirable one of reconciliation, together with the recovery of a past in which Irish people of whatever stripe can find common meaning. The reconciling power of shared war service is a theme which has recurred repeatedly since the war itself, though often it has seemed more of a pious hope than a genuine possibility. Now that the actual participants are all gone (or very nearly so), we seem to have another opportunity to test this supposition. If the Tower can advance the cause of healing, then we shall all be mightily in debt to the two prime movers, the Irish nationalist (Fine Gael) politician, Paddy Harte, and the former loyalist paramilitary leader, Glenn Barr. It is a deeply significant project. When I visited it in September 1998, a few weeks before its completion, I saw the youth trainee workers (deliberately drawn from both Irish traditions) dig some munitions, a shell and a bullet, out of the Belgian earth. It is a common occurrence to find such still-dangerous mementoes all along the line of the Western Front. These armaments were put to one side to be destroyed – one might say decommissioned – after eighty years: a pattern, perhaps, for more recent Irish history?

Bibliographical essay: recent writing about Ireland and the First World War

(Full titles and publication details of the works cited are provided in the bibliography.)

An indispensable starting point for any understanding of Ireland during the period of the great war is David Fitzpatrick's massive and seminal *Politics and Irish Life 1913–1921*. It is subtitled *Provincial Experience of War and Revolution*, and is essentially a study of popular politics and social attitudes, in which a wonderfully lucid local investigation of County Clare is integrated into the broader 'national' picture. One of the most impressive features of the work is the extraordinarily wide range of source material employed by Fitzpatrick, and the enviable ease with which he melds together conventional official documentary sources with private papers, oral testimony and statistical evidence. Although one might have hoped that this work would stimulate additional detailed studies of other localities, the sheer brilliance of Fitzpatrick's work may ironically have discouraged other scholars from trying to emulate his achievement.[1]

David Fitzpatrick, nevertheless, has himself promoted further studies, initially arising from an undergraduate course which he taught at Trinity College, Dublin, on the impact of the First World War. In 1986, under the imprint of 'Trinity History Workshop', he edited a series of essays by his students under the title *Ireland and the First World War*. 'No previous work', declared Fitzpatrick in his introduction, 'has explored the War's many-faceted impact upon Ireland.' The 'general reader', he asserted,

remains dependent upon the sketchy and thinly documented references to the War as an external factor which
did little more than modify the terms of political debate
and redefine political alignments in Ireland. Its overwhelming importance in the life (and sometimes death) of
ordinary Irish people is largely ignored, so reducing a
social catastrophe, which left few people untouched, to the
status of a minor if unfortunate disturbance.[2]

The collection itself testifies to the wide range of possible
studies. Four chapters cover aspects of military involvement, including the Catholic chaplaincy, recruiting and
responses in Waterford, voluntary aid organisations (such
as the Red Cross and the St John's Ambulance Association)
and Trinity College. Three other chapters investigate the
impact of the war on child welfare, the Labour movement
and nationalism in East Down, while two essays are inter-
estingly based on non-literary sources: one on war memorials and the other on a marvellous collection of wartime
recruiting posters held in the library of Trinity College,
Dublin.

David Fitzpatrick went on to edit a further Trinity
History Workshop volume – *Revolution?: Ireland 1917–
1923* – which straddles Ireland's experience of both the
Great War and the violence which followed it. He has
investigated the recruitment contribution of Ireland to the
British war effort in an essay, 'The overflow of the deluge:
Anglo-Irish relationships, 1914–1922' and, with stimulating forensic detail, in an important article, 'The logic of
collective sacrifice: Ireland and the British army,
1914–1918'. Timothy Bowman has also written about the
recruitment of Ulster and National Volunteers in an article
entitled 'Composing divisions'. In a posthumously published essay, 'Irish recruiting and the Home Rule crisis',
drawing on Josephine Howie's sadly uncompleted Ph.D.
on Britain and the Irish Question during the First World
War, David and Josephine Howie demonstrate that
throughout August 1914 both unionists and nationalists

'jockeyed for position and attempted to extract every ounce of political advantage from the new political situation created by the war'.[3] Exploiting his own doctoral research, which investigated recruiting and the various administrative approaches adopted, Patrick Callan has written two articles ('British recruitment in Ireland, 1914–1918', and 'Recruiting for the British army in Ireland') covering the broad picture. Putting the phenomenon in a longer chronological perspective, I have discussed the issue of Irish enlistment in the British army before, during and after the Great War in an essay of my own: 'The Irish military tradition and the British Empire'.

Another study by Fitzpatrick also places the wartime experience in a rather longer and wider perspective. This is his chapter, 'Militarism in Ireland, 1900–1922', in the *Military History of Ireland*. This piece identifies the prevalence of militaristic thought and organisation in early twentieth-century Ireland, from the Ulster and Irish Volunteers to such apparently benign outfits as the Boys' Brigade and the Girl Guides. The chapter also usefully summarises the extent of Irish enlistments between 1914 and 1918 and examines the revival of physical-force nationalism in the Easter Rising and the growth of militant republicanism, especially accompanying the anti-conscription campaign of 1918. Here he confirms that specifically wartime circumstances crucially affected political developments in Ireland. A book by Thomas Hennessey, *Dividing Ireland*, lends weight to this conclusion, arguing that, although partition was already inevitable before 1914, the Great War created circumstances 'which led to a form of psychological partition which could not have been predicted before the war'.[4] In an outline review of some Irish historians' approaches to the First World War ('Southern Ireland, historians and the First World War'), Thomas Dooley has also argued that the conflict 'crystallised differences between the two nationalist traditions', that is to say, the separatists and the constitutionalists.[5]

In the introduction to the original Trinity History Workshop volume, David Fitzpatrick observed that the history of Ireland and the First World War was too important to be left exclusively to academic historians. There is, indeed, a very lively amateur interest in the history of the conflict, and one of the most exciting developments in recent years has been the increasing investigation of local, and even family, histories of the Great War experience, coming frequently from outside the formal academic environment. Two outstanding such studies are Philip Orr's *The Road to the Somme: Men of the Ulster Division Tell Their Story* and Terence Denman's *Ireland's Unknown Soldiers: the 16th (Irish) Division in the Great War.*

Orr's admirable work certainly seems to confirm Fitzpatrick's emphasis on the importance of pre-war associations. Orr explicitly draws a parallel between the 36th (Ulster) Division and the so-called pals battalions raised in Great Britain – close-knit units of friends and neighbours who enlisted together in the autumn of 1914. The Ulster Division carried over 'the closely territorial – almost tribal – bonding' of the Ulster Volunteer Force. Thus the impact, both within the formation itself and at home, of the terrible casualties suffered on the first two days of the Battle of the Somme in July 1916 – some 5,500 killed, wounded or missing out of 17,000 – hit particularly hard. Orr used official records and the published histories and memoirs of the Great War for his book. But he gave his account a tremendous added richness by drawing on a wide range of personal testimony and memorabilia from the soldiers themselves. Seventy years on, he was even able to interview a handful of survivors. His use of this material – some of it notoriously difficult for the historian to handle – was exemplary and drew out some unexpected social aspects of the time. One striking feature was the extreme localism of the men who joined up. For most of them, indeed, the army gave them their first experience of travel, even within Ireland. The men of the 107th Brigade, drawn predominantly from the working-class back streets of

Belfast, were sent to County Donegal for training where they were struck by the squalid living conditions of the local inhabitants. As one recalled:

> We halt one day beside a house well off the beaten track, and go to explore the place. The primitive state of the dwelling amazes us. A woman appears, apparently in a state of terror, and we ask for a drink. She has no bread but proceeds to make scones like pancakes, baked on a flat affair over some burning twigs in the open hearth. Not a word does she say. Has she heard of War? Probably not. Maybe she thinks this country is invaded.

When they went further afield to England the (mostly) God-fearing Ulstermen were dismayed to discover that the people of Seaford in Sussex had been dreading the arrival of 'wild Irishmen'. A few months later the inhabitants of Picardy in France similarly worried about '20,000 wild Protestants' descending upon them.[6]

The Road to the Somme is both a monument to the mythology of Ulster's role at the Somme and a corrective to that myth. It provides historical chapter and verse for the sacrifices made, but it is 'revisionist' history in that it does not ignore the realities of the wartime experience. The book persuasively suggests that in France the individual soldiers of the Ulster Division were not in any real sense fighting for 'Ulster', or the British crown, or against Home Rule. Like most other soldiers condemned to the horrors of the Western Front, their motives were mixed, and in the heat of battle such loyalty as they had was mostly reserved for their immediate comrades or, in some cases, only for themselves. Orr presents us with 'honest witnesses of the Somme' who do not gloss over 'the absurdities, obscenities and immoralities' of the conflict, and he eloquently urges us to listen to 'the mundane but authentic voice of the ordinary human being whom circumstances thrust into the crucible of violence'.[7]

The history of the other two 'New Army' divisions raised in Ireland at the start of the war, the 10th and 16th

Divisions, far less unionist in complexion than the 36th, has understandably been much more obscure – hence Terence Denman's choice of *Ireland's Unknown Soldiers* as the title for his study of the 16th (Irish) Division. Denman has done a great deal to recover the complex and human reality of a formation largely composed of Catholic Irish nationalists. The fate of the two most outstanding nationalist recruits to the 16th Division – Tom Kettle and Willie Redmond – epitomised that of the wider constitutional nationalist movement. Kettle, who was killed in September 1916, towards the end of the Battle of the Somme, had reflected after the Easter Rising on his probable fate: 'These men will go down in history as heroes and martyrs; and I will go down – if I go down at all – as a bloody British officer.'[8] Redmond's fate was, if anything, more poignant, and his life is the subject of another excellent book by Terence Denman: *A Lonely Grave: the Life and Death of William Redmond*. Although Redmond was not an Irish politician of the first rank, he was an important confidant of his older brother John, the leader of the Irish Parliamentary Party, and he was a representative of the more radical tendency within what was socially a rather conservative grouping. Denman follows Redmond's career as a Nationalist MP from 1883, and his enlistment into the army in 1914, although by this stage he was over fifty years old. The circumstances of his death in action side by side with the Ulster Division prompted some observers to hope that it would help bring North and South closer together. These hopes, however, were not to be fulfilled and, in an intensely interesting review of the ways in which Redmond was remembered, and the efforts to raise a public memorial to him, Denman demonstrates the extent to which in the new post-war Ireland the life of a constitutional nationalist like Redmond came to be regarded simply as a tragic failure.

Detailed local studies of the Great War period can help to put human flesh on the bare bones of the wider story. *Donegal, Ireland and the First World War*, by Niall Mac

Fhionnghaile, is an informative and stimulating account of both the general course of the war and its impact, especially in north Donegal. In an essay in David Fitzpatrick's *Ireland and the First World War*, Pauline Codd has examined 'Recruiting and responses to the war in Wexford'. In a volume devoted to the history of Cavan, Eileen Reilly has looked at the county during the era of the Great War. A short article in the journal of the Military History Society of Ireland by Martin Staunton ('Kilrush, Co. Clare and the Royal Munster Fusiliers') shows what can be done for even a small town using an admirably wide range of sources. This article represents in microcosm what Staunton has done in his admirable master's thesis on the Munster Fusiliers. One of the most productive sources is contained in the official War Office publication, *Soldiers Died in the Great War* which lists all the fatal casualties by regiment.[9] In the journal of the Western Front Association Staunton has outlined how this work might be used: ('*Soldiers Died in the Great War 1914–1919* as historical source material'). By using this source Patrick J. Casey in 'Irish casualties in the first world war' has attempted to calculate a definitive figure of Irish losses. But, having carefully extracted 29,739 men of Irish birth from the 667,000 individuals listed in *Soldiers Died*, he then rather casually inflates the figure 'to be in the region of 35,000' by estimating 'that there are approximately 5,000 further Irish casualties from the ranks of the armies of the British colonies and the United States of America'.[10] Neither sailors nor airmen were included in the original figure.

Specific studies can be based on either location or unit. An example of the former is *Bushmills Heroes 1914–1918*, compiled and edited by Robert Thompson, which consists of a hundred or so copiously illustrated biographies of local men who perished in the war. The latter category is represented by two studies of units from the same regiment: Gardiner S. Mitchell, '*Three Cheers for the Derrys!*': *a History of the 10th Royal Inniskilling Fusiliers in the 1914–1918 War*, and W. J. Canning, *Ballyshannon, Belcoo,*

Bertincourt: the History of the 11th Battalion The Royal Inniskilling Fusiliers (Donegal & Fermanagh Volunteers) in World War One. Other local studies include the 1990–1 volume of *Times Past*, journal of the Ballincollig Community School Local History Society, which includes an excellent article on recruiting in County Cork by Eoin McCarthy and Gerard O'Sullivan, along with a comprehensive listing of Cork-born soldiers who died in the Great War. *Deeds Not Words*, by David Robertson, tells the story of the ninety-three young men from Wilson's Hospital Church of Ireland School at Multyfarnham, County Westmeath, who served in the war while Doreen Corcoran ('County Antrim war memorial at the Knockagh') has produced a neat and revealing study of one local commemoration.

The most comprehensive recent local investigation is Thomas P. Dooley's *Irishmen or English Soldiers?* By focusing on one ordinary individual – James English – a working-class Catholic recruit from Waterford City, the author has succeeded magnificently in the aim of rescuing one of history's 'inarticulate' from the obscurity of even the relatively recent past, and has also made the whole exercise accessible to the non-academic reader. The fascinating investigation of the particular pressures acting on one person gives the opportunity to test, and in some cases correct, generalisations made by other historians and commentators. The work also provides particularly valuable insights into the nature and working of Redmondite Nationalism, especially at a local level.

The military side of the Irish involvement in the Great War has been covered in Tom Johnstone, *Orange, Green and Khaki: the Story of the Irish Regiments in the Great War, 1914–1918*. This work is both comprehensive and limited. On the one hand it is a handy compendium of information concerning virtually all the fighting which involved Irish units, drawn from regimental and other unit histories, with some additional material from memoirs and unpublished records. On the other, it says nothing about the domestic context of that service, nor does it consider the social, political and economic circumstances of the time. Thus, much of 'the story of the Irish regiments in the Great War' is, in fact, left out. Myles Dungan's two volumes of gleamings from memoirs and unpublished archives, *Irish Voices from the Great War* and *They Shall Not Grow Old*, also concentrate largely on the battlefield experience. These fascinating compilations include material from interviews with veterans preserved in the Radio Telefís Éireann Sound Archive. Dungan's admirable intention has been 'to keep before the public eye a neglected area of historical research and evaluation and to bring some more anecdotal material into the public domain in an edited, organised and palatable form'.[11] The same author's broader review of Irish military service, *Distant Drums: Irish Soldiers in Foreign Armies*, contains a useful chapter on the First World War.

But the mere chronicling of Irish actions in battle is not in itself very revealing without some consideration of how their very *Irishness* affected behaviour or the way in which, for example, the military high command treated them. Another part-time historian, Nicholas Perry, has very professionally 'number-crunched' his way through the evidence to estimate how Irish the nominally Irish units were during the war ('Nationality in the Irish infantry regiments in the First World War'). As Irish recruiting declined during the conflict, and in the absence of conscription, there were fewer and fewer drafts to replace casualties at the Front, and so Irish formations were gradually 'diluted' with soldiers from other parts of the British Isles.

In an important article, 'The Catholic Irish soldier in the First World War: the "racial environment"', Terence Denman has examined the attitudes which, for example, characterised Irish soldiers as terrific 'shock troops', excellent in attack but suspect in defence, and 'patronised for their supposed limited intellectual capacity and their childlike qualities'. While conceding that 'it would be surprising . . . if there were not particular characteristics which distinguished Catholic Irish soldiers', Denman's careful conclusion is that in matters of discipline and effectiveness, whether in attack or defence, they were not markedly different from other units of the British army.[12] Similarly, Joanna Bourke in '"Irish Tommies"' has examined the way Irish experiences in the war were interpreted by journalists and other commentators, concluding that 'the Irish soldier was little different from his English counterpart'.[13] In another publication Denman has provided a vivid picture of life on active service drawing on the correspondence of one officer ('An Irish battalion at war: from the letters of Captain J. H. M. Staniforth, 7th Leinsters, 1914–1918'). Denman has complemented this 'microcosmic' view of army life with an examination of Irish military service in a broader national context: 'The 10th (Irish) Division 1914–15: a study in military and political interaction'. The difficulties of Irish politics also crop up in Jane Leonard's essay 'The reaction of Irish officers in the British army to the Easter Rising of 1916'.

A beginning has been made on the cultural impact of the war in Ireland. I have written three preliminary essays on the subject: 'The Great War in modern Irish memory', which also touches on the topic of war memorials; 'Irish culture and the Great War'; and 'Irish prose writers of the First World War', which examines some twenty novels covering various aspects of the war from an Irish perspective. These are supplemented by an illustrated article, 'Irish artists and the First World War', which was published in *History Ireland*. The growing interest in the Great War is demonstrated by other recent articles in *History Ireland*, including George Boyce, 'Ireland and the First World War', and David Officer, 'Re-presenting war: the Somme Heritage Centre'. Boyce's article (which drew on his wide-ranging inaugural lecture at the University of Wales, Swansea, in 1993, *The Sure Confusing Drum: Ireland and the First World War*) itself provoked a critical letter (to which Boyce responded) in the subsequent number of the magazine.[14]

A start has also been made on the social and economic
dimension of the war and its aftermath, although the economic side of things is gravely understudied. One exception is Peter Murray's study of Power's distillery in the
journal of the Irish Labour History Society: 'The First
World War and a Dublin distillery workforce'. Other
aspects of Ireland's economic life during the war are
covered in two essays by Philip Ollerenshaw: 'Textile business in Europe during the First World War' and 'The business and politics of banking in Ireland 1900–1943'. A
civilian tragedy of the war, the loss of the Royal Mail
Steamer *Leinster* in October 1918, is covered in Roy
Stokes, *Death in the Irish* Sea. As demonstrated with essays
by Tierney, Bowen and Fitzpatrick on 'Recruiting posters'
and Jane Leonard on war memorials, '"Lest we forget"' in
David Fitzpatrick's *Ireland and the First World War*, visual
sources can be very rewarding. Pictures can certainly help
to illuminate the social context of military service. One
interesting selection of wartime photographs taken by the
pioneer Irish photographer, Father Frank Browne, SJ, is
contained in E. E. O'Donnell, *Father Browne: a Life in
Pictures*. Browne served as a chaplain with the Irish
Guards on the Western Front. An essay by Jane Leonard
on the Catholic chaplaincy (which is in fact not restricted to
Catholics) and another by Patrick Callan ('Ambivalence
towards the Saxon shilling') on the attitudes of the
Catholic Church in general are the only studies so far
specifically devoted to religious matters. A recent study of
state housing and British policy up to 1922 (Murray Fraser,
John Bull's Other Homes) details the highly politicised
scheme to provide housing for ex-servicemen, and demonstrates the conjunction of war service, social policy, architectural history and the political changes of the immediate
postwar period. Judith Hill's *Irish Public Sculpture* contains fifty fascinating pages on post-war memorial-build-
ing, both to the Great War and the Irish War of
Independence. A rather grimmer aspect of these years is
covered in Jane Leonard, 'Getting them at last: the IRA

and ex-servicemen'. Leonard has also investigated the interesting and revealing topic of war remembrance ceremonies in independent Ireland: 'The twinge of memory: Armistice Day and Remembrance Sunday in Dublin since 1919' and the general issue of commemoration in a thoughtful pamphlet, *The Culture of Commemoration*, published by the Cultures of Ireland Group.

The eightieth anniversary of the Battle of the Somme stimulated work which examined both that terrible engagement itself and also its longer-term memory, particularly that of the 36th (Ulster) Division. Timothy Bowman, 'The Irish at the Somme', neatly traces the involvement during the battle of Irish units, including the 16th (Irish) Division, as well as the 36th, and the Tyneside Irish Brigade composed of Irish emigrants from the north-east of England. In an issue which coupled the Somme anniversary with that of the Easter Rising, the Northern Ireland 'Cultural Traditions Journal' *Causeway* included Philip Orr's 'Lessons of the Somme for an era of change', Alan MacFarland's detailed account of the action, 'Spectacular heroism and devastating losses', and Peter Collins's 'Ripples from the Rising'.

Despite the growing body of literature now being produced, what still needs to be done? Local studies, covering any number of topics, including recruitment, employment, economic developments during the war, returning ex-servicemen, and the design and dedication of war memorials are all fertile fields for investigation. We still know very little about the detail of who among the Irish Volunteers and Ulster Volunteers actually joined up. Industrial mobilisation for war products – textiles for uniforms, engineering for munitions, agriculture for military and civilian foodstuffs, or horses for the army – provide further rich topics for investigation. The role of women, both at home and serving, nearer the battlefront, for example as nurses, has scarcely been touched, though part of a chapter on the Ulster Women's Unionist Council by Diane Urquhart ('"The female of the species is more deadlier than the male"?'), points the way to further work on the political and social reaction of women to the conflict, and an essay by Margaret Downes on 'The civilian voluntary aid effort' covers much 'women's work'. The medical history of the wartime years in Ireland remains almost completely uncharted. The literary response to the war also demands further work. Many local newspapers regularly published poems about the war, not, to be sure, necessarily of high literary quality, but no doubt heart-felt all the same, and undoubtedly revealing of popular attitudes. The response of nationalists, especially in Ulster, requires to be recovered and documented, and the role of local churches, Catholic and Protestant, in supporting or opposing the war, and in dealing with the unhappily common tragedy of bereavement, is another fascinating, and largely neglected, area of study. So, there remains much yet to be done. The beauty (perhaps the 'terrible beauty'?) of a topic such as Ireland and the Great War is that it lends itself abundantly to research at many levels of intensity, from the purest and most abstruse academic approach to the much more personal and local – and for many the most engrossing and satisfying – sphere of community, family or school classroom history.[15]

Notes

Citations of both published and unpublished secondary sources in the notes consist of the surname(s) of the author(s) and a short title, with full information being provided in the bibliography. Citations for primary sources are given in full.

INTRODUCTION

1 Martin, '1916', p. 68.
2 See the bibliographical essay, pp. 144–56.

I OBLIGATION

1 Hayes-McCoy, 'Foreword', to Harris, *Irish Regiments in the First World War*, p. x.
2 Harris, *Irish Regiments in the First World War*, pp. 26–32; Harris, 'The other half million'.
3 Curtis, *A History of Ireland*, p. 406.
4 Lee, *Ireland 1912–1985*, p. 23 n. 88.
5 Fitzpatrick, 'Militarism in Ireland', p. 388.
6 *Hansard*, 8 Jan. 1915, 18 H.L. 5s, cols. 351–2; see also Simkins, *Kitchener's Army*, p. 112.
7 Callan, 'Recruiting for the British army in Ireland', pp. 42–3; see also Callan, 'British recruitment in Ireland' and 'Voluntary recruiting for the British army'.

8 Alan Ward, 'Lloyd George and the 1918 Irish conscription crisis', pp. 120–2.

9 Quoted in Holmes, *The Little Field Marshal*, p. 326.

10 Callan, 'British recruitment in Ireland', p. 48.

11 Orr, *Road to the Somme*, p. 38.

12 See the view of Edwin Montagu quoted in Jeffery, *British Army and Crisis of Empire*, p. 99.

13 Kettle, *Poems and Parodies*, p. 15.

14 See Grigg, 'Nobility and war'; Bond, 'British "anti-war" writers'; Trevor Wilson, *Myriad Faces of War*, pp. 851–3.

15 Quoted in Harris, *Irish Regiments in the First World War*, p. 14.

16 Recruiting pamphlet, c. Sep. 1914 (in the possession of the author).

17 23 Sep. 1914 (quoted in Lucey, 'Cork public opinion', p. 38).

18 Callan, 'Ambivalence towards the Saxon shilling', p. 101.

19 17 Oct. 1914 (quoted in Bew, *Ideology and the Irish Question*, p. 131).

20 *Cork Constitution*, 3 Sep. 1914 (quoted in Lucey, 'Cork public opinion', p. 47).

21 12 Sep. 1914 (quoted in Orr, *Road to the Somme*, p. 50).

22 Denis Gwynn, *Life of John Redmond*, p. 391.

23 Bew, *Ideology and the Irish Question*, pp. 118–52.

24 Martin, *The Irish Volunteers*, p. 148.

25 Stephen Gwynn, *The Charm of Ireland*, p. 279.

26 Howie and Howie, 'Irish recruiting', p. 8.

27 Ibid., p. 15.

28 By F. S. Boas, *Newtownards Chronicle*, 31 Oct. 1914 (quoted in Orr, *Road to the Somme*, p. 54).

29 Quoted in Philip Ollerenshaw, 'Businessmen and the development of Ulster Unionism, 1886–1921', *Journal of Imperial and Commonwealth History* (forthcoming).

30 Colvin, *Carson*, vol. III, pp. 33–4. See also Howie and Howie, 'Irish recruiting'.

31 Simkins, *Kitchener's Army*, p. 187.

32 Respectively, 324, 311 and 310 men. Totals calculated from figures in Staunton, 'The Royal Munster Fusiliers', pp. 57–8.

[33] Ibid.: 1,734 as opposed to 1,543.

[34] Fitzpatrick, 'The logic of collective sacrifice', p. 1020, fig. 1.

[35] Dungan, *Distant Drums*, p. 54.

[36] Mitchell, *'Three Cheers for the Derrys'*, p. 3.

[37] Dooley, *Irishmen or English Soldiers*, p. 124.

[38] See Tierney, Bowen and Fitzpatrick, 'Recruiting posters', pp. 53, 56.

[39] *Workers' Republic*, 18 Dec. 1915 (reprinted in Connolly, *A Socialist and War*, p. 102).

[40] Fitzpatrick, 'The logic of collective sacrifice'.

[41] Hynes, *The Soldiers' Tale*, p. 111. Hynes also speaks from personal experience, having been a United States Marine pilot during the Second World War.

[42] Wallace Lyon, typescript memoirs (IWM).

[43] Barry, *Guerrilla Days*, p. 8.

[44] Lee, *Ireland 1912–1985*, p. 270.

[45] Macardle, *The Irish Republic*, p. 114. Macardle perhaps wrote from personal knowledge: her brother Richard served in France during the war (*Irish Press*, 24 Dec. 1958).

[46] Sir Henry Robinson, *Memories*, pp. 232–3.

[47] *Ireland's Cause*, probably published early in 1916. There is a copy of the pamphlet in the Library of the Royal Irish Academy, and an illustration of a page in Vaughan, *New History of Ireland*, vol. VI, plate 60, where it is dated as 1915. There is an account by Redmond of his visit to the front (19–23 Nov. 1915) in Kerr, *What the Irish Regiments Have Done*, pp. 7–22.

[48] Martin, *The Irish Volunteers*, p. 168.

[49] *The Irish Volunteer*, 22 May 1915 (quoted in Martin, *The Irish Volunteers*, p. 190).

[50] 'Peace and the Gael' (published anonymously in *Spark*, Dec. 1915), in Pearse, *Political Writings*, p. 216.

[51] *Workers' Republic*, 25 Dec. 1915 (quoted in Ruth Dudley Edwards, *Pearse*, p. 245).

[52] R. H. Foster, 'Irish Methodism and war', p. 76.

[53] *Report of Diocesan Council of Meath for 1914*, p. 14.

[54] Coogan, *Collins*, pp. 31–2.

[55] Bew, *Ideology and the Irish Question*, p. 122.

[56] Martin, '1916', p. 95; Stephens, *The Insurrection in Dublin*, p. 19; St John Ervine, 'The story of the Irish rebellion', p. 28. Ervine recycled some of this journalistic account in his semi-autobiographical novel, *Changing Winds*.

[57] Hart, *The IRA and Its Enemies*, p. 171.

[58] Related by veteran Terence Poulter in Shane McElhatton, 'Dublin Fusiliers put raw soldiers into early action', *Irish Times*, 24 Apr. 1984.

[59] Linklater, *The Man on My Back*, pp. 40–1.

[60] Gibbon, *Inglorious Soldier*, pp. 289–90.

[61] Margaret Ward, *Unmanageable Revolutionaries*, pp. 107–17.

[62] See, for example, Winter, *The Experience of World War I*, pp. 173–5; A. J. P. Taylor, *The First World War*, plates 63–4, the latter with an inimitable Taylorian caption: 'Lloyd George casts an expert eye over munition girls'.

[63] Very little modern historical work has been devoted to the Irish economy during the First World War. Unless otherwise noted, the economic information in the following paragraphs has been drawn from E. J. Riordan's *Modern Irish Trade and Industry*; his article 'The war and Irish industry'; Branagan, 'Ireland and war contracts'; and Russell *et al.*, 'Four years of Irish economics'.

[64] Moss and Hume, *Shipbuilders to the World*, pp. 175–206. Another 10,000 workers were employed at Belfast's second shipyard, Workman Clark & Co.

[65] For an overview, see Ollerenshaw, 'Textile business'.

[66] There is a 1917 drawing by the Belfast artist William Conor of 'Miss Madeleine Ewart working a turret lathe for 18lb shells' (reproduced in Judith Wilson, *Conor*, p. 16).

[67] Kelleher, 'Gunpowder to guided missiles', p. 220.

[68] Ibid., pp. 182–9.

[69] Mason, 'Dublin opticians', pp. 147–8. Sir Howard Grubb had invented the submarine periscope and his pattern had been copied by the Germans before 1914. Grubb's was one of the twenty or so most important optical manufacturers in the United Kingdom. For the general context, see MacLeod and MacLeod, 'War and economic development'.

70 Lysaght in Russell *et al.*, 'Four years of Irish economics', p. 318.

71 Irish whitefish landings 1914: 336,448 cwts, value £138,960; 1918: 561,000, value £599,461 (Pollock, 'The seafishing industry', pp. 76, 213, 723, 745); *Report on the Sea and Inland Fisheries of Ireland for 1918*, iii–vi [Cmd 601], H. C. 1920, xvi, 903–6.

72 Sixty crew and Post Office staff (of 102 on board), 376 of 489 servicemen and 115 of 180 civilians (Stokes, *Death in the Irish Sea*, p. 130). For a full list of sinkings in Irish waters, see Lloyd's of London, *Lloyd's War Losses*.

73 Kelleher, 'Gunpowder to guided missiles', p. 220.

74 *The Turret Lathers*, Dec. 1916 (Somme Heritage Centre, Newtownards, County Down).

75 Clarke, *The Royal Victoria Hospital*, p. 107.

76 British Red Cross Society, *Report by the Joint War Committee*, pp. 726, 728.

77 For a preliminary study, see Downes, 'The civilian voluntary aid effort'.

78 Numbers calculated from the (imperfect) lists in the Weekly Irish Times, *1916 Rebellion Handbook*, pp. 56–8.

79 Margaret Ward states that 'Margaretta Keogh' was a member of Cumann na mBan and implies that she was an active participant on the Volunteer side. She cites the *Catholic Bulletin*, May 1918, and *An Phoblacht*, 25 June 1932, as authority (*Unmanageable Revolutionaries*, pp. 113, 275 n. 54). Other sources, including the republican memorial listing compiled by Donnelly, *The Last Post* (p. 26), Weekly Irish Times, *1916 Rebellion Handbook* (p. 277), Desmond Ryan, *The Rising* (pp. 178–9), and O'Farrell, *Who's Who in the Irish War of Independence* (p. 82), give no indication whatsoever that she was a political activist.

80 British Red Cross Society, *Report by the Joint War Committee*, p. 727; Urquhart, '"The female of the species"', pp. 104–5.

81 Belfast Citizens' Committee, *The Great War*, p. 102.

82 Lucey, 'Cork public opinion', pp. 69–71.

83 Margaret Ward, *Unmanageable Revolutionaries*, p. 119.

[84] Irish National War Memorial, *Ireland's Memorial Records*, vol. I, p. i.

[85] It is possible that one or two names of still-living men may have been included in the *Memorial Records*. There are occasional stories of such names being inscribed on war memorials, though they are not often substantiated. One example concerns Robert John Cooke who appears on the war memorial of Methodist College, Belfast. Far from being dead, he had, in fact, emigrated to South Africa after the war as a Congregationalist minister. A photograph of the war memorial included in a school history published in 1939 was doctored to remove Cooke's name from the tablet, which, presumably because of the cost, was not itself altered (see Henderson, *Methodist College Belfast*, p. 479, and Fry, *The Methodist College Belfast Register*, p. 110).

[86] See, for example, 'An Irishman's Diary', *Irish Times*, 2 July 1994.

[87] Casey, 'Irish casualties in the First World War'.

[88] This does not include officers (Saorstát Éireann, *Census of Population 1926*, vol. x, *General Report* (Dublin, 1934), p. 12).

[89] Fitzpatrick, 'Militarism in Ireland', p. 501 n. 50.

[90] Biographical details of the Hackett brothers in Ron Edwards, 'My First CO', an article about Robert Hackett.

2 PARTICIPATION

[1] David Williamson, 'The Screenplay', in Gammage, *The Story of Gallipoli*, p. 144.

[2] A notable exploration of this theme is Clark, *The Donkeys*. The phrase 'lions led by donkeys' is attributed to the German General Max Hoffman in conversation with Field Marshal Erich von Ludendorff.

[3] The numbers were 40,000 ('British Expeditionary Force') as opposed to 8,000 ('Egyptian Expeditionary Force') (Grey, *Military History of Australia*, p. 118).

[4] For a thoughtful exploration of the Great War resonance of such places, see Winter, *Sites of Memory, Sites of Mourning*.

5   There is an enormous literature on the 'Anzac tradition'. An especially good collection of essays is in Inglis, *Anzac Remembered*.

6   Reflecting on the Australian casualties of that day, Bill Gammage, the military adviser to the film, wrote: 'All the tragic waste of the Great War was contracted into their passing, for as they died the *English* [emphasis added] troops at Suvla, plainly visible from the Nek, were making tea' (Gammage, 'ANZAC: trial by ordeal', in Gammage, *The Story of Gallipoli*, p. 34). See Prior, 'The Suvla Bay tea-party', for a shrewd assessment of the Suvla Bay landing.

7   These difficulties are especially well covered in Denman, *Ireland's Unknown Soldiers*, ch. 2.

8   Ibid., p. 23.

9   Denman, 'The 10th (Irish) Division', p. 20.

10   Falls, 'Maxwell, 1916, and Britain at war', p. 205.

11   Cooper, *The Tenth (Irish) Division*, p. 13.

12   1 May 1915 (quoted in Hanna, *The Pals at Suvla Bay*, p. 29).

13   Cooper, *The Tenth (Irish) Division*, p. viii (foreword by Redmond).

14   MacDonagh, *The Irish at the Front*, p. 6 (introduction by Redmond).

15   De Montmorency, *Sword and Stirrup*, p. 245.

16   Hanna, *The Pals at Suvla Bay*, pp. 61, 74, 113.

17   Curtayne, *Ledwidge*, p. 127.

18   Cooper, *The Tenth (Irish) Division*, pp. 179–80.

19   Tynan, *The Years of the Shadow*, p. 178; Tynan, *The Wandering Years*, pp. 10–11. There was some public concern that the exploits of the division had been insufficiently recognised in official despatches. See Stephen Gwynn, *Redmond's Last Years*, pp. 195–7.

20   St John Ervine, *Changing Winds* (New York edn), p. 498. In the novel one of the closest friends of the protagonist Henry Quinn, Gilbert Farlow, a playwright and theatre critic, dies at Gallipoli.

21   Phillips, *The Revolution in Ireland*, p. 88.

22   Gibbon, *Inglorious Soldier*, pp. 31–2.

23 Norway, *The Sinn Fein Rebellion*, p. 68. For the context of this memoir, see my introduction to Norway and Norway, *The Sinn Fein Rebellion*.

24 Ruth Dudley Edwards, *Pearse*, p. 285.

25 Taillon, *The Women of 1916*, p. 63.

26 Brennan, *Allegiance*, p. 66.

27 Sweeny, 'In the GPO', p. 104.

28 Griffith and O'Grady, *Curious Journey*, p. 78.

29 [Casement], *Ireland, Germany and the Freedom of the Seas*, p. 1. Casement is identified as the author of the pamphlet in Brennan, *Allegiance*, p. 37.

30 *Irish Worker*, 8 Aug. 1914 (reprinted in Connolly, *A Socialist and War*, p. 36).

31 Pearse to Joe McGarrity, 19 Oct. 1914 (quoted in Ruth Dudley Edwards, *Pearse*, p. 225).

32 Townshend, *Political Violence in Ireland*, p. 288.

33 Norway, *The Sinn Fein Rebellion*, p. 4.

34 There are – and were – no steps at the GPO. The 'steps of the GPO', so often cited (for example in Macardle, *The Irish Republic*, p. 155), is one of those 'mythopoeic realities' which populates Irish popular memory. F. X. Martin cites a bystander describing Pearse 'as standing on what seemed to be a chair between the columns of the GPO' (Martin, '1916', p. 9 n. 7).

35 Desmond Ryan, *The Rising*, pp. 142–3.

36 Townshend, *Political Violence in Ireland*, p. 302: see also Hayes-McCoy, 'A military history of the Rising', pp. 287–90.

37 R. F. Foster, *Modern Ireland*, p. 483.

38 [Smyly], 'Experiences of a VAD', p. 817. Smyly is identified as the author of this anonymously published article in Finkelstein, *An Index to Blackwoods Magazine*.

39 Desmond Ryan, *The Rising*, p. 148.

40 Johnstone, *Orange, Green and Khaki*, pp. 209–12.

41 [Smyly], 'Experiences of a VAD', p. 839.

42 O'Connor, *Gogarty*, p. 163.

43 O'Halpin, *The Decline of the Union*, p. 118; see also Townshend, 'The suppression of the Easter Rising'.

44 Robertson to Kitchener, 26 Apr. 1916 (PRO PRO 30/57/55).

[45] Arthur, *Maxwell*, p. 195.

[46] Ó Broin, *Wylie and the Irish Revolution*, p. 3.

[47] Macready, *Annals of an Active Life*, vol. I, p. 241. Macready had been nominated to be military governor at Belfast in 1914 if civil disorder had broken out. He was later GOC Ireland, 1920–3.

[48] Lee, *Ireland 1912–1985*, pp. 28–36.

[49] Diary of Sir Henry Wilson, 26 Apr. 1916 (IWM). Quotation from the Wilson Papers is by permission of the Trustees of the Imperial War Museum.

[50] Denman, *A Lonely Grave*, p. 97.

[51] Ledwidge to Bob Christie, 4 May 1916 (quoted in Curtayne, *Ledwidge*, p. 149). Thomas MacDonagh, poet and literary scholar, was one of the signatories of the Proclamation.

[52] Stephen Gwynn, *Redmond's Last Years*, p. 230.

[53] McCance, *Royal Munster Fusiliers*, vol. II, pp. 197–8. See also Staunton, 'The Royal Munster Fusiliers', pp. 229–30.

[54] Denman, *Ireland's Unknown Soldiers*, p. 144. See also Leonard, 'The reaction of Irish officers'.

[55] For example Capt. Sir Basil Brooke (Barton, *Brookeborough*, p. 25).

[56] MacDonagh, *The Irish on the Somme*, p. 39.

[57] The calendar was abolished in 1752 when eleven days were added, the Battle of the Boyne subsequently being celebrated on 12 July.

[58] S[amuels] and S., *With the Ulster Division*, p. 52.

[59] Orr, *Road to the Somme*, pp. 164–5. *Reliable* authority for these stories is hard to come by, and they have certainly multiplied with the telling.

[60] S[amuels] and S., *With the Ulster Division*, p. 62. It seems unlikely that, above the noise of the battle, *The Times* reporter actually heard the cries of 'No Surrender!', but they are a persistent feature in the retelling of the story of 1 July 1916. Like the 'steps of the GPO', perhaps they are another Irish 'mythopoeic reality'.

[61] Falls, *36th (Ulster) Division*, pp. 12–13.

[62] Stewart, *Ulster Crisis*, pp. 241–2.

[63] MacDonagh, *The Irish on the Somme*, pp. 24–5.

[64] Published in the *Sentinel*, 15 July 1916 (quoted in Mitchell, *'Three Cheers for the Derrys!'*, pp. 111–12). The places mentioned are all Derry localities.

[65] The poem was also published in Logan, *Ulster in the X-Rays*, pp. 146–7, and as a song with music by W. Hamilton Burns (Belfast, n.d.).

[66] A. J. P. Taylor, *English History*, p. 95.

[67] Mitchell, *'Three Cheers for the Derrys!'*, p. 108. Of 263 fatalities in total over the whole war, 123 from this battalion died on 1 July 1916 (figures from the United Kingdom War Office publication, *Soldiers Died in the Great War 1914–1919*, part 32).

[68] S[amuels] and S., *With the Ulster Division*, pp. 5–6.

[69] This was first proposed by the General Purposes Committee on 13 July and passed by the full council on 19 July (Belfast Corporation Miscellaneous Committee Minute Book, July 1915–May 1919, pp. 191–2, 195–6 (Belfast City Council Archives)).

[70] It comprised 5th and 6th Royal Inniskilling Fusiliers, and 5th and 6th Royal Irish Rifles.

[71] *Meath Chronicle*, 15 May 1916 (quoted in Curtayne, *Ledwidge*, p. 155).

[72] Falls, *Military Operations: Macedonia*, pp. 64–82.

[73] Denman, *Ireland's Unknown Soldiers*, p. 16.

[74] Mary S. Kettle, 'Memoir', in Thomas Kettle, *The Ways of War*, pp. 31–2.

[75] Denman, *Ireland's Unknown Soldiers*, p. 145.

[76] Harris, *Irish Regiments in the First World War*, p. 102.

[77] Johnstone, *Orange, Green and Khaki*, p. 281.

[78] Leslie, *The Irish Tangle*, p. 246.

[79] 'The Irish MP's Advice', in O'Higgins, *The Voice of Banba*, p. 75.

[80] Denman, *A Lonely Grave*, p. 85.

[81] *The Times*, 11 June 1917 (quoted in Denman, *A Lonely Grave*, p. 130).

[82] Denman, *Ireland's Unknown Soldiers*, title of ch. 5.

[83] Sir Philip Gibbs's phrase (quoted in O'Rahilly, *Doyle*, p. 550).

[84] Ibid., p. 555.

[85] Johnstone, *Orange, Green and Khaki*, p. 295.

[86] Ibid., p. 298.

[87] Mitchell, *'Three Cheers for the Derrys!'*, p. 200.

[88] Rex Taylor, *Assassination*, pp. 160–2.

[89] The best guide to the crown forces is Townshend, *The British Campaign in Ireland*. Recruitment into the IRA is illuminatingly explored in Hart, *The IRA and Its Enemies*.

[90] A suggestion advanced in Jeffery, *British Army and Crisis of Empire*, pp. 73–4.

[91] Details about John Kipling from George Webb, 'Foreword', to Kipling, *The Irish Guards*, vol. I, pp. 7–19.

[92] Ibid., vol. II, pp. 24, 28.

3 IMAGINATION

[1] Lennox Robinson, *The Big House*, pp. 9–46.

[2] This is a not uncommon conflation in recollections of the war. In the family of Willie Hackett the 'memory' is that the news of his death (on 5 November) came on 11 November. His death notice was published in the *Irish Times*, 13 Nov. 1918.

[3] Lennox Robinson, *Cooper*, p. 88.

[4] See Winter, *The Great War and the British People*, for a thorough analysis.

[5] Emphasis in original; quoted in Hyam, *Britain's Imperial Century*, pp. 378–9.

[6] Cooper, *The Tenth (Irish) Division*, p. 253.

[7] Arnold, *Jellett*, p. 41.

[8] O'Connell et al., *Jellett*, p. 55.

[9] See, for example, Eksteins, *Rites of Spring*, and, for a contrary view, Winter, *Sites of Memory, Sites of Mourning*.

[10] The best biographical source for Lavery is McConkey, *Lavery*.

[11] Lavery, *Life of a Painter*, p. 138.

[12] Ibid.

[13] Harries and Harries, *The War Artists*, p. 2; Griffin, *Wild Geese*, p. 243.

[14] Lavery, *Life of a Painter*, p. 139.

[15] For biographical details, and a wonderfully lucid critique of Orpen's work, see Arnold, *Orpen*. See also Arnold's 'Introduction' to the 1986 new edition of Orpen's *An Onlooker in France*.

[16] Konody and Dark, *Orpen*, p. 166. After some vicissitudes, including an attack on the painting itself with an 'indelible aniline pencil', the picture ended up in the Mildura Arts Centre, Victoria, Australia (see Hamilton and Beyer, *The Elliott Collection*, pp. 81–7).

[17] McConkey, *A Free Spirit*, p. 63.

[18] Keating, 'Orpen', p. 26.

[19] Arnold, *Orpen*, p. 345.

[20] McConkey, *Lavery*, pp. 152–3. McConkey erroneously identifies Darling as the Lord Chief Justice.

[21] Lavery, *Life of a Painter*, p. 207.

[22] McCoole, *Hazel*, p. 60.

[23] McConkey, *Lavery*, pp. 153–4.

[24] Harries and Harries, *The War Artists*, p. 30.

[25] Orpen, *An Onlooker in France* (1924 edn), p. v.

[26] Konody and Dark, *Orpen*, pp. 85–6.

[27] Orpen, *An Onlooker in France* (1924 edn), p. v.

[28] Arnold, 'Introduction', to Orpen, *Onlooker in France* (1996 edn), p. xi.

[29] Keating, 'Orpen', p. 24.

[30] Jeffery, 'The Great War', pp. 140–1.

[31] Falls, *36th (Ulster) Division*, p. 126.

[32] Orpen, *An Onlooker in France* (1924 edn), plates XIX and LXX.

[33] Imperial War Museum, *Catalogue*, pp. 227–8, nos. 2973, 2984; Hobart and Hobart, *an Ireland . . . imagined*, p. 54.

[34] Arnold, *Orpen*, p. 340.

[35] Orpen, *An Onlooker in France* (1924 edn), pp. 16–17.

[36] Lavery, *Life of a Painter*, p. 148.

[37] *Manchester Guardian*, 4 Dec. 1918 (IWM World War I artists press cuttings book).

[38] The Ulster Museum captions the painting *Daylight Raid from My Studio Window, 7 July 1917*, but the shorter title

(which appears on the back of the work) seems definitive. See McConkey, *Lavery RA*, p. 83.

39 McConkey, *Lavery*, p. 130. An alternative explanation is that Lavery painted out the Madonna not so much to spare his wife's feelings as to avoid offending the good Protestant burghers of Belfast.

40 Orpen, *An Onlooker in France* (1924 edn), plate XI. The painting is in the Imperial War Museum.

41 Orpen to Alfred Yockney (Ministry of Information), 3 July 1918 (Imperial War Museum Department of Art 1st World War archive: Sir William Orpen (henceforth IWM: Orpen) 78-3, fol. 109); R. Langton Douglas to Yockney, 25 June 1918 (IWM Department of Art archives, file 47/2).

42 This rule was occasionally broken. *The Liffey Swim* was acquired while Jack Yeats was still alive (see Arnold, *Yeats*, pp. 251–2).

43 Lavery, *Life of a Painter*, p. 144.

44 *Evening Standard*, 7 May 1923 (IWM World War I artists press cuttings book).

45 Pedants will claim that this is a Union *Flag*. So it is, but it is also, correctly, a Union Jack. See Crawford, 'The Union Jack'.

46 Konody and Dark, *Orpen*, p. 101.

47 Orpen, *An Onlooker in France* (1924 edn), plate LXXV.

48 Caption to a reproduction of the painting in Orpen, *The Outline of Art*, p. 377.

49 Charles ffoulkes (curator and secretary, IWM) to Sir Martin Conway (director-general, IWM), 3 Jan. 1923 (IWM: Orpen, 78C-3, fol. 90).

50 *Daily Herald*, 8 May 1923 (IWM World War I artists press cuttings book).

51 Quoted in Harries and Harries, *The War Artists*, p. 149.

52 *Patriot*, 10 May 1923 (IWM World War I artists press cuttings book).

53 Orpen to ffoulkes, 20 Feb. 1928 (IWM: Orpen, 78D-3, fol. 61). Haig died on 29 Jan. 1928.

54 Laffin, *British Butchers and Bunglers of World War One*.

[55] Stradling and Hughes, *The English Musical Renaissance*, p. 72.

[56] 'Music and the war', in Stanford, *Interludes, Records and Reflections*, p. 102.

[57] Stradling and Hughes, *The English Musical Renaissance*, p. 74.

[58] For Stanford's works, see Hudson, 'Catalogue'. I am grateful to my colleague at the University of Ulster, Dr Desmond Hunter, who has recorded the organ sonatas, for additional information about Stanford.

[59] Greene, *Stanford*, p. 195. For an unsympathetic critique, see Joseph Ryan, 'Nationalism and music in Ireland', pp. 261–4.

[60] Concert information extracted from the *Musical Times* and Ruthven, *Belfast Philharmonic Society*.

[61] Biographical details from Greer, *Harty*.

[62] *Belfast News-Letter*, 27 Nov. 1919.

[63] For Robert Graves's professed Irishness, see Graves, *Goodbye to All That*, pp. 30, 229.

[64] This is an elusive work. It is not listed in Hudson, 'Catalogue', which otherwise seems definitive. There is a copy in the Cambridge University Library music collection.

[65] Leonard, 'The twinge of memory', p. 102.

[66] Stewart, *Ulster Crisis*, p. 135; Moore, *Elgar*, p. 664.

[67] Stanford and Forsyth, *A History of Music*, p. 322.

[68] Bax, *Farewell My Youth* (London, 1943), pp. 27–8 (quoted in Joseph Ryan, 'Nationalism and music in Ireland', p. 258).

[69] Stradling and Hughes, *The English Musical Renaissance*, p. 74, where the piece is erroneously identified as a Rhapsody.

[70] Foreman, *Bax*, pp. 140, 346. Bax's was not the only nationalist response to the events of 1914–18, or 1916. I have argued elsewhere that John F. Larchet's *The Legend of Lough Rea* could be seen in this light (Jeffery, 'The Great War', p. 138).

[71] Hogan and O'Neill, *Joseph Holloway's Irish Theatre*, pp. 46–7; notes extracted from Lord Chamberlain's Office submissions, 1900–68, card index (British Library Manuscripts Room).

[72] J. C. Trewin, 'Introduction', to O'Casey, *Three More Plays*, p. xi.

[73] MacGill, 'Suspense: A Play in 3 Acts' (typescript version, Lord Chamberlain's Collection, 1930/14 no. 9608 (British Library Manuscripts Room)); *The Times*, 9 Apr. 1930. In addition to the works mentioned above, Irish plays about the Great War include George Bernard Shaw's *O'Flaherty VC* and *Going West*, by Louis J. Walsh, which is briefly discussed in my essay, 'Irish culture and the Great War', pp. 91–2.

[74] The verse is in MacGill, *Soldier Songs*; *The Amateur Army*, *The Great Push* and *The Diggers* are semi-autobiographical reportage; the novels are: *The Red Horizon*, *The Brown Brethren*, *The Dough-Boys* and *Fear!*. Owen Dudley Edwards, 'MacGill', is an indispensable source for this writer. The following passage draws on my essay, 'Irish prose writers of the First World War', where some of the works cited are discussed at greater length.

[75] See O'Sullivan, 'MacGill'.

[76] Esher to his son, Oliver Brett, 25 Oct. 1915 (quoted in Owen Dudley Edwards, 'MacGill', p. 96 n. 6).

[77] Ibid., p. 75.

[78] MacGill, *The Red Horizon*, pp. 39, 41, 83–4.

[79] Orpen, *An Onlooker in France* (1924 edn), p. 20.

[80] Sales figure taken from an advertisement in a 1918 printing of *The Brown Brethren*.

[81] MacGill, *The Red Horizon*, pp. 119, 300.

[82] MacGill, *Fear!*, p. 2.

[83] Ibid., pp. 139, 246.

[84] Onions, *English Fiction and Drama of the Great War*, p. 52.

[85] Noted in the fourth printing (n.d.) copy in Belfast Central Library.

[86] Sheeran, *The Novels of Liam O'Flaherty*, p. 67.

[87] Onions, *English Fiction and Drama of the Great War*, p. 54.

[88] Cecil, 'The literary legacy of the war', p. 220.

[89] *Times Literary Supplement*, 21 Nov. 1929, p. 938.

[90] This is the theme of Samuel Hynes's important *A War Imagined*.

[91] St John Ervine, *Changing Winds*, pp. 457, 458.

[92] Quotations taken from the Penguin edition (Harmondsworth, 1946).

[93] Hinkson, *The Ladies' Road*, p. 72. Under the pseudonym Peter Deane, Hinkson wrote another novel, *The Victors*, and a volume of short stories, *Harvest*. See Cecil, *The Flower of Battle*, pp. 282–306.

[94] Smithson, *The Marriage of Nurse Harding*, pp. 104–5.

[95] In my possession.

[96] Hinkson, *The Ladies' Road*, p. 80.

[97] Tynan, *The Years of the Shadow*, p. 310.

[98] Tynan, *The Golden Rose*, p. 99.

[99] Emphasis added. David R. Woodward, 'The Home Front in the First World War', in Jordan, *British Military History*, p. 300.

[100] For a stern critique, see Prior and Wilson, 'Paul Fussell at war'.

[101] W. B. Yeats (though very difficult to characterise as a 'war poet') and Patrick MacGill have already been mentioned. Others include Thomas Kettle, Katharine Tynan, Thomas MacGreevy, Harry Midgley, Dora Sigerson Shorter and Lord Dunsany.

[102] 'In memoriam Francis Ledwidge', in Heaney, *Field Work*, pp. 130–1.

[103] For Dunsany, see Amory, *Dunsany*; for Ledwidge, see Curtayne, *Ledwidge*.

[104] Curtayne, *Ledwidge*, p. 83.

[105] Ledwidge, 'The Irish in Gallipoli', in Cooper, *The Tenth (Irish) Division*, p. xxvi.

[106] 'Thomas McDonagh [*sic*]', in Ledwidge, *Complete Poems*, p. 210. This volume does not include 'The Irish in Gallipoli'.

[107] Note the 'even': Curtayne, *Ledwidge*, p. 164.

[108] Ledwidge was not in France at all. He was in Belgium, but neither 'Belgium' nor 'Flanders' provides as satisfactory a rhyme as 'France'. Thus the imperative of art overrode historical precision, and thus, too, is weight added to David Woodward's already noted warning against using literary sources as documentary evidence. There is a similar difficulty with Seamus Heaney's poem 'In memoriam Francis Ledwidge' (cited in n. 102 above). Heaney, recalling a childhood walk along the seafront at Portstewart, writes that 'the

bronze soldier hitches a bronze cape'. But the Portstewart war memorial soldier has no cape.

[109] Ledwidge, 'Soliloquy', in his *Complete Poems*, p. 260.

[110] Heaney, *Field Work*, p. 131.

4 COMMEMORATION

[1] *Belfast News-Letter*, 18 Nov. 1919.

[2] *Irish Builder*, 6 Dec. 1919.

[3] See papers relating to the Ulster Division memorial, Oct.–Dec. 1919 (PRO WO 32/5868, nos. 6, 10, 10A and 11).

[4] Diary of Sir Henry Wilson, 18 Nov. 1921 (IWM).

[5] *Seanad Éireann Official Report* (henceforth *Seanad Report*), vol. 8, 9 Mar. 1927, col. 422. During this Senate debate Andrew Jameson, himself a trustee of the Irish National War Memorial, outlined the history of the fund. Unless otherwise indicated quotations concerning the early history of the memorial are taken from Jameson's speech (cols. 421–32). See also the account in Leonard, '"Lest we forget"', pp. 64–7.

[6] There is now a considerable literature on this topic. The best includes: Inglis, *Sacred Places*; Maclean and Phillips, *The Sorrow and the Pride*; and Shipley, *To Mark Our Place*.

[7] *Irish Builder*, 6 Sep. 1919; 31 Jan. 1920.

[8] There was a scheme to have Lutyens's cenotaph adopted as a universal imperial war memorial, with replicas being put up throughout the empire (see the *Press* (Christchurch, New Zealand), 15 Aug. 1919). In some places, such as Auckland, New Zealand, Hong Kong and Hamilton, Bermuda, this was done.

[9] This is almost precisely what was originally proposed for the Queensland State memorial in Brisbane, where Sir Bertram Mackennal prepared designs including a cenotaph based on Lutyens's design, but 'surmounted by a huge bronze soldier with a banner in one hand and leading with the other a horse ridden by a female Victory'. This proved too expensive, and eventually a circular Greek colonnade was erected (Inglis, *Sacred Places*, pp. 290–2).

[10] *Irish Builder*, 6 Sep. 1919.

[11] Irish National War Memorial, *Ireland's Memorial Records*, vol. I, p. iii; Bowe, *Clarke*, p. 141.

[12] *Seanad Report*, vol. 8, 9 Mar. 1927, cols. 413–19.

[13] Ibid., cols. 419–20. For Gogarty's attitude to the war, see O'Connor, *Gogarty*, pp. 160–2.

[14] *Seanad Report*, vol. 8, 9 Mar. 1927, col. 451.

[15] Cosgrave to MacNeill (IFS high commissioner, London), 8 Apr. 1926 (NAI Department of the Taoiseach papers (henceforth DT) S.4156A).

[16] White, *O'Higgins*, p. 13.

[17] Emphasis added. *Dáil Éireann Official Report* (henceforth *Dáil Report*), vol. 29, 29 Mar. 1927, cols. 400–3. For Hickie, see Jeffery, 'The Great War', p. 149.

[18] *Dáil Report*, vol. 29, 29 Mar. 1927, cols. 407–13.

[19] *Seanad Report*, vol. 8, 7 Apr. 1927, col. 721.

[20] See Leonard, 'The twinge of memory'.

[21] *Belfast News-Letter*, 12 Nov. 1919.

[22] *Belfast Telegraph*, 10 Nov. 1925.

[23] See correspondence between the Ministry of Finance and the Executive Council, June–July 1928 (NAI DT S.4156A). For Frank Scarlett, see 'Notes on Edward Lutyens' (Alfred Jones Biographical Index, Irish Architectural Archive (Dublin), L91) and Rothery, *Ireland and the New Architecture*, pp. 62–4.

[24] Note from president to Executive Council, 2 Mar. 1929 (NAI DT S.4156A).

[25] The information in this paragraph is drawn from Fraser, *John Bull's Other Homes*, pp. 240–71.

[26] *Seanad Report*, vol. 8, 9 Mar. 1927, cols. 431, 421.

[27] Jameson to Cosgrave, 29 July 1929; 'Proposal outlined at meeting of Cabinet by Mr T. J. Byrne, Principal Architect, Board of Works', 29 Oct. 1929 (NAI DT S.4156A).

[28] *Sunday Times*, 31 Aug. 1930 (NAI DT S.4156B).

[29] See notes and correspondence, Dec. 1929 (NAI DT S.4156B).

[30] Jameson to Cosgrave, 12 Dec. 1929 (NAI DT S.4156B)

[31] Hussey, *Lutyens*, pp. 6, 113–17, 231–4. Stephen Gwynn described Lutyens's Liverpool cathedral commission as

being 'for the Irish overseas' (Stephen Gwynn, *The Charm of Ireland*, p. 280).

[32] Lutyens to May Lutyens (his wife), 4 Aug. 1924 (Royal Institute of British Architects (RIBA) Library, Lutyens Family Papers, LuE/18/13/6).

[33] Report by T. J. Byrne, 23 Oct. 1930 (NAI DT S.4156B).

[34] In my essay 'The Great War', I erroneously identified the cross at Islandbridge as Bloomfield's design (pp. 146, 155 n. 53).

[35] Butler, *The Architecture of Sir Edwin Lutyens*, vol. II, pp. 23–4.

[36] President of the Executive Council to secretary, Department of Finance, 19 Dec. 1931 (NAI DT S.4156B). There was criticism in the Dublin Corporation of unemployment relief money being spent on the war memorial (see *Irish Times*, 5 Jan. 1932 (clipping in NAI DT S.4156B)). For the national financial crisis of 1931, see Fanning, *The Irish Department of Finance*, pp. 206–15. In fact, by 1939 the state contribution amounted to only £37,836 9s. 8d. (extract from parliamentary debates, 7 Mar. 1939, NAI DT S.4156B).

[37] *British Legion Annual 1941*, a special number devoted to the Irish National War Memorial.

[38] Byrne, among others, is quoted in a lengthy report about the circumstances of the war memorial in the *Irish Times*, 16 Apr. 1937 (clipping in NAI DT S.4156B).

[39] Lutyens to Mary Lutyens, 6 Aug. 1935 (RIBA Library, Lutyens Family Papers, LuE/20/7/1).

[40] See correspondence and papers, Mar. 1939–Oct. 1940 (NAI DT S.4156B).

[41] Sir Plunket Barton (first chairman of the executive council of the Irish National War Memorial), quoted in the *Irish Times*, 16 Apr. 1937 (clipping in NAI DT S.4156B).

[42] See correspondence and papers, Dec. 1938–Apr. 1939 (NAI DT S.4156C).

[43] Bhreathnach-Lynch, 'Public sculpture in independent Ireland', pp. 44–5.

[44] Hill, *Irish Public Sculpture*, p. 155.

[45] Ibid., pp. 157–60; see also Ireland, Republic of, Department

of External Affairs, *Cuimhneachán*, p. 45. Even in 1966 the scheme was incomplete. A sculpture by Oisin Kelly, *The Children of Lir*, was not added until 1971.

46 Desmond Fitzgerald, the minister for external affairs, was in the GPO; Cosgrave was second-in-command at the South Dublin Union.

47 Baldwin to Cosgrave and reply, 8 and 13 Oct. 1926; Amery to Cosgrave, 15 Oct. 1926; press clippings, Oct. 1926 (NAI DT S.5276-1).

48 This problem of grieving was even more acute in more distant parts of the British Empire, such as Australia and New Zealand. See the general discussion in Winter, *Sites of Memory, Sites of Mourning*, esp. ch. 4.

49 See notes and correspondence about British war graves, Dec. 1940–Dec. 1950 (NAI DT S.12244A–B). For the Imperial War Graves Commission, see Gibson and Ward, *Courage Remembered*.

50 Lyons, *The Enigma of Tom Kettle*, pp. 305–6.

51 Various war memorial schemes are discussed in Jeffery, 'The Great War in modern Irish memory', pp. 146–52. I am grateful to my former student Mr Aidan Barry for details about the history of Lurgan war memorial.

52 Corcoran, 'County Antrim war memorial'.

53 *Irish Builder*, 28 Nov. 1925; *Belfast Telegraph*, 10 June 1926.

54 *Irish Builder*, 11 Jan. 1919; *Cork Weekly Examiner*, 21 Nov. 1925.

55 *Belfast Telegraph*, 10 Nov. 1925.

56 Hill, *Irish Public Sculpture*, p. 165. This work also narrates the circumstances and vicissitudes of nationalist monument-building (see pp. 152–60, 162–201).

57 One letter was added to this inscription after the Second World War. It now reads 'Erected to the memory of those of Nenagh and District who fell in the Great Wars'.

58 *Nenagh Guardian*, 17 Nov. 1928.

59 *Belfast Telegraph*, 14 Nov. 1925.

60 *New Society*, vol. 57, no. 975 (23 July 1981), p. 136. Fifty thousand has evidently become a canonical number. In November 1998 it was widely cited as the number of Irish

deaths in the war. An editorial in the *Irish Times*, for example, asserted that 'more than 50,000' died, even though (on the same page) the columnist Kevin Myers suggested that the figure was 'upwards of 35,000' (11 Nov. 1998, p. 15 cols. 1 and 5).

61 A number are illustrated in Rolston, *Politics and Painting*, plates between pp. 32 and 33.

62 See report in the *Irish Independent*, 12 Nov. 1956.

63 Harris, *Irish Regiments in the First World War*, p. 212.

64 Andrews, *Dublin Made Me*, pp. 78–9.

65 Leonard, 'The twinge of memory', p. 111.

66 Boydell, 'A Terrible Beauty is Born', Op. 59 (composer's manuscript copy, courtesy of the Contemporary Music Centre, Dublin). The piece received its premiere in the Gaiety Theatre, Dublin, on Easter Monday, 11 Apr. 1966 (Ireland, Republic of, Department of External Affairs, *Cuimhneachán*, p. 47).

67 O'Neill, *Autobiography*, p. 78; Budge and O'Leary, *Belfast*, pp. 162–3.

68 Minutes of the inaugural meeting, 25 Jan. 1997 (*The Blue Cap* (Journal of the Royal Dublin Fusiliers Association), no. 4 (Feb. 1997), p. 1).

69 Quotations from Somme Association Development Appeal brochure. The admirable cross-community objectives of the association are slightly undermined by the membership structure, which includes specific categories for Orange Lodges.

70 For example, Heaney's 'In memoriam Francis Ledwidge' (Heaney, *Field Work*, pp. 130–1) and Longley's 'In memoriam' and 'Wounds', which draw on his father's service in the 36th (Ulster) Division (Longley, *Selected Poems*, pp. 18, 36).

71 A more explicitly loyalist exploration of the Somme is provided by Brian Ervine in his unpublished play 'Somme Day Mourning', which was first staged, by the Shankill Community Theatre Company, in Belfast in November 1994. See also Billy Ervine, *Gone But Not Forgotten: the Somme*.

72 There is some evidence that in a cultural context the political situation in Northern Ireland might have made First World

War-related art more, rather than less, problematic. Ulster Television, who have an extensive art collection, sold William Conor's *The Cenotaph, Belfast 1919* in June 1995 'as we did not have a suitable place to display it' (letter to the author from Theo Snoddy, UTV Art Adviser, 24 Oct. 1996).

[73] Barker, *Regeneration, The Eye in the Door* and *The Ghost Road*; Faulks, *Birdsong*.

[74] Freeland, *Canberra Cosmos*, p. 80.

[75] Denman, *Ireland's Unknown Soldiers*, p. 16.

[76] *Irish Times*, 24 Sep. 1998.

[77] *Irish Builder*, 25 Jan. 1919.

[78] Some £200,000 came from the Trust (*Irish Times*, 26 May 1999).

[79] Philip Johnston, 'Peace tower unites islands in homage' (*Daily Telegraph*, 12 Nov. 1998). John Ezard in the *Guardian*, 12 Nov. 1998, p. 3, ascribes this erroneous assertion to the British Embassy in Brussels. See also Katharine Butler, 'Queen and President open Anglo-Irish peace tower' (*Independent*, 12 Nov. 1998); Alan Hamilton, 'Side by side, in tribute to the fallen' (*The Times*, 12 Nov. 1998).

[80] *Irish Times*, 14 Nov. 1998.

BIBLIOGRAPHICAL NOTE

[1] Fitzpatrick's pupil Peter Hart, however, has triumphantly taken up the challenge in his study of County Cork between 1916 and 1923: *The IRA and Its Enemies*.

[2] Fitzpatrick, *Ireland and the First World War*, p. vii.

[3] Howie and Howie, 'Irish recruiting', p. 22.

[4] Hennessey, *Dividing Ireland*, p. 235.

[5] Dooley, 'Southern Ireland, historians and the First World War', p. 5.

[6] Orr, *Road to the Somme*, pp. 61, 79, 104.

[7] Ibid., p. 227.

[8] Denman, *Ireland's Unknown Soldiers*, p. 145.

[9] Eighty parts originally published in 1921; republished by Picton Publishing Facsimile Reprints (1988).

[10] Casey, 'Irish casualties in the First World War', p.197.

11 Dungan, *They Shall Not Grow Old*, p. 9.

12 Denman, 'The Catholic Irish soldier in the First World War',
    pp. 356, 364, 365.

13 Bourke, '"Irish Tommies"', p. 24.

14 See *History Ireland*, 2/4 (Winter 1994), pp. 9–10.

15 This is a revised version of an essay prepared for a privately
    published volume dedicated to the memory of Dr Austin
    Logan (1951–95), teachers' adviser for Environment and
    Society at the Western Education and Library Board,
    Northern Ireland.

Bibliography

Amory, Mark, *Biography of Lord Dunsany* (London, 1972).

Andrews, C. S., *Dublin Made Me* (Dublin and Cork, 1979).

Arnold, Bruce, 'Introduction', to Orpen, *An Onlooker in France* (new edn, 1996), pp. ix–xiii.

Jack Yeats (New Haven and London, 1998).

Mainie Jellett and the Modern Movement in Ireland (New Haven and London, 1991).

Orpen: Mirror to an Age (London, 1981).

Arthur, Sir George, *General Sir John Maxwell* (London, 1932).

Barker, Pat, *The Eye in the Door* (London, 1993).

The Ghost Road (London, 1995).

Regeneration (London, 1991).

Barry, Tom, *Guerrilla Days in Ireland* (pbk edn, Tralee, 1962).

Bartlett, Thomas, and Jeffery, Keith (eds.), *A Military History of Ireland* (Cambridge, 1996).

Barton, Brian, *Brookeborough: the Making of a Prime Minister* (Belfast, 1988).

Belfast Citizens' Committee, *The Great War 1914–1918: Ulster Greets Her Brave and Faithful Sons and Remembers Her Glorious Dead* (Belfast, 1919).

Bew, Paul, *Ideology and the Irish Question: Ulster Unionism and Irish Nationalism 1912–1916* (Oxford, 1994).

Bhreathnach-Lynch, Sighle, 'Public sculpture in independent Ireland 1922–1972', *The Medal*, no. 21 (1992), pp. 44–52.

Bond, Brian, 'British "anti-war" writers and their critics', in Cecil and Liddle, *Facing Armageddon*, pp. 817–30.

Bourke, Joanna, '"Irish Tommies": the construction of a martial manhood 1914–1918', *Bullán*, 3/2 (Winter 1997/Spring 1998), pp. 13–30.

Bowe, Nicola Gordon, *The Life and Work of Harry Clarke* (Dublin, 1989).

Bowman, Timothy, 'Composing divisions: the recruitment of Ulster and National Volunteers into the British army in 1914', *Causeway*, 2/1 (Spring 1995), pp. 24–9.

'The Irish at the Somme', *History Ireland*, 4/4 (Winter 1996), pp. 48–52.

Boyce, George, 'Ireland and the First World War', *History Ireland*, 2/3 (Autumn 1994), pp. 48–53.

The Sure Confusing Drum: Ireland and the First World War (Swansea, 1993).

Branagan, W. J., 'Ireland and war contracts', *Studies*, 4 (Sept. 1915), pp. 470–7.

Brennan, Robert, *Allegiance* (Dublin, 1950).

British Red Cross Society, *Report by the Joint War Committee and the Joint War Finance Committee of the British Red Cross Society and the Order of St John of Jerusalem in England on Voluntary Aid Rendered to the Sick and Wounded at Home and Abroad and to British Prisoners of War, 1914–1919* (London, 1921).

Budge, Ian, and O'Leary, Cornelius, *Belfast: Approach to Crisis. A Study of Belfast Politics 1613–1970* (London, 1973).

Butler, A. S. G., *The Architecture of Sir Edwin Lutyens* (3 vols., London, 1950).

Callan, Patrick, 'Ambivalence towards the Saxon shilling: the attitudes of the Catholic church in Ireland towards enlistment during the First World War', *Archivum Hibernicum*, 41 (1986), pp. 99–111.

'British recruitment in Ireland, 1914–1918', *Revue Internationale d'Histoire Militaire*, 63 (1985), pp. 41–50.

'Recruiting for the British army in Ireland during the First World War', *Irish Sword*, 17 (1987), pp. 42–56.

'Voluntary recruiting for the British army in Ireland during the First World War' (Ph.D. thesis, University College, Dublin, 1984).

Canning, W. J., *Ballyshannon, Belcoo, Bertincourt: the History of the 11th Battalion The Royal Inniskilling Fusiliers (Donegal & Fermanagh Volunteers) in World War One* (published by the author, Dunsilly Lodge, Co. Antrim, 1996).

[Casement, Sir Roger], *Ireland, Germany and the Freedom of the Seas: A Possible Outcome of the War of 1914* (?New York, n.d. [c. Aug. 1914]).

Casey, Patrick J., 'Irish casualties in the First World War', *Irish Sword*, 20 (1997), pp. 193–206.

Cecil, Hugh, *The Flower of Battle: British Fiction Writers of the First World War* (London, 1995).

'The literary legacy of the war: the post-war novel – a select bibliography', in Peter Liddle (ed.), *Home Fires and Foreign Fields: British Social and Military Experience in the First World War* (London, 1985), pp. 205–30.

Cecil, Hugh, and Liddle, Peter H. (eds.), *Facing Armageddon: the First World War Experienced* (London, 1996).

Clark, Alan, *The Donkeys* (London, 1961).

Clarke, Richard, *The Royal Victoria Hospital Belfast: a History 1797–1997* (Belfast, 1997).

Codd, Pauline, 'Recruiting and responses to the war in Wexford', in Fitzpatrick, *Ireland and the First World War*, pp. 15–26.

Collins, Peter, 'Ripples from the Rising', *Causeway*, 3/2 (Summer 1996), pp. 22–7.

Colvin, Ian, *The Life of Lord Carson*, vol. III (London, 1936).

Connolly, James, *A Socialist and War, 1914–1916*, ed. P. J. Musgrove (London, 1941).

Coogan, Tim Pat, *Michael Collins* (London, 1990).

Cooper, Bryan, *The Tenth (Irish) Division in Gallipoli* (London, 1918).

Corcoran, Doreen, 'County Antrim war memorial at the Knockagh', *Carrickfergus & District Historical Journal*, 2 (1986), pp. 17–19.

Crawford, J. R., 'The Union Jack', in A. C. Fox-Davies, *A Complete Guide to Heraldry* (revised edn, London, 1969), pp. 474–8.

Curtayne, Alice, *Francis Ledwidge: a Life of the Poet* (London, 1972).

Curtis, Edmund, *A History of Ireland* (pbk edn, London, 1961).

De Montmorency, Hervey, *Sword and Stirrup: Memories of an Adventurous Life* (London, 1936).

Deane, Peter [Pamela Hinkson], *Harvest* (London, n.d. [1926]).

The Victors (London, 1925).

Denman, Terence, 'The Catholic Irish soldier in the First World War: the "racial environment"', *Irish Historical Studies*, 27 (1991), pp. 352–65.

Ireland's Unknown Soldiers: the 16th (Irish) Division in the Great War (Dublin, 1992).

'An Irish battalion at war: from the letters of Captain J. H. M. Staniforth, 7th Leinsters, 1914–1918', *Irish Sword*, 17 (1989), pp. 165–73.

A Lonely Grave: the Life and Death of William Redmond (Dublin, 1995).

'The 10th (Irish) Division 1914–1915: a study in military and political interaction', *Irish Sword*, 17 (1987), pp. 16–25.

Donnelly, Mary, *The Last Post: Glasnevin Cemetery. Being a Record of Ireland's Heroic Dead in Dublin City and County* (Dublin, n.d. [1932]).

Dooley, Thomas P., *Irishmen or English Soldiers?: the Times and World of a Southern Catholic Irish Man (1876–1916) Enlisting in the British Army During the First World War* (Liverpool, 1995).

'Southern Ireland, historians and the First World War', *Irish Studies Review*, 4 (Autumn 1993), pp. 5–9.

Downes, Margaret, 'The civilian voluntary aid effort', in Fitzpatrick, *Ireland and the First World War*, pp. 27–37.

Dungan, Myles, *Distant Drums: Irish Soldiers in Foreign Armies* (Belfast, 1993).

Irish Voices from the Great War (Dublin, 1995).

They Shall Not Grow Old: Irish Soldiers and the Great War (Dublin, 1997).

Edwards, Owen Dudley, 'Patrick MacGill and the making of a historical source: with a handlist of his works', *Innes Review* (Scottish Catholic Historical Association), 37/2 (1986), pp. 73–99.

Edwards, Ron, 'My First CO', *Journal of the Military Collectors' Club of Canada* (Summer 1992), pp. 52–62.

Edwards, Ruth Dudley, *Patrick Pearse: the Triumph of Failure* (pbk edn, London, 1979).

Eksteins, Modris, *Rites of Spring: the Great War and the Birth of the Modern Age* (pbk edn, London, 1990).

Ervine, Billy, *Gone But Not Forgotten: the Somme* (talk given to Ballymacarrett Arts and Cultural Society) (Bilfawast, 1999).

Ervine, St John G., *Changing Winds* (Dublin, 1917; New York, 1920).

'The story of the Irish rebellion', *Century Magazine* (1917), pp. 22–39.

Falls, Cyril, *The History of the 36th (Ulster) Division* (Belfast, 1922).

'Maxwell, 1916, and Britain at war', in Martin, *Leaders and Men*, pp. 202–14.

Military Operations: Macedonia (Official History of the War), vol. I, *From the Outbreak of War to the Spring of 1917* (London, 1933).

Fanning, Ronan, *The Irish Department of Finance 1922–1958* (Dublin, 1978).

Faulks, Sebastian, *Birdsong* (London, 1994).

Finkelstein, David, *An Index to Blackwoods Magazine, 1901–1980* (Aldershot, 1995).

Fitzpatrick, David, 'The logic of collective sacrifice: Ireland and the British army, 1914–1918', *Historical Journal*, 38 (1995), pp. 1017–30.

'Militarism in Ireland, 1900–1922', in Bartlett and Jeffery, *A Military History of Ireland*, pp. 379–406, 498–502.

'The overflow of the deluge: Anglo-Irish relationships, 1914–1922', in Oliver MacDonagh and W. F. Mandle (eds.), *Ireland and Irish-Australia: Studies in Cultural and Political History* (London, 1986), pp. 81–94.

Politics and Irish Life 1913–1921: Provincial Experience of War and Revolution (Dublin, 1977).

Fitzpatrick, David (ed.), *Ireland and the First World War* (Dublin, 1986).

Revolution?: Ireland 1917–1923 (Dublin, 1990).

Foreman, Lewis, *Bax: a Composer and His Times* (London, 1983).

Foster, R. F., *Modern Ireland 1600–1972* (London, 1988).

Foster, R. H., 'Irish Methodism and war', in Alexander McCrea (ed.), *Irish Methodism in the Twentieth Century* (Belfast, 1931), pp. 68–84.

Fraser, Murray, *John Bull's Other Homes: State Housing and British Policy in Ireland, 1883–1922* (Liverpool, 1996).

Freeland, Guy, *Canberra Cosmos: the Pilgrim's Guide to Sacred Sites and Symbols of Australia's Capital* (Sydney, 1995).

Fry, Paul, *The Methodist College Belfast Register, 1868–1984* (Belfast, n.d. [1985]).

Fussell, Paul, *The Great War and Modern Memory* (Oxford, 1975).

Gammage, Bill, *The Story of Gallipoli: the Film About the Men Who Made a Legend* (Ringwood, Vic., 1981).

Gibbon, Monk, *Inglorious Soldier* (London, 1968).

Gibson, T. A. Edwin, and Ward, G. Kingsley, *Courage Remembered: the Story Behind the Construction and Maintenance of the Commonwealth's Military Cemeteries and Memorials to the Wars of 1914–1918 and 1939–1945* (London, 1989).

Graves, Robert, *Goodbye to All That* (Harmondsworth, 1960).

Greene, Harry Plunket, *Charles Villiers Stanford* (London, 1935).

Greer, David (ed.), *Hamilton Harty: His Life and Music* (Belfast, 1979).

Grey, Jeffrey, *A Military History of Australia* (Cambridge, 1990).

Griffin, Gerald, *The Wild Geese: Pen Portraits of Famous Irish Exiles* (London, n.d.).

Griffith, Kenneth, and O'Grady, Timothy E., *Curious Journey: an Oral History of Ireland's Unfinished Revolution* (Cork, 1998).

Grigg, John, 'Nobility and war: the unselfish commitment', *Encounter* (March 1990), pp. 21–7.

Gwynn, Denis, *The Life of John Redmond* (London, 1932).

Gwynn, Stephen, *The Charm of Ireland* (London, 1934).

    John Redmond's Last Years (London, 1919).

Hamilton, Ian, and Beyer, Anjelie, *The Elliott Collection, Mildura Arts Centre* (Mildura, Vic., 1998).

Hanna, Henry, *The Pals at Suvla Bay: Being the Record of 'D' Company of the 7th Royal Dublin Fusiliers* (Dublin, 1917).

Harries, Meirion, and Harries, Susie, *The War Artists: British Official War Art of the Twentieth Century* (London, 1983).

Harris, Henry, *The Irish Regiments in the First World War* (Cork, 1968).

'The other half million', in O. D. Edwards and F. Pyle (eds.), *1916: The Easter Rising* (London, 1968), pp. 101–15.

Hart, Peter, *The IRA and Its Enemies: Violence and Community in Cork* (Oxford, 1998).

Hayes-McCoy, G. A., 'A military history of the Rising', in Kevin B. Nowlan (ed.), *The Making of 1916: Studies in the History of the Rising* (Dublin, 1969), pp. 253–338.

Heaney, Seamus, *Field Work* (London, 1979).

Henderson, J. W., *Methodist College Belfast, 1868–1938* (Belfast, 1939).

Hennessey, Thomas, *Dividing Ireland: World War I and Partition* (London, 1998).

Hill, Judith, *Irish Public Sculpture: a History* (Dublin, 1998).

Hinkson, Pamela, *The Ladies' Road* (Harmondsworth, 1946).

Hobart, Alan, and Hobart, Mary, *an Ireland . . . imagined* [exhibition catalogue] (London, 1993).

Hogan, Robert, and O'Neill, Michael J. (eds.), *Joseph Holloway's Irish Theatre* (Dixon, Cal., 1969).

Holmes, Richard, *The Little Field Marshal: Sir John French* (London, 1981).

Howie, David, and Howie, Josephine, 'Irish recruiting and the Home Rule crisis of August–September 1914', in Michael Dockrill and David French (eds.), *Strategy and Intelligence: British Policy During the First World War* (London, 1996), pp. 1–22.

Hudson, Frederick, 'A revised and extended catalogue of the works of Charles Villiers Stanford (1852–1924)', *Music Review*, 37 (1976), pp. 106–29.

Hussey, Christopher, *The Life of Sir Edwin Lutyens* (London, 1950).

Hyam, Ronald, *Britain's Imperial Century 1815–1914: a Study of Empire and Expansion* (London, 1976).

Hynes, Samuel, *The Soldiers' Tale: Bearing Witness to Modern War* (Pimlico edn, London, 1998).

A War Imagined: the First World War and English Culture (London, 1990).

Imperial War Museum, *A Concise Catalogue of Paintings, Drawings and Sculpture of the First World War 1914–1918* (London, 1963).

Inglis, K. S., *Anzac Remembered: Selected Writings of K. S. Inglis*, ed. John Lack (Melbourne, 1998).

Sacred Places: War Memorials in the Australian Landscape (Melbourne, 1998).

Ireland, Republic of, Department of External Affairs, *Cuimhneachán 1916–1966: a Record of Ireland's Commemoration of the 1916 Rising* (Dublin, 1966).

Irish National War Memorial, *Ireland's Memorial Records 1914–1918* (8 vols., Dublin, 1923).

Jeffery, Keith, *The British Army and the Crisis of Empire, 1918–1922* (Manchester, 1984).

'The Great War in modern Irish memory', in T. G. Fraser and Keith Jeffery (eds.), *Men, Women and War (Historical Studies XVIII)* (Dublin, 1993), pp. 136–57.

'Irish artists and the First World War', *History Ireland*, 1/2 (Summer 1993), pp. 42–5.

'Irish culture and the Great War', *Bullán*, 1/2 (Autumn 1994), pp. 87–96.

'The Irish military tradition and the British Empire', in Keith Jeffery (ed.), *'An Irish Empire'?: Aspects of Ireland and the British Empire* (Manchester, 1996), pp. 94–122.

'Irish prose writers of the First World War', in Kathleen Devine (ed.), *Modern Irish Writers and the Wars* (Gerrards Cross, 1999), pp. 1–17.

Johnston, Jennifer, *How Many Miles to Babylon?* (London, 1974).

Johnstone, Tom, *Orange, Green and Khaki: the Story of the Irish Regiments in the Great War, 1914–1918* (Dublin, 1992).

Jordan, Gerald (ed.), *British Military History: a Supplement to*

Robin Higham's Guide to the Sources (New York and London, 1988).

Keating, Seán, 'William Orpen: a tribute', *Ireland Today*, 2/8 (Aug. 1937), pp. 21–6.

Kelleher, George D., 'Gunpowder to guided missiles: Ireland's war industries' (MA thesis, University College, Cork, 1983).

Kennedy, S. B., *Irish Art and Modernism, 1880–1950* (Belfast, 1991).

Kerr, S. Parnell, *What the Irish Regiments Have Done* (London, 1916).

Kettle, Thomas M., *Poems and Parodies* (Dublin, 1916).

The Ways of War (Dublin and London, 1917).

Kipling, Rudyard, *The Irish Guards in the Great War* (Spellmount edn, 2 vols., Staplehurst, 1997).

Konody, P. G., and Dark, Sidney, *Sir William Orpen: Artist and Man* (London, 1932).

Laffin, John, *British Butchers and Bunglers of World War One* (Gloucester, 1988).

Lavery, John, *The Life of a Painter* (London, 1940).

Ledwidge, Francis, *The Complete Poems of Francis Ledwidge* (London, 1919).

Lee, J. J., *Ireland 1912–1985: Politics and Society* (Cambridge, 1989).

Leonard, Jane, 'The Catholic chaplaincy', in Fitzpatrick, *Ireland and the First World War*, pp. 1–14.

The Culture of Commemoration: The Culture of War Commemoration (Dublin, 1996).

'Getting them at last: the IRA and ex-servicemen', in Fitzpatrick, *Revolution?: Ireland 1917–1923*, pp. 118–29.

'"Lest we forget"', in Fitzpatrick, *Ireland and the First World War*, pp. 59–67.

'The reaction of Irish officers in the British army to the Easter Rising of 1916', in Cecil and Liddle, *Facing Armageddon*, pp. 256–68.

'The twinge of memory: Armistice Day and Remembrance Sunday in Dublin since 1919', in Richard English and Graham Walker (eds.), *Unionism in Modern Ireland: New*

Perspectives on Politics and Culture (London, 1996), pp. 99–114.

Leslie, Shane, *The Irish Tangle for English Readers* (London, n.d. [1946]).

Linklater, Eric, *The Man on My Back: an Autobiography* (London, 1941).

Lloyd's of London, *Lloyd's War Losses: the First World War. Casualties to Shipping Through Enemy Causes, 1914–1918* (London, 1990).

Logan, James, *Ulster in the X-Rays* (London, 1923).

Longley, Michael, *Selected Poems* (London, 1998).

Lucey, Dermot J., 'Cork public opinion and the First World War' (MA thesis, University College, Cork, 1972).

Lyons, J. B., *The Enigma of Tom Kettle: Irish Patriot, Essayist, Poet, British Soldier, 1880–1916* (Dublin, 1983).

Macardle, Dorothy, *The Irish Republic* (pbk edn, London, 1968).

McCance, S., *History of the Royal Munster Fusiliers*, vol. II, *From 1861 to 1922 (Disbandment)* (Aldershot, 1927).

McCarthy, Eoin, and O'Sullivan, Gerard, 'Recruiting and recruits in County Cork during the First World War, 1914–1918', *Times Past* (Journal of the Ballincollig Community School Local History Society), 7 (1990–1), pp. 7–18.

McConkey, Kenneth, *A Free Spirit: Irish Art 1860–1960* (London, 1990).

Sir John Lavery (Edinburgh, 1993).

Sir John Lavery RA, 1856–1941 [exhibition catalogue] (Belfast, 1984).

McCoole, Sinéad, *Hazel: a Life of Lady Lavery, 1880–1935* (Dublin, 1996).

MacDonagh, Michael, *The Irish at the Front* (London, 1916).

The Irish on the Somme (London, 1917).

MacFarland, Alan, 'Spectacular heroism and devastating losses', *Causeway*, 3/2 (Summer 1996), pp. 18–21.

Mac Fhionnghaile, Niall, *Donegal, Ireland and the First World War* (Leitirceannain, 1987).

MacGill, Patrick, *The Amateur Army* (London, 1915).

The Brown Brethren (New York, 1918; London, 1919).

The Diggers: the Australians in France (London, 1919).

The Dough-Boys (London, 1918).

The Great Push: an Episode of the Great War (London, 1916).

Fear! (London, 1921).

The Red Horizon (London, 1916).

Soldier Songs (London, 1917).

McGuinness, Frank, *Observe the Sons of Ulster Marching Towards the Somme* (London, 1986).

Maclean, Chris, and Phillips, Jock, *The Sorrow and the Pride: New Zealand War Memorials* (Wellington, 1990).

MacLeod, Roy, and MacLeod, Kay, 'War and economic development: government and the optical industry in Britain, 1914–1918', in J. M. Winter (ed.), *War and Economic Development: Essays in Memory of David Joslin* (Cambridge, 1975), pp. 165–203.

Macready, Sir Nevil, *Annals of an Active Life* (2 vols., London, 1924).

Martin, F. X. (ed.), *The Irish Volunteers, 1913–1915* (Dublin, 1963). *Leaders and Men of the Easter Rising: Dublin 1916* (London, 1967).

'1916 – myth, fact and mystery', *Studia Hibernica*, 7 (1967), pp. 7–124.

Mason, Thos. H., 'Dublin opticians and instrument makers', *Dublin Historical Record*, 6 (1944), pp. 133–49.

Midgley, Harry, *Thoughts from Flanders* (Belfast, 1924).

Mitchell, Gardiner S., *'Three Cheers for the Derrys': a History of the 10th Royal Inniskilling Fusiliers in the 1914–1918 War, Based on the Recollections of Veterans Jim Donaghy & Leslie Bell* (Derry, 1991).

Moore, Jerrold Northrop, *Edward Elgar: a Creative Life* (Oxford, 1987).

Moss, Michael, and Hume, John R., *Shipbuilders to the World: 125 Years of Harland and Wolff, Belfast, 1861–1986* (Belfast, 1986).

Murray, Peter, 'The First World War and a Dublin distillery workforce: recruiting and redundancy at John Power & Son, 1915–1917', *Saothar*, 15 (1990), pp. 48–56.

Norway, Mrs Hamilton, *The Sinn Fein Rebellion as I Saw It* (London, 1916).

Norway, Mary Lousia, and Norway, Arthur Hamilton, *The Sinn Fein Rebellion as They Saw It*, ed. Keith Jeffery (Dublin, 1999).

Ó Broin, León, *W. E. Wylie and the Irish Revolution, 1916–1921* (Dublin, 1989).

O'Casey, Sean, *Three More Plays* (pbk edn, London, 1965).

O'Connell, Daire, *et al.*, *Mainie Jellett 1897–1944* [exhibition catalogue] (Dublin, 1991).

O'Connor, Ulick, *Oliver St John Gogarty: a Poet and His Times* (London, 1964).

O'Donnell, E. E., *Father Browne: a Life in Pictures* (Dublin, 1994).

O'Farrell, Padraic, *Who's Who in the Irish War of Independence, 1916–1921* (Dublin and Cork, 1980).

Officer, David, 'Re-presenting war: the Somme Heritage Centre', *History Ireland*, 3/1 (Spring 1995), pp. 38–42.

O'Flaherty, Liam, *Return of the Brute* (London, 1929).

O'Halpin, Eunan, *The Decline of the Union: British Government in Ireland, 1892–1920* (Dublin and New York, 1987).

O'Higgins, Brian, *The Voice of Banba: Songs, Ballads and Satires* (2nd edn, Dublin, 1931).

Ollerenshaw, Philip, 'The business and politics of banking in Ireland 1900–1943', in P. L. Cottrell, Alice Teichova and Takeshi Yuzawa (eds.), *Finance in the Age of the Corporate Economy* (Aldershot, 1997), pp. 52–78.

'Textile business in Europe during the First World War: the linen industry, 1914–1918', *Business History*, 41 (1999), pp. 63–87.

O'Neill, Terence, *The Autobiography of Terence O'Neill* (London, 1972).

Onions, John, *English Fiction and Drama of the Great War, 1918–1939* (London, 1990).

O'Rahilly, Alfred, *Father William Doyle: a Spiritual Study* (3rd edn, London, 1925).

Orpen, Sir William, *An Onlooker in France, 1917–1919* (London, 1921; revised edn 1924).

An Onlooker in France (new edn, Dublin, 1996).

Orpen, Sir William (ed.), *The Outline of Art* (London, n.d. [1923]).

Orr, Philip, 'Lessons of the Somme for an era of change', *Causeway*, 3/2 (Summer 1996), pp. 14–17.

The Road to the Somme: Men of the Ulster Division Tell Their Story (Belfast, 1987).

O'Sullivan, Patrick, 'Patrick MacGill: the making of a writer', in Seán Hutton and Paul Stewart (eds.), *Ireland's Histories: Aspects of State, Society and Ideology* (London and New York, 1991), pp. 203–22.

Pearse, P. H., *Political Writings and Speeches*, ed. Desmond Ryan (Dublin, n.d.).

Perry, Nicholas, 'Nationality in the Irish infantry regiments in the First World War', *War and Society*, 12 (1994), pp. 65–95.

Phillips, W. Alison, *The Revolution in Ireland 1906–1923* (London, 1923).

Pollock, Vivienne, 'The seafishing industry in Co. Down, 1880–1939' (DPhil thesis, University of Ulster, 1988).

Prior, Robin, 'The Suvla Bay tea-party: a reassessment', *Journal of the Australian War Memorial*, 7 (Oct. 1985), pp. 25–34.

Prior, Robin, and Wilson, Trevor, 'Paul Fussell at war', *War in History*, 1 (1994), pp. 63–80.

Reilly, Eileen, 'Cavan in the era of the Great War, 1914–1918', in Raymond Gillespie (ed.), *Cavan: Essays in the History of an Irish County* (Dublin, 1995), pp. 177–95.

Riordan, E. J., *Modern Irish Trade and Industry* (London, 1921).

'The war and Irish industry', *Studies*, 4 (Mar. 1915), pp. 115–19.

Robertson, David, *Deeds Not Words* (published by the author, Multyfarnham, County Westmeath, 1998).

Robinson, Sir Henry, *Memories: Wise and Otherwise* (London, 1924).

Robinson, Lennox, *The Big House: Four Scenes in Its Life* (London, 1928).

Bryan Cooper (London, 1931).

Rolston, Bill, *Politics and Painting: Murals and Conflict in Northern Ireland* (London, 1991).

Rothery, Sean, *Ireland and the New Architecture 1900–1940* (Dublin, 1991).

Russell, George, Riordan, E. J., Lysaght, Edward E., and Malone, Andrew E., 'Four years of Irish economics, 1914–1918', *Studies*, 7 (June 1918), pp. 301–27.

Ruthven, Malcolm, *Belfast Philharmonic Society, 1874–1974* (Belfast, 1973 [*sic*]).

Ryan, Desmond, *The Rising* (Dublin, 1949).

Ryan, Joseph J., 'Nationalism and music in Ireland' (Ph.D. thesis, St Patrick's College, Maynooth, 1991).

S[amuels], A. P. I., and S., D. G., *With the Ulster Division in France: A Story of the 11th Battalion Royal Irish Rifles (South Antrim Volunteers) from Bordon to Thiepval* (Belfast, n.d. [c. 1920]).

Sheeran, Patrick F., *The Novels of Liam O'Flaherty* (Dublin, 1976).

Shipley, Robert, *To Mark Our Place: a History of Canadian War Memorials* (Toronto, 1987).

Simkins, Peter, *Kitchener's Army: the Raising of the New Armies, 1914–1916* (Manchester, 1988).

Smithson, Annie M. P., *The Marriage of Nurse Harding* (Dublin, 1935).

[Smyly, Vivienne], 'Experiences of a VAD', *Blackwoods Magazine*, 200 (July–Dec. 1916), pp. 814–40.

Stanford, Charles V., *Interludes, Records and Reflections* (London, 1922).

Stanford, Charles V., and Forsyth, Cecil, *A History of Music* (London, 1916).

Staunton, Martin, 'Kilrush, Co. Clare and the Royal Munster Fusiliers', *Irish Sword*, 16 (1986), pp. 268–72.

    'The Royal Munster Fusiliers in the Great War, 1914–1919' (MA thesis, University College, Dublin, 1986).

    '*Soldiers Died in the Great War 1914–1919* as historical source material', *Stand To!*, 27 (Winter 1989), pp. 6–8.

Stephens, James, *The Insurrection in Dublin* (Dublin and London, 1916).

Stewart, A. T. Q., *The Ulster Crisis* (London, 1967).

Stokes, Roy, *Death in the Irish Sea: the Sinking of RMS Leinster* (Cork, 1998).

Stradling, Robert, and Hughes, Meirion, *The English Musical Renaissance, 1860–1940* (London, 1993).

Sweeny, Joseph A., 'In the GPO: the fighting men', in F. X. Martin (ed.), *The Easter Rising, 1916 and University College Dublin* (Dublin, 1966), pp. 96–105.

Taillon, Ruth, *The Women of 1916* (Belfast, 1996).

Taylor, A. J. P., *English History 1914–1945* (pbk edn, Harmondsworth, 1970).

    The First World War: an Illustrated History (pbk edn, Harmondsworth, 1966).

Taylor, Rex, *Assassination: the Death of Sir Henry Wilson and the Tragedy of Ireland* (London, 1961).

Thompson, Robert (ed.), *Bushmills Heroes 1914–1918* (published by the author, Coleraine, n.d. [c. 1994]).

Tierney, Mark, Bowen, Paul, and Fitzpatrick, David, 'Recruiting posters', in Fitzpatrick, *Ireland and the First World War*, pp. 47–58.

Townshend, Charles, *The British Campaign in Ireland: the Development of Political and Military Policies* (Oxford, 1975).

    Political Violence in Ireland: Government and Resistance Since 1848 (Oxford, 1983).

    'The suppression of the Easter Rising', *Bullán*, 1/1 (Spring 1994), pp. 27–47.

Tynan, Katharine, *The Golden Rose* (London, 1924).

    The Wandering Years (London, 1922).

    The Years of the Shadow (London, 1919).

United Kingdom, War Office, *Soldiers Died in the Great War 1914–1919*, 80 parts (London, 1921; facsimile edn, London, 1988).

Urquhart, Diane, '"The female of the species is more deadlier than the male"?: The Ulster Women's Unionist Council, 1911–1940', in Janice Holmes and Diane Urquhart (eds.), *Coming into the Light: the Work, Politics and Religion of Women in Ulster 1840–1940* (Belfast, 1994), pp. 93–123.

Vaughan, W. E. (ed.), *A New History of Ireland*, vol. VI, *Ireland Under the Union, II (1870–1921)* (Oxford, 1996).

Walker, Graham, *The Politics of Frustration: Harry Midgley and the Failure of Labour in Northern Ireland* (Manchester, 1985).

Ward, Alan J., 'Lloyd George and the 1918 Irish conscription crisis', *Historical Journal*, 17 (1974), pp. 107–29.

Ward, Margaret, *Unmanageable Revolutionaries: Women and Irish Nationalism* (new edn, London, 1989).

Weekly Irish Times, *1916 Rebellion Handbook* (new edn, Dublin, 1998).

White, Terence de Vere, *Kevin O'Higgins* (pbk edn, Tralee, 1966).

Wilson, Judith C., *Conor 1881–1968: the Life and Work of an Ulster Artist* (Belfast, 1981).

Wilson, Trevor, *The Myriad Faces of War: Britain and the Great War, 1914–1918* (Cambridge, 1986).

Winter, J. M., *The Experience of World War I* (pbk edn, London, 1989).

The Great War and the British People (London, 1985).

Sites of Memory, Sites of Mourning: the Great War in European Cultural History (Cambridge, 1995).

Index

Abbey Theatre, Dublin, 26, 69, 95
agriculture, 31
Ahern, Bertie, Irish government
    minister, 135
Albert, King of the Belgians, 141
All Quiet on the Western Front, 99
Amery, Leopold, British politician,
    126
Ancient Order of Hibernians, 133
Anderson, Sir John, British
    bureaucrat, 117
Anglo-Irish ascendancy class, impact
    of war on, 70, 72–3
Anglo-Irish War (1919–21), 69, 71
Antrim, county war memorial, 129,
    151
Anzac (Australian and New Zealand
    Army Corps), 37–8
Arklow, Co. Wicklow, 31
Armistice and Remembrance Day,
    69–70
    in Dublin: (1919) 115, (1924) 93,
        115–16, (1940) 123, (1939–45)
        135, (since 1945) 135
    exploitation by unionists, 113–14
    place of bereaved at, 126–7

Seán Lemass on, 131
Seán MacBride on, 131
    interdenominational service, 142
Armistice Night, Amiens, 81–3
Army Service Corps, 76
Arnold, Bruce, art historian, 78
artistic responses to the war, 71–90
Artists' Rifles, 73–4
Asquith, Herbert, British prime
    minister, 15
Atkinson, Professor George, head of
    Dublin Metropolitan School of
    Art, 124
Australia, and First World War, 37–8
Austria, 12
Auxiliary Division of Royal Irish
    Constabulary, 65

Baldwin, Stanley, British prime
    minister, 125
Ballincollig, Co. Cork, 151
Barbusse, Henri, writer, 79
Baring, Cecil, failed banker, 119
Barker, Pat, novelist, 138
Barr, Glenn, former loyalist
    paramilitary leader, 143

Barry, Tom, British soldier and IRA
    commander, 21, 27
Bather's Pool, The, 72
Battle Exploits Memorials
    Committee, 109
Bax, Sir Arnold ('Dermot O'Byrne'),
    composer and quondam Irish
    nationalist, 93–4
Beadle, James Prinsep, war artist, 134
Bean, Charles, historian, 20
Belfast, impact of Somme losses in, 59
    St Patrick's church, 76
    Presbyterian War Memorial, 129
    St Anne's Cathedral, 132
    unveiling of cenotaph, 132
Belfast Philharmonic Society, 91, 92
Belgium, 61, 109
    violation of, influencing
        recruitment, 10–12, 21, 59
    courage of, 24
    destruction compared with Dublin,
        45
    Peace Tower at Mesen, 138–43
bereaved, place of in war
    commemoration, 126–7
bereavement, 36
Bew, Paul, historian, 14, 26
Big House, The, 69–70
Black and Tans, paramilitary force,
    66, 69
Bloomfield, Sir Reginald, architect,
    119
Blown Up: Mad, 86
Boer War memorials, 116, 129
Boland, Michael, 1916 Volunteer, 50
Bond, Brian, historian, 10
Bourke, Joanna, historian, 153
Bowen, Elizabeth, novelist, 69

Bowen, Paul, historian, 154
Bowman, Timothy, historian, 145,
    155
Boyce, George, historian, 138, 153
Boydell, Brian, composer, 136
Boyne, Battle of the (1690), 56, 133
Brahms, Johannes, composer, 92
Bray war memorial, 131
Brennan, Robert, 1916 Volunteer, 46
Browne, Father Frank, army chaplain
    and photographer, 154
    photographs by, 43, 46
Browning, F. H., rugby player and
    part-time soldier, 41, 44
Buchan, John, writer and
    propagandist, 77
Bulgarian army, 59
Bushmills, Co. Antrim, 150
Byrne, T. J., architect, 119–21

Canning, W. J., military historian, 150
Carson, Sir Edward, unionist leader,
    14–15, 16
Casement, Sir Roger, nationalist
    leader, 47–8, 50, 76
Casey, Patrick J., military historian,
    35, 150
Callan, Patrick, historian, 6, 7, 146,
    154
Castlemaine, Lord, landowner, 140
casualties: civilian, 31, 32–3
    military, 33–5, 150
Cavan, in the war, 150
    memorial operating theatre, 129
Cenotaph
    London, 110–11
    Belfast, 132
    Dublin, 115

Central Council for the Organisation
of Recruiting in Ireland, 17
*Charge of the 36th (Ulster) Division,
Somme, 1st July 1916*, 134
Children of the Dead End, 96
Clan na Gael, 47
Clarke, Harry, artist, 62, 111
Clarke, Kathleen, nationalist leader,
33
Codd, Pauline, historian, 150
Collins, Michael, Irish revolutionary
leader, 26, 75
memorial to, 124
Collins, Peter, historian, 155
Connaught Rangers, 41, 54, 133
Connolly, Capt. A. P., British Legion
official, 123
Connolly, James, revolutionary
socialist
on recruitment to British
army, 19, 47
calls Pearse a 'blithering idiot', 24
optimism during Rising, 51
Conor, William, artist, 34, 40
conscription, 26
effect on recruitment, 8
Cookstown war memorial, 128
Cooper, Bryan, unionist, British
soldier and Irish senator
on 10th (Irish) Division, 41
at Gallipoli, 42–3
on effect of war on the Big Houses,
70
faith in reconciling power of war
service, 71
Corcoran, Doreen, local historian,
151
Cork
war memorial, 129–30

women workers, 29
Women's Emergency Committee, 33
Cosgrave, William, head of Irish
government, 142
on unionist exploitation of Poppy
Day, 113–14
and proposals for war memorials,
116, 118, 124
admirable views on war
commemoration, 125–6
Cowan, Maj. Samuel K., loyalist
versifier, 58
Craig, Sir James, unionist leader, 106,
133
Cullen, Mr R. M., Catholic ex-
soldier, 133
Cumann na mBan, 28
Curragh incident (1914), 15–16
Curtis, Edmund, historian, 5

Dairmuid and Grania, 93
Dalton, Canon John, patron of
Patrick MacGill, 96
Dark, Sydney, journalist, 78
Darling, Mr Justice, 76
de Valera, Eamon head of Irish
government, 125
and Irish National War Memorial,
121–3
and Irish nationalist memorial, 125
Dead Germans in a Trench, 76
Denman, Terence, historian, 55, 61,
139, 149, 152–3
Department of Recruiting in Ireland, 17
Derry/Londonderry, parallel with
Mesen/Messines, 138
Dillon, John, Ulster Division recruit,
27

divisions
  10th (Irish), 39, 70, 71, 104
    formation, 39–42
    at Suvla Bay, 38, 42–3
    at Salonika, 59
    historiography, 153
  11th, 38
  12th (Eastern), 39
  16th (Irish), 39, 105
    on Western Front, 61–4, 138–9, 140
    veterans at Belfast Cenotaph, 132
    historiography, 149, 155
  36th (Ulster), 39, 79
    on Western Front, 55–9, 61, 64, 138–9, 140
    Thiepval memorial, 107–9, 137
    history of (frontispiece), 108
    incorporation into loyalist tradition, 133–4
    historiography, 147–8
Donaghy, Jim, British soldier, 19, 58, 64
Donegal, 149–50
Dooley, Thomas, historian, 19, 146, 151
Douglas, Robert Langton, Director of National Gallery, 85
Downes, Margaret, historian, 156
Doyle, Father Willie, army chaplain, 64
Drogheda war memorial, 131
Dublin, 73, 74, 93
  economic impact of war in, 26, 30 32
  effect of Gallipoli losses, 44
  see also Easter Rising; Irish National War Memorial

Duffin, Adam, Belfast businessman, 16
Dungan, Myles, broadcaster and author, 18, 152
Dunne, Reggie, British ex-serviceman and assassin, 65
Dunsany, Lord, patron of Francis Ledwidge, 104

Easter Rising (1916), 2, 7, 36, 44, 76, 77
  youth of rebels, 26–7
  female rebels, 28, 32–3
  popular attitudes towards, 45–7
  events of, 49–52
  government's response to 52–4
  impact on soldiers in British army, 45, 54–5, 153
  effect on C. V. Stanford, 91
  impact on Francis Ledwidge, 104
  commemoration of, 125, 135, 136
economic impact of war, 30–2
Elgar, Sir Edward, composer and unionist, 92, 93
Elizabeth II, Queen, 136, 140
engineering industry, 30
England, recruiting compared to Ireland, 6
English, James, Irish soldier in British army, 19
enlistment, in British army, 5–10
  estimates of, 5–6
  motives for, 9–22
  'Big Words', 10–14, 65
  naive patriotism, 9, 16
  economic factors, 18–20
  social factors, 20–1
  supposed Irish military tradition, 21–2

enlistment, in British army (*cont.*)
  historiography, 145–6, 150
  see also conscription
enlistment, in separatist cause, 22–8
Enniscorthy, Co. Wicklow, 45
Ervine, St John, writer, 26–7, 44,
  100
Esher, Lord, royal servant, 96, 97
explosives production, 31
ex-servicemen
  associations, 90, 93, 111–12, 122–3,
    129
  nationalist, 121, 129
  housing for, 117, 154

Falls, Cyril, unionist and military
    historian, 39, 108
fascists, at Belfast Cenotaph, 132
Faulks, Sebastian, novelist, 95, 138
Fear!, 98
fishing industry, 31–2
FitzGerald, Garrett, former
    taoiseach, 142
Fitzpatrick, David, historian, 1
  on recruitment, 6, 18, 19–20, 26
  on casualties, 35
  historical works, 144–7, 150, 154
Fitzwilliam Square, Dublin, possible
    site for war memorial, 115
France, 12, 63, 67, 69
  Ledwidge mistakenly in, 105, 172
    n. 108
  see also Guinchy; Somme, Battle of
    the
Fraser, Murray, historian, 154
French, Viscount, viceroy of Ireland,
    109
Fussell, Paul, literary critic, 102

Gallipoli, 37–8, 42, 53, 139
Garden of Remembrance, Dublin, 125
Gaza, 59, 138
George V, King, 55
German Planes Visiting Cassel, 85
Germany, 12, 47–8, 49–50, 52, 123
Gibbon, Monk, writer, 28
Gleanings from a Navvy's Scrap Book,
  96
Glenavy, Lord, unionist and Irish
    senator, 113
Gogarty, Oliver St John, wit,
    surgeon, poet and senator
  on the Rising, 52
  on war memorials, 112
  friend of Lutyens, 119
'Gorgeous Wrecks', volunteer corps, 44
Graves, Alfred Perceval, poet, 93
Graves, Robert, poet, 93
Great War in Modern Memory, The, 102
Greece, 59
Griffith, Arthur, nationalist leader,
    memorial to, 124
Grigg, John, historian, 10
Grubb, Thomas, periscope maker, 31,
    160 n. 69
Guinchy, 61, 128
  Irish memorial cross at, 60, 111
Gwynn, Stephen, writer and
    nationalist MP, 14, 54

Hackett, William Lumley (Willie),
    casualty of war, 3–4, 35–6
Haig, Field Marshal Earl, soldier,
    89–90
  Earl Haig Park, 117
Hamilton, Sir Ian, British general,
    rejected for Irish command, 53

Hanna, Henry, Dublin lawyer, 42

Harris, Henry, military historian, 5, 23, 33

Hart, Peter, historian, 27

Harte, Paddy, Fine Gael politician, 143

Harty, Sir Hamilton, composer, 90, 92

Hayes-McCoy, G. A., historian, 5

Heaney, Seamus, poet, 104, 105, 137, 172 n. 108

Henley, W. E., lesser poet, 91

Hennessey, Thomas, historian, 146

Hickie, Sir William, British soldier and Irish senator, 60, 112, 114, 140

Hill, Judith, art historian, 154

Hinkson, Pamela, writer, 100, 101–2

Historial de la Grande Guerre, France, 138

Hobson, Bulmer, revolutionary leader, 49

Holy Well, The, 75

housing for ex-servicemen, 117, 154

How Many Miles to Babylon? 137

Howie, David and Josephine, historians, 15, 143–4

Hughes, Herbert, musician, 74

Hulluch, gas attack at, 51

Hynes, Samuel, literary historian, 20–1

Imperial War Graves Commission, 127–8

'In Flanders Fields' Museum, Belgium, 138

Information, Department of, British propaganda bureau, 77

Iper, see Ypres

Ireland's Memorial Records, 5, 33, 35, 67, 111, 119
  illustrated, 62

Irish Builder, critical of replicas, 109
  on Lutyens' Cenotaph, 110–11

Irish Citizen Army (ICA), 28, 32, 47

Irish Guards, 43, 65, 66–7, 91, 99

Irish Land (Provision for Sailors and Soldiers) Act, 1919, 117

Irish National Aid and Volunteer Dependants' Fund, 33, 77

Irish National War Memorial, 5, 33, 139, 142
  tortuous history of, 109–23
  illustrated, 120, 122
  partial completion of, 135
  crosses in Belgium, France and Macedonia, 60, 111, 140
  see also Ireland's Memorial Records

Irish Republican Army (IRA), 28, 65, 117

Irish Republican Brotherhood (IRB), 26, 47

Irish Rugby Football Union, 41

Irish Sailors' and Soldiers' Land Trust, 117, 141–2

Irish Volunteers, pledged to war effort, 13
  propensity to enlist, 20
  separatist wing, 22–4, 44–6
  split in, 47, 48–9

Island of Ireland Peace Tower, see Peace Tower

Jacob's biscuit factory, 36, 45, 104

Jagger, Charles Sergeant, sculptor, 74

Jameson, Andrew, whiskey distiller and senator, 119, 128

Jameson, Andrew (*cont.*)
    on Irish National War Memorial,
        112–13, 115, 118–19
Jellett, Mainie, artist, 71–3
Jellett, Sir William, Unionist MP, 72
Jerusalem, 59, 138
Johnston, Jennifer, novelist, 69, 137
Johnstone, Tom, military historian,
    151–2

Keating, Seán, artist, 75–6, 77, 79
Keene, James Bennett, bishop, 24
Keogh, Margaret, nurse, 33
Kettle, Tom, poet, nationalist MP
    and British soldier, 48, 55
    reasons for enlistment, 9–12
    foresees being remembered as 'a
        bloody British officer', 61, 149
    entry in *Ireland's Memorial Records*, 62
    memorial to, 128
    verse used in 1916 commemoration
        cantata, 136
Kilkeel war memorial, 132
Kilrush, Co. Clare, 150
Kipling, Lieut. John, soldier, 66–7
Kipling, Rudyard, writer, 66–8, 79
Kitchener, Lord, British soldier and
    war minister
    and volunteer 'New Army', 15, 16,
        38, 39, 50
    unsuitable nominee for Irish
        command, 53
Kut (Iraq), British surrender at, 52

Ladies' Road, The, 100, 101–2
Lambay Castle, Co. Dublin, 119
Lane, Sir Hugh, art connoisseur, 75,
    119

Langemarck/Langemark, Belgium,
    64, 99, 139
Larkin, James, labour activist, 42, 74
Lavery, Hazel, society hostess and
    iconic beauty, 74, 76, 83–4
Lavery, Sir John, artist
    response to war, 73–4
    and Irish nationalist sympathies,
        76–7
    as war artist, 83–5
    on Orpen, 86
    criticised as an Irishman, 88
    friend of Lutyens, 119
Ledwidge, Francis, poet and Irish
    soldier in British army, 136
    at Gallipoli, 42
    response to Easter Rising, 54
    and Serbia, 59
    representative character of, 102–4
Lee, J. J., historian, 6, 54
Legion of Irish Ex-Servicemen, 111
Leinster, RMS, sinking of, 32, 154
Leinster Regiment, 153
Lemass, Seán, Fianna Fail politician
    and taoiseach, 131, 135
Leonard, Jane, historian, 153, 154–5
Leslie, Shane, writer, 61
Limerick, 44
linen industry, 30, 154
Linklater, Eric, Scottish writer, 27–8
literary responses to the Great War,
    66–70, 97–106, 137–8
Logue, Michael, cardinal and
    archbishop of Armagh, 12
London Irish Rifles (18th battalion
    County of London Regiment), 96
Londonderry, 57–8, 138
Longford war memorial, 130–1

illustrated, 132
Longley, Michael, poet, 137
Loos, Battle of, 67
Lurgan war memorial, 128–9
Lusitania, sinking of, 32, 75, 119
  use of in propaganda, 17
Lutyens, Sir Edwin, architect, 137
  designs frame for Lavery painting,
    76
  and cenotaph, 110
  and Irish National War Memorial,
    118–22, 135
  Irish mother, 118–19
Lyon, Wallace, pig-sticker and
  soldier, 21
Lysaght, Edward, writer, 31

Macardle, Dorothy, historian, 21
MacDonagh, Thomas, poet and
  republican leader, 54, 104, 105,
    136
MacDonald, Ramsay, pacifist and
  British politician, 73
Macedonia, 59, 60, 138
  Irish war memorial in, 111
MacFarland, Alan, sometime director
  of Somme Heritage Centre, 155
MacFhionnghaile, Niall, local
  historian, 149–50
MacGill, Patrick, writer, 95–8,
    99–100
Mackenzie, Sir Alexander, Scottish
  composer, 92
MacNeill, Eoin, chief-of-staff of
  Irish Volunteers, 23–4, 26
MacNeill, James, diplomat, 113
Macready, Sir Nevil, British soldier,
    53

Mahon, Sir Bryan, British soldier
  and Irish senator, 112
Markiewicz, Constance, Irish
  revolutionary, 28
  breeches and puttees criticised, 47
Marriage of Nurse Harding, The,
    100–1
Martin, F. X., historian, 1
Masterman, Charles F. G., British
  propagandist, 74
Maxwell, Sir John, British soldier, 53
Mayo, 100, 101
McAleese, Mary, president of
  Ireland, 141
McCarthy, Eoin, local historian, 151
McConkey, Kenneth, art historian,
    75
McGrath, Raymond, sculptor, 125
McGuinness, Frank, playwright, 137
Men of the South, 76
Men of the West, 76
  illustrated, 77
Merrion Square, Dublin, 124
  possible site for war memorial,
    112–14
Mesen/Messines, Belgium, Island of
  Ireland Peace Tower, 3, 138–43
  Battle of, 61, 63
Messines Park, Derry, 117
Methodist College, Belfast, war
  memorial, 162 n. 85
Middleton, Lord, unionist politician,
    6
Midgley, Harry, versifier and
  Northern Ireland politician, 103
Mitchell, Gardiner S., military
  historian, 150
Moneymore memorial hall, 129

Monkstown, Co. Antrim, Somme mural at, 134
Mullingar, Co. Westmeath, 140
Multyfarnham, Co. Westmeath, 151
Mundow, Harry, chairman Office of Public Works, 135
munitions production, 30–1, 32
murals depicting Somme scenes, 133–4
Murray, Peter, labour historian, 154
musical responses to the Great War, 90–4, 136
Myers, Kevin, journalist, 35

Nash, John, artist, 74
Nash, Paul, artist, 74
National Gallery of Ireland, 75, 85
nationalists
    attitudes to war, 10–14
    and Easter Rising, 47–52, 54–5
    impact of war on, 75–6, 146
    and commemoration of war, 114, 122–6, 131, 136
nationality of Irish military formations, 152, 153
Nenagh war memorials, 131
New Zealand, 38
    memorial at Messines, 140
Newtownards, Co. Down, 137
Norway, Mrs Hamilton, wartime Dublin eyewitness, 49, 101
Nugent, Sir Oliver, commander of Ulster Division, 56, 64
nursing, 32, 33

O'Brien, William, nationalist MP, 12
Observe the Sons of Ulster Marching Towards the Somme, 137
O'Byrne, Dermot, see Bax, Sir Arnold

O'Casey, Sean, playwright, 44, 49
    and The Silver Tassie, 95
O'Donnell, E. E., compiler of historic photographs, 154
O'Donnell, Patrick, archbishop of Armagh, 133
O'Flaherty, Liam, writer, 99
O'Higgins, Kevin, Irish government minister, 114–15, 126, 142
Ollerenshaw, Philip, historian, 154
Onlooker in France, An, 78
Orange Order, 57, 133
Orpen, Sir William, artist
    response to war, 74–83, 85–90
    friend of Lutyens, 119
Orr, Philip, historian, 9, 147–8, 155
O'Sullivan, Gerard, local historian, 151
O'Sullivan, Joseph, British ex-serviceman and assassin, 65
Owen, Wilfred, poet, 79

Parnell Square, Dublin
    possible site for Great War memorial, 115
    nationalist memorial in, 125
Passchendaele/Passendale, Battle of, 64
Peace Conference at the Quai d'Orsay, A, 86
Peace Tower (at Mesen/Messines), 3, 138–43
    illustrated, 141
Pearse, Patrick, republican visionary, 23, 43, 54
    response to Great War, 24
    and Easter Rising, 47–9, 164 n. 34
    'In Memoriam Padraig Pearse', 94
    parallel with Francis Ledwidge, 105

Perry, Nicholas, military historian, 152
Phoenix Park, Dublin
  possible site for war memorial,
    112–13, 115
  remembrance ceremonies at, 116
pictures, usefulness of as historical
    evidence, 154
Plough and the Stars, The, 44
Poland, 59
Pollock, H. M., unionist government
    minister, 129
Portadown war memorial
  ecumenical dedication of, 133
  Garvaghy Road Somme
    commemoration, 133
Power, Albert, sculptor, 124
Presbyterian War Memorial Hostel,
    Belfast, 129
propaganda, 74
  recruiting, 11, 13, 17, 21–2
  anti-recruiting, 25
Purce, Margaret, medical doctor, 32

Radio Telefís Éireann, 136, 152
recruitment, *see* enlistment
Red Horizon, The, 96–8
Redmond, John, nationalist leader,
    24, 48, 54, 55
  Woodenbridge, Co. Wicklow,
    speech, 13–14, 21, 23, 47, 104
  visit to Front, 22
  favours formation of 'Irish
    Brigade', 39, 61
  and 10th (Irish) Division, 41
Redmond, William Archer, member
    of Dail, 114–15
Redmond, Willie, nationalist MP and
    British soldier, 106

reaction to Easter Rising, 54
enlistment and death in action, 61,
    63–4
study of, 149
religious denominations
  Church of Ireland, 21, 24
  Methodists, 24
  Protestants, 56, 57, 129, 131–4, 148
  Presbyterians, 129
  Roman Catholics, 12, 20, 56, 64, 77,
    129, 132–3
Remarque, Erich Maria, writer, 79
remembrance ceremonies, *see*
    Armistice and Remembrance
    Day
Return of the Brute, 99
Richardson, Sir George, UVF
    commander, 56
Roberts, Lord, Irish soldier and
    British field marshal, 67
Robertson, David, local historian, 151
Robertson, Sir William, British
    general, 53
Robinson, Sir Henry, vice-president
    of Irish Local Government
    Board, 21–2, 117
Robinson, Lennox, playwright,
    69–70, 71
Rodin, Auguste, sculptor, 80
Ross, Florence, munitions worker, 32
Royal Academy, 88, 107
Royal British Legion, 90, 93, 129
  and Irish National War Memorial,
    111–12, 122–3
Royal Dublin Fusiliers, 18, 27
  at Gallipoli, 41–2, 44
  song, celebrating, 92–3
  Boer War memorial in Dublin, 116

Royal Dublin Fusiliers Association, 137
Royal Hibernian Academy, 74, 76
Royal Inniskilling Fusiliers, 58, 150–1
Royal Irish Dragoon Guards, 64
Royal Irish Fusiliers, 133
Royal Irish Lancers, 65
Royal Irish Rifles, 27, 58
Royal Munster Fusiliers, 65, 150
    recruiting, 18, 28
    at Gallipoli, 44–5
    response to Easter Rising, 55
Russell, George ('AE'), savant, writer
    and artist, 74
Russia, 12
Ryan, Major, British Legion
    representative, 123
Ryan, Desmond, 1916 Volunteer, 50

St Stephen's Green, Dublin
    insurgent trenches in, 51
    Boer War memorial, 116
    Tom Kettle memorial, 128
Salonika, 59, 70, 104, 111
Scarlett, Frank, architect, 116
Scotland, recruiting compared to
    Ireland, 6
Second World War, impact on Great
    War commemoration, 134–5
'separation women', 45–6
Serbia, 59, 104, 111
Shamus O'Brien, 91
Shaw, George Bernard, writer, 73
Shillington, Maj. D. G., unionist MP,
    133
shipbuilding, 30
Signing of the Peace in the Hall of
    Mirrors, Versailles, 28 June 1919, 86

Silver Tassie, The, 95
Simkins, Peter, historian, 16, 18
Simpson, Revd Frederick, Anglican
    clergyman, 70
Simthson, Annie M. P., popular
    novelist, 100–1
Sinn Fein, 25, 31, 88, 117, 142
Smyly, Vivienne, nurse, 51
Soloheadbeg ambush, 71
Somme, Battle of the, 55–7, 147–8,
    155
    impact of 1 July losses in Ulster,
    57–9
    16th (Irish) Division at, 61
    commemoration of, 107–9, 133–4,
    136–7
    proposed bridge as memorial, 136
Somme Association, 137
Somme Heritage Centre, 137
South Irish Horse, 28
Sowing the Seed for the Board of
    Agriculture and Technical
    Instruction in Ireland, 75
Spender, Col. Wilfrid, unionist
    bureaucrat, 106
Stanford, Charles Villiers, composer,
    90–1, 93
Staniforth, Capt. J. H. M., soldier,
    153
Staunton, Martin, historian, 150
Stephens, James, writer, 26
Stewart, A. T. Q., historian, 57
Stokes, Roy, maritime historian, 154
Strauss, Richard, composer, 92
Studio Window, 7 July 1917, The,
    83–5
Súlleabháin, Tomás Ó, librettist, 136
Suspense, 95

Suvla Bay, 58, 71, 104
  British (or Irish) troops drink tea on
    beach, 37–8
  10th (Irish) Division at, 42
  impact of losses in Ireland, 44, 70

Taylor, A. J. P., historian, 58
Taylor Art Prize, 72
Thinker on the Butte de Warlencourt,
  The, 76, 79–81
Thomas, Corporal E., Irish soldier,
  64
Thompson, Robert, local historian,
  150
Thornton, Brighid Lyons, republican
  activist, 46
Tierney, Mark, historian, 154
To the Unknown British Soldier in
  France, 86–90
Townshend, General, surrender at
  Kut, 52
Townshend, Charles, historian, 49,
  50
Trinity College Dublin students,
  provocative behaviour of, 115
Trinity History Workshop, 144
Tynan, Maj. J. J., British Legion
  official, 123
Tynan, Katharine, *littérateuse*, 43–4,
  100, 101–2

Ulster Volunteer Force (UVF), offer
  of service in British army, 15
  propensity to enlist, 20
  hospital work, 33–4
  and Ulster Division, 39, 56, 147
Ulster Women's Unionist Council, 33
Unemployment Relief Act, 1931, 121

unionists
  attitudes to war, 14–16
  response to Easter Rising, 55
  and commemoration of war, 106–7,
    114, 131–4, 136
United Kingdom, recruiting
  compared to Ireland, 7–8
Urquhart, Diane, historian, 155–6

Verdun, Battle of, 52
Virginia war memorial, 131
voluntary war work, 33

war, purifying effects of, 24
war memorials, 107–35
war service, alleged reconciling
  power of, 55, 63–4, 71, 133, 149
Weir, Peter, Australian film director,
  37, 38
Wellington House, British
  propaganda bureau, 74
Western Front Association, 137, 150
Western Wedding, The, 75
Wexford, recruiting in, 150
Whitman, Walt, poet, 92
Widor, Charles Marie, composer, 91
Wilson, Sir Henry, Irish soldier in
  British army
  reaction to Easter Rising, 54
  assassinated by ex-servicemen, 65
  aesthetic judgment of Thiepval
    memorial, 109
Wilson, Trevor, historian, 10
women
  republican volunteers, 28
  war workers, 28–31, 32–4
  historiography, 155–6
  see also 'separation women'

Woodward, David, historian, 102
Wytschaete/Wijtschate, Belgium, 43,
    61
    Irish memorial at, 111, 140

Yeats, William Butler, poet and
    senator, 71, 85, 93, 95

on commemorating the Great War,
    113
Ypres/Iper, 45, 46, 106, 138
    'Ypres on the Liffey', 52
    Third Battle of, 64
Yugoslavia, 111